Lewis E. Daniell

Personnel of the Texas State Government

Texans Embracing the Executive and Staff, Heads of the Departments, United States Senators and Representatives, Members of the 20th Legislature. 1887

Lewis E. Daniell

Personnel of the Texas State Government
Texans Embracing the Executive and Staff, Heads of the Departments, United States Senators and Representatives, Members of the 20th Legislature. 1887

ISBN/EAN: 9783744727686

Printed in Europe, USA, Canada, Australia, Japan

Cover: Foto ©Suzi / pixelio.de

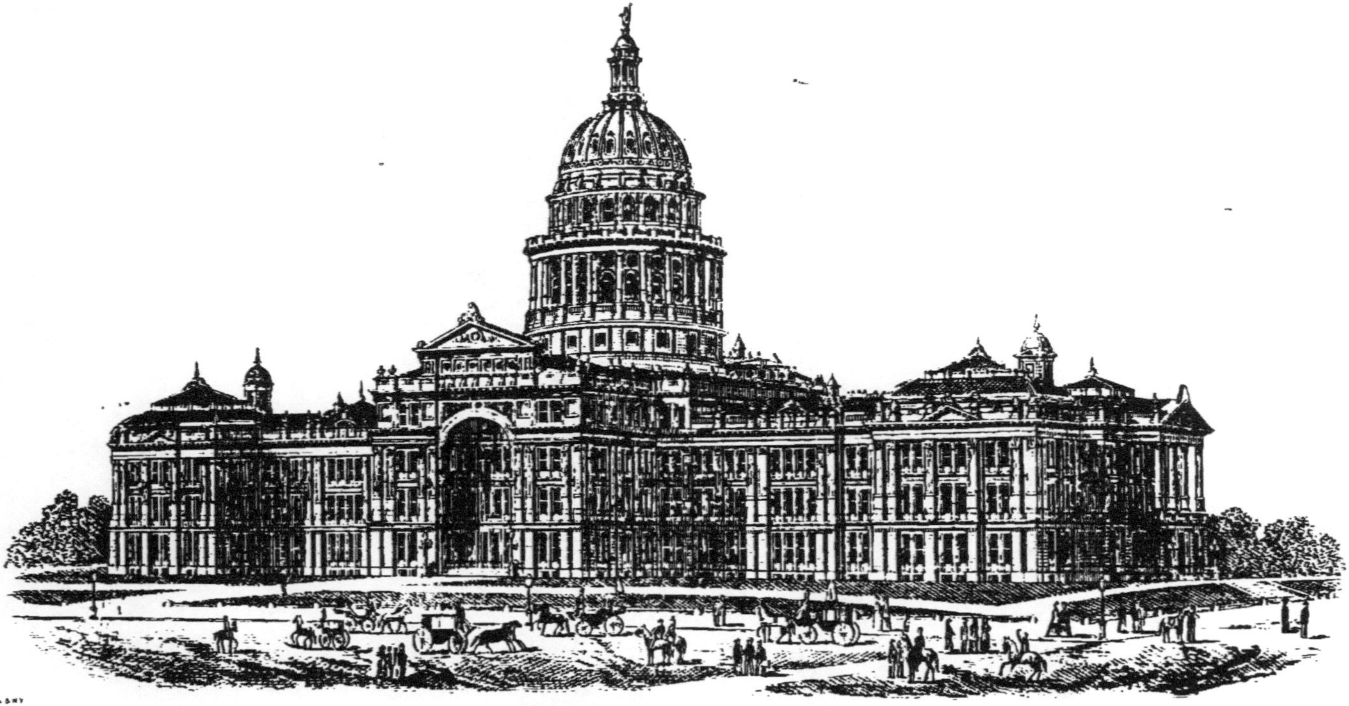

TEXAS STATE CAPITOL BUILDING

E.E. Myers Architect

Perspective
No. 1

PERSONNEL

OF THE

Texas State Government,

WITH

SKETCHES OF DISTINGUISHED TEXANS,

EMBRACING

*The Executive and Staff, Heads of the Departments,
United States Senators and Representatives,
Members of the XXth Legislature.*

COMPILED AND PUBLISHED BY L. E. DANIELL.

AUSTIN:
PRESS OF THE CITY PRINTING COMPANY.
1887.

PREFACE.

DR. BURLESON has graphically remarked, that "Texas has the material for a grander epic than Homer's immortal Iliad or the more beautiful epic of the Æneid of Virgil." If this be true of the youthful past of the State and her already realized grandeur, what will be the accummulated material to fill up the thrilling pages to be written by the historian fifty years hence? Without biography, there can be no truthful history. Man is the architect and builder of states and nations. He is the soul of the body politic; and as the body without the spirit is dead, so all intellectual and material essence is lifeless without the inspiration of his active and creative being. Biography must carry into its record of eloquence demonstrated or worked out problems of human origination; and, if it fails to do so, it will be thrown aside as the offspring of insincerity, and prove a mythical or hurtful delusion. He is indeed brave who records the comminglings—noble and ignoble—of the living actors of his time.

January, 1889, will, perhaps, witness the last inauguration of the State's chief magistrate whose usefulness and distinction lay in achievements of the sword as much as from the work wrought by his civil service. We have reached the utilitarian epoch of Texas. She needs and calls for that patriotism and statesmanship the glories of whose achievements must conceive and develop in the womb of peace, and at birth be heralded as good will to man, and the promise of a secure highway to happiness.

It is proposed simply to tell the inquiring reader and student of the times who the representative men are. They are well known at home, but should be introduced everywhere. We comply with the demand of a curious citizenship when we write up the personnel of the State's officials and representatives. The people will sit in judgment and reward merit, and place the true value upon well directed exertion. It is our duty to inform the rising generation of all those distinguished and useful public servants whose wisdom and virtues lay in the creation of measures most fruitful of good and promotive of social and public virtue, education and religion.

L. S. ROSS.

PERSONNEL

OF THE

TEXAS STATE GOVERNMENT.

STATE EXECUTIVE DEPARTMENT.

GOVERNOR LAWRENCE SULLIVAN ROSS.

THE State of Texas is truly honored by the line of her chieftains, and tablet and monument will continue to perpetuate their memory. By their deeds of heroic daring and self-sacrificing patriotism, they gave to her independence, and established the boundaries for a great empire. It is ever glorious to contemplate the history of our nation's independence, through the union of Thirteen States, but it is not less glorious when we contemplate the achievements of Texas' sons in their defiance and resistance of Mexico. It was a matchless conflict and a grand triumph. It was one against many States.

The subject of this sketch, L. S. Ross, occupies an honored place among those who wrought out the results which give such importance to the Lone Star State in her history and position among the sisterhood of our Union of States; for he was of the generation of those who succeeded to no less daring and effective effort in maintaining the perpetuity of the rich inheritance bequeathed by living and dead fathers—the heritage of our freedom. To the sons of these noble men was handed down a patriotic legacy, which must be inviolate and perpetual. There were the murderous savages on the one hand, and on the other the resentful Mexicans across the Rio Grande. These foes to domestic security had to be driven back or be captured in their incursions of crime and theft.

L. S. Ross' father was Captain S. P. Ross, who immigrated to Texas in 1839. He will ever live in Texas history as the slayer of "Big Foot," the Comanche chief. Following the death of this dreaded chief, was the sleepless and effective crusade against the rapacious and treacherous tribes of the Comanche and Kiowa Indians. He was the leader of the pioneers who destroyed their power to do evil, and who will ever be held in grateful memory by Texans.

Governor Ross was born at Benton's Post, Iowa, in the year 1838, and came to Texas with his father. His mind was familiarized with his father's recitals of Indian warfare, and his heart was inspired to vigilance and action against that foe wherever occasion demanded, and well did he execute the inborn mandate, when mounting his war-steed, with sword and rifle in hand, he marshaled his command against the foe of his brave sire. This was an inherited antagonism.

We now enter upon his life as a soldier. He was, in a mythological sense, a son of Mars. At about twenty years of age, we find him a student of Florence Wesleyan University, Alabama. The Indians in Texas exhibiting hostile intentions, young Ross abandoned the classic halls of the student to take the field in defense of the people of Texas. Major Van Dorn, of the United States Army, had to lead an expedition against the hostile Comanches of the Wichita mountains. Ross commanded one hundred and thirty-five friendly Indians, when his power of influence to command men was signally manifested over the red men of the forest. Van Dorn precipitated a conflict, October, 1858, with the hostile Comanches at Wichita mountains. The author of "Ross' Texas Brigade" informs us that it was a most hotly contested engagement. It is said: "Through the prodigies of valor, and to the sagacity, skill and bravery of Ross, was the complete annihilation of the hostiles."

In this engagement he received two wounds. His innate,

knightly chivalry in this conflict, no doubt, impelled him to distinguished daring. In the heat of battle, among those savage foes, he saw a young daughter of his race—the offspring of a Texan mother. Her release and restoration to the home of civilzation wes his inspiration in that hour. It was the motive, no doubt, intensifying the bravery of the man to the deadening of all fear. Like a knight of old, he rescued this fair maid from the savages, and gave her, by adoption, all the advantages of a christian education. The story of Lizzie Ross' rescue will occupy a page in history which will render immortal the name of Ross. This first service of his on the field of battle inspired the brave Van Dorn and the gallant Second U. S. Cavalry, which he commanded, to recommend his being promoted to a position in the United States service. And we are informed that General Winfield Scott, commander of the United States Army, in an autograph letter, made proper and honorable acknowledgment of his conduct, and proffered his "friendship and assistance."

The brave youth was superior to the seductions of flattery and military honor thus thrust upon him. He modestly accepted the expression of so distinguished mention, and returned to finish his collegiate course at Florence and thus terminated his first brilliant campaign.

The year following, soon after his return home, Governor Sam Houston signified his remembrance of Captain Ross' services upon the field under Van Dorn, and in 1860 commissioned him a captain of sixty rangers for the frontier protection.

A remaining large body of Comanches had made a destructive raid through Parker county. Captain Ross successfully executed a descent upon them, resulting in almost their extermination. By this soldier-like dash and surprise, the prestige of the Comanches as implacable foes was broken. The savage tribe of warriors had witnessed the slaying of their daring chief, Peta Nocona, by Captain Ross, in a hand to hand fight. Of those surviving this carnage of blood, many perished upon the plains in seeking their allies upon the waters of the Arkansas river. Their spirit of resistance and hatred to the whites seemed to have been extinguished. They felt that the spirit of their god had departed from them. Their chief had been slain, and hundreds of their force either killed or wounded.

Captain Ross' success in this border engagement is thus acknowledged by Governor Houston:

"Your success in protecting the frontier gives me great satisfaction. I am satisfied, with the same opportunities, you would rival, if not excel, the greatest exploits of McCulloch or Jack Hays. Continue to repel, pursue and punish every body of Indians coming into the State, and the people will not withhold their praise." * * *

Having, with such wonderful dispatch, so intimidated the savage invaders as to render them hopefully pacific, wonted security was felt on the borders of the State. This mission being accomplished, Captain Ross tendered his resignation as commander of the Rangers, and was, in grateful appreciation, made aid-de-camp, with the rank of colonel, on the staff of Governor Houston.

The following letter from Governor Houston should not be omitted in this connection:

EXECUTIVE DEPARTMENT,
AUSTIN, TEXAS, February 23, 1861.

Captain L. S. Ross, Commanding Texas Rangers:

SIR—Your letter of 13th, tendering your resignation in the ranging service of Texas, has been received. The Executive regrets that you should think of resigning your position, as the State frontier requires good and efficient officers. He is, therefore, unwilling to accept your resignation. * * * * The Executive has always had confidence in your capacity as an officer; and your deportment as a soldier and gentleman has met with his entire approval. It is his desire that you at once increase your command to eighty-three, rank and file, and take the field again.

Very respectfully,

[Signed] SAM HOUSTON.

Executive Department.

The late war of sections was at this time fully inaugurated; the stage of frenzied hate and strife was reached, and States had fallen into line for battle. All through this beautiful land were heard the voices of men and women clamoring for war.

We have now to record his acumen, forethought and diplomacy in the interests of the South, to which he was allied. He felt the importance of making allies of the Indians in Texas and on the borders, and to anticipate any movement in that direction by the government at Washington. The estrangement of the Indians in Texas and on the border, they now being friendly, would be attended with danger and greatly enfeeble the efficiency of Texas in her relations to the Confederate government. He interviewed Governor Clark at once upon the proper policy to be pursued. It is said Major Van Dorn sustained Captain Ross in this matter, and also pressed it upon the consideration and action of the Executive. The wisdom of the suggested treaty stipulation was accepted and approved by his Excellency, as the following letter sets forth:

AUSTIN, July 13, 1861.

Captain L. S. Ross:

DEAR SIR—When you were here a few days ago, you spoke of the disposition of the Indians to treat with the people of Texas. At the time you did so, I was so crowded with business I was unable to give to the subject the consideration its importance demanded. I nevertheless concluded and determined to adopt and carry out your suggestions. I would be pleased for you to inform me whether it may now be in time to accomplish the objects you spoke of, and, if so, whether you would be willing to undertake its execution. You mentioned, I believe, that a day was fixed by the Indians for the interview, but that you informed them that by that time Texas could not be ready.

Very respectfully,

[Signed] EDWARD CLARK.

Captain Ross was promptly commissioned by the Governor, and was about to enter upon the embassy, accompanied by Mr. Downs, of the Waco Examiner, and a few other chosen friends, when it was heard that General Pike was en route for a like purpose by authority of the Confederate government. Captain Ross had anteceded General Pike through his friends, Shirley, Jones and Pickle, by correspondence with them, and General Pike found the Indians ready to enter the Confederate service.*

This company of braves was consolidated with the Sixth Regiment of Texas Cavalry, at the city of Waco.

Captain Ross now entered upon the Confederate service. He was possessed of no vain intoxication because of the remembrance of the honors achieved, as narrated in this history. Like every patriotic soldier, he stood ready to be assigned any post of duty. We find him enlisted as a private in the company of his brother, Captain P. F. Ross, but he was taken from the ranks and promoted to major as early as September 12, 1861. This regiment was officered as follows: B. Warren Stone, colonel; J. L. Griffith, lieutenant-colonel. Ex-Governor Throckmorton served as captain of Company K. This regiment was assigned to the command of General Ben McCulloch, then in Missouri. The regiment, with all possible dispatch, repaired to the headquarters of General McCulloch. It fought with great gallantry in the battle of Chuitennela (Creek Nation), and in the three days' fights at Elk Horn and Pea Ridge, Arkansas.

A new role was assigned him just previous to this battle, that of a raider to the rear of the Federal army. He was given three hundred men from Companies Third and Sixth, Texas Cavalry; and well did he execute this delicate and dangerous move. It was managed with daring and consummate skill. Besides capturing a good many prisoners, he destroyed large supplies—both of commissaries and quarter-

*The author of "Ross' Texas Brigade" must be credited with bringing to light of record this important service.

masters. The command was known as the "Army of the West," and was commanded by Generals McCulloch and Price. It was transferred to the Cis-Mississippi Department, to reinforce General Beauregard, who was defending Corinth. The Sixth Regiment was dismounted after serving on outpost before Corinth, and soon reorganized, Major Ross being made colonel, commanding the brigade to which his regiment was attached. This was a summary promotion, as per order:

> Colonel L. S. Ross will immediately assume command of Rouns' Brigade, Jones' Division, Army of the West.
>
> L. JONES, Major-General.
>
> CHARLES S. STRINGFELLOW, A. A. G.

As is characteristic of the man, Colonel Ross declined the honor, and, as desired, was restored to the command of his regiment, General Phifer succeeding to the command of the brigade.

Then followed the storming of Corinth and the conflict at Hatchie Bridge, in which he commanded his regiment.

General Dabney H. Maury thus writes in an official letter to General Jackson:

> No regiment can have a more honorable name on its flag than "Hatchie," and, to my certain knowledge, no regiment can more justly and proudly bear that name on its colors than the Sixth Texas Cavalry.

In defending the Hatchie Bridge, Colonel Ross commanded the shattered brigade of General Phifer.

General Pryor thus refers to that defense, which was the salvation of the Army of the West:

> Withdrawing from the east bank of the Hatchie, and taking position upon a little ridge two or three hundred yards distant, the little brigade then made a gallant stand for several hours, to which General Maury so complimentarily alludes to Colonel Ross: "Whether in advance or retreat, distinguished ability characterized him as a com-

mander. After his regiment was remounted and joined to other cavalry regiments, triumphant successes attended him, whether in command or executing the orders of his superiors."

The First Mississippi Cavalry thus refers to him:

In conclusion, allow us to say, we are proud to have served under you and with your gallant Texans, and hope yours and theirs and our efforts in behalf of our bleeding country will at length be crowned with success.

W. V. Lister, Captain Company K.
J. E. Turner, Captain Company I.
J. A. King, Captain Company G.

The defeated Confederate Army had fallen back upon Grenada, Mississippi. The four remounted Texas regiments, under General Ross, in the Holly Springs raid, led to forcing General Grant to fall back upon Memphis, Tennessee, delaying his further advance upon Vicksburg for twelve months.

After the fall of Vicksburg, the retreat of the Confederate forces upon Jackson, in their failure to succor the beleaguered Vicksburg, received one of the most distinguished supports ever rendered by a body of cavalry. He successfully resisted the advance of Sherman. For this service, he was placed in command of a brigade composed of the First Mississippi and Sixth Texas.

The continued recurring successes which attended him just antecedent to his promotion to a brigadier general, on the field of battle at Yazoo City, excited the attention of Lieutenant General Stephen D. Lee, General D. H. Maury, who a second time made honorable mention of him, Ex-Governor Francis R. Lubbock, a member of President Davis' staff, General W. H. Jackson and General Joseph E. Johnston, who not only urged his promotion, but enumerated the elements of character and mind which had established his prestige, and demanded the bestowal of the highest military recognition. It was accorded; he occupied an exalted position in the judgment of those high in authority, and it was decided that he should be enrolled on the lists of advancing elevation and honor.

The defense and protection he gave to Yazoo City called forth the recorded expressions of more than fifty of her leading citizens in sentiments of praise and gratitude. The month of October, 1863, in which this distinguished mention was made of the young hero, was indeed replete in voicing his deeds of valor, ability and augmenting usefulness.

His relations to Johnston's Georgia campaign, and Hood's in Tennessee, did not lessen the confidence and esteem of the respective commanders. The author of Ross' Texas Brigade has most happily portrayed the soldier when he says, "Ross and Armstrong were the eyes of Hood, and, in his defeat and retreat, their brigades absolutely saved the army from annihilation."

Gen. Ross was most unpretending, which is the essence of manly worth and conscious rectitude. His every honor sought him, which he rather repelled than invited. Had the government of his love and allegiance been established, he would have succeeded, no doubt, to the highest military preferment.

The life and deeds of this man, while still on the threshold of manhood, were almost phenomenal. His volunteer beginning or entrance upon the trial of arms recalls the dash and success of the young Napoleon, in his furious dispersion of the Paris mob, which gave the impress that he was the man of noble destiny. Success brought to the latter that glory which defeat disappointed in the former.

It is a relief for the reader to turn his thoughts from the fields of battle to the peaceful pastoral plains of our sunny land. We shall now follow the subject of this narrative to the retirement and sequestered walks of his country home. Like Regulus, of Rome, the pacificator and statesman, who only left his farm by invitation to adjust the threatening disaffections and factions of the Roman senate, which he repeatedly accomplished, and retired to his country home, he had never sought military promotion, and ignored the invitations and attractions of civil position.

The voters of Texas, when their freedom was unawed by the bayonet, have shown a wise preferment and discrimination in selecting their chief officer.

General Ross, when chosen Governor of the State, had served his constituency in the capacity of sheriff of his county, and again in the constitutional convention of 1875, and in the Senate of 1881 and 1883. In both capacities he exhibited ability and gave unmistakable evidences of as efficient and distinguished success as attended his military career. His record, while a member of the convention, was such as to command the respect and admiration of the people. It was expected that he would become, at no distant date, prominent to fill the higher positions of state. The surprise is, that his nomination and election has been postponed so long. Had he possessed less modesty and more demonstrative ambition, his present elevation would have been reached years ago. The distinguished gentleman and honored official whose adherents had opposed General Ross' nomination, too lightly estimated the affection, admiration and confidence so unusual, in which he was held by the men and women of the State. All these emotions of mind and heart had lost none of their effective power and energy, when called into action, although latent so long. The remembrance of his heroic achievements, long ere he had reached the meridian of life, attracted and lent enthusiasm to his political followers. The noble comrades of his brigade and their allies were determined that he, who had never been vanquished in war, should not be in this civil struggle. Many condemned and not a few ridiculed the scenes and tactics which controlled the votes which nominated him. The prophecy was fulfilled, that thirty thousand ex-soldiers, who knew his deeds, would send up one grand shout for Sul. Ross. It was a feeling allied to resentment towards his opponents, that was aroused to

J. B. Wheeler.

carry by storm the fortified castles of the opposition. General Ross is worthy of the gubernatorial chair of this great State. Added to his unquestionable ability to fill acceptably the high office, the wisdom characteristic of his conduct in war, as a commander, will no doubt be exercised, commanding those aids and agencies which will give his administration success and honor.

THOMAS BENTON WHEELER.

THE achievements of great men are an inheritance of the rising youth of the land. Possibilities are illustrated by their lives, inspiring emulation and arousing the highest energies and efforts of the ambition. Biographies of individuals, whether their lives were for good or evil, last by example through generations. The stores of experience are thereby unlocked, and even the plow-boy may walk in and gather inspiration of a life devoted to the good of his kind.

In this brief biography of the life of Lieutenant Governor Wheeler, there are impressive lessons of the triumph of determination and fixed purpose over every kind of obstacles.

T. B. Wheeler had the misfortune to lose his father when he was five years of age, and, impressed with the knowledge that his mother would finally depend upon his exertions, he soon developed the capacity to undertake and successfully accomplish that responsibility. His mother, with her two sons, immigrated to Texas in 1854, settling in Hays county. Young Wheeler, from this time until the war commenced between the States, labored with his own hands, with a double purpose, to support his mother in her declining years and obtain an education that would fit him for the contests in life with men of noble and patriotic purpose, and by energy and application attained both objects.

His education was only fairly begun when he entered the Confederate army. At the school of Mountain City, about twelve miles from San Marcos, he laid the foundation of a broad and practical education, upon which he has since been able to build and accomplish brilliant practical results.

He made his first political speech against secession, because he disbelieved in secession upon the ground of policy. When, though, his State seceded from the Union he entered the army as a private in Company "A" of Wood's regiment. Serving thus for eighteen months, he was given a commission to raise a company of volunteers for cavalry service. He was then assigned to duty at points in Louisiana and Texas, and on all occaiions behaved himself with that gallantry which is inseparable from his nature.

At the close of the war, he returned home without means and commenced teaching, devoting all his spare time to the study of the law, and improved both his literary and legal education.

Having obtained a license to practice law, in 1866 he was elected county attorney of Travis county under the constitution of that year, from which office he was removed by the Federal General Reynolds, on the ground of his being an "impediment to reconstruction."

In 1872, Mr. Wheeler was elected, as a Democratic candidate, mayor of the city of Austin, and re-elected in 1873 and 1875, by an increased majority each time.

In the capacity of mayor of the city of Austin, more than in any other, perhaps, the metal of the man was fully tested. In 1874, the Democratic party of the State elected, under the reconstruction laws, the Honorable Richard Coke governor, with a large Democratic majority in the Legislature, but Governor Edmund Davis, who was the Republican governor of the State, refused to yield the office and papers to his successor, and for the purpose of holding the office assembled about him the negro militia, and held the capitol building with his armed troops. On the other hand, the people of the State organized and armed themselves in sufficient force to expel the usurpers. Under these circumstances Mayor Wheeler, seeing the imminent danger, exercised all his influence and diplomacy to avert the conflict of arms, and by his conciliation and determination, on many eventful and critical occasions, and his wise counsels, he succeeded in quieting the turbulent and pacifying the belligerent, and by him, as much or perhaps more than any other man, a conflict was avoided and the legal representatives of the people took possession of the State government. Mayor Wheeler was, on that occasion, requested by Governor Coke to take possession of the State arsenal on Pecan street. When he got there he was arrested by Davis' troops, and but for the judicious advice of the mayor a general engagement would have occurred. The man was equal to the emergency, and although the most violent passions of men were rampant, the settlement of all difficulties was effected without the shedding of one drop of blood. As an expression of the approval of the heroic conduct of Mayor Wheeler in these trying times, the Fourteenth Legislature voluntarily passed a vote of thanks to him for his wise counsel, judicious action and influence in allaying the storm of local conflict.

In 1877 he resigned the mayoralty of Austin, for the purpose of entering fully into the practice of law.

He removed to Brackenridge, Stephens county, Texas, and in 1880 he was elected district judge, of what at that time was known as the Twelfth Judicial District, by a large majority of votes. In 1884, he was re-elected, without opposition, and was filling that high and responsible office in the (now) Thirty-fifth Judicial District, when he was chosen Lieutenant-Governor of the State of Texas.

During Judge Wheeler's incumbency of the district judgeship, the trouble arose in his jurisdiction, on account of illegal fence cutting, so disturbing the peace of the State. His charge to the grand jury against the fence cutters aroused the most bitter feelings among the lawless classes,

Executive Department.

but true to duty and unflinching in courage, he administered the laws with a firm hand, and to him, more than any other man, are the people of that district indebted for the suppression of lawlessness and the protection and safety of property. In every emergency of life, T. B. Wheeler has proved himself equal to the occasion, and well may it be said of him, "*Mens agnea et arduis.*"

Governor Wheeler was born in Marshall county, Alabama, on the 7th day of June, 1840. He has been married twice. In 1866 he was married to Miss Kittie G. Manor, who died in 1881. His second marriage was to Miss Ida DeBerry, daughter of the Hon. A. W. DeBerry.

Governor Wheeler is of average height and weight, with a handsome figure and an open, intellectual face. He is easy and graceful in manners and speech. He has close analytical powers, readily discriminating, and quick to appreciate character. He is eminently social and sympathetic, and possesses the charm of easy approach, making the plainest man composed in his presence. He excels as an orator, thinking rapidly and connectedly on his feet, and is ready in debate. As a presiding officer he is an eminent success, being quick, fair and impartial. He is a devoted Texan, and will never do anything which will militate against the fair name or the interest of his adopted State.

STATE OFFICERS.

JOHN MARKS MOORE.

SECRETARY OF STATE.

THE Secretary of State, was born in Houston county, Texas, on the twenty-third day of January, 1853. His education was begun in the common schools of the State. He was for a time a student of Washington and Lee University, Virginia, and graduated from the law school of Cumberland University, Lebanon, Tennessee. In his chosen profession, he has attained a good degree of success and prominence. His public life began by election to the office of district attorney of the Twelfth Judicial District. He was also a member of the Eighteenth Legislature of the State of Texas, from the Forty-second Representative District. His present position is Secretary of State under Governor Ross, in which office he gives evidence of adaptability and public approval. Mr. Moore's religious predilections are with the Episcopal Church. He is also a Royal Arch Mason. He was married to Miss Estelle Grace, of Eastland county, on the eighteenth day of March, 1884. He is five feet eight inches high, and weighs one hundred and sixty pounds. His complexion is dark, black hair and eyes, and his person stout and robust. He thinks for himself, and deals in positives, not negatives. He is not wanting in the elements of a true American gentleman, and does not discard true politeness in the midst of business.

State Officers.

JOHN DODD McCALL.

COMPTROLLER.

NATURE always preserves a just equilibrium. Proportioned to the degree of responsibility is the capacity to meet it. Opportunities of supply are, by an eternal law, made to quadrate to the measure of demand arising out of the extremities of human experience.

When, in 1866, Dr. J. R. McCall died and left to John D., his son, of only twenty summers, the onerous care of a helpless family, the ability to meet the responsibility was was present, and only needed to be elicited in order to be manifest. This untimely weight was heroically borne by young McCall, and proved, in fact, the befitting means to call forth and develop the elements of a noble manhood.

Mr. McCall is a native of Tennessee, born on the ninth day of August, 1846, in Paris, Henry county, of that State. Paternally, his lineal descent is Scotch-Irish. His mother's name was America P. Cooke, and her ancestry of English and Welch extraction. Maternally, his genealogical record, on this continent, reaches back to the colonial period.

In the early part of the Seventeenth Century, Rev. Devereux Jarrett, a clergyman of the church of England, was sent over as a commisioner by the church to Virginia. Rev Mr. Jarrett was the grand-nephew of Walter Devereux, the first Earl of Essex. The remarkable, romantic marriage of Miss Elizabeth Patterson, of Baltimore, Maryland, to Jerome Bonaparte, is a link in one line of the genealogical chain of this family. Only two generations back, Jarrett, Patterson and Devereux are names of hereditary descent. Six generations, reaching back through two hundred and fifty years. link Comptroller McCall with the English clergymen.

Comptroller McCall was educated at the schools at Austin and Waco, Texas. Largely, the course of his educational preparation has been directed to business, rather than literature for its own sake. His information, derived both from school and experience, has not tended to variety, but to unity, and that in the line of the business engagement to which he has been elected.

He began public life as a door-keeper for the Senate of the Tenth Legislature. In 1865, he was given a clerkship under Hon. R. J. Downs, the Secretary of State. He served as warrant clerk in 1871 under Comptroller Bledsoe—his political faith being well known to the Comptroller. He was retained in this department of State government under the administration of Hon. Stephen H. Darden and also of Hon. W. M. Brown. When Colonel W. J. Swain was elected Comptroller, Mr. McCall was made chief clerk, which position he held up to the time of his elevation to be the Comptroller of the State of Texas.

Comptroller McCall is a man of indomitable energy, pleasant manners, and quick movement. Not having been trained to oratory, he makes no pretentions in that way. There are boldness and dash in what he does. He is rather tall, having a vigilant eye, and shows a commendable degree of patience and executive ability in the government of the force under him. He is often impelled by an exhileration of vital force, that nerves the athlete, approaching the arena of honored conflict.

Having emigrated from the romantic hills of his boyhood, early in the year 1853, he is by length of citizenship a Texan.

Though too young to have filled a place in the long service of the war between the States, he entered the army toward the close, and under command of Colonel J. S. Ford, was engaged in the last battle of the war, fought near Brownsville, Texas. In this engagement, the gallant young soldier behaved valiantly, and was a principal actor in the last Confederate victory.

State Officers.

FRANCIS RICHARD LUBBOCK.

STATE TREASURER.

THE fabric of a nation's history is woven largely from the material of individual biography. Personal experiences and exploits, that in absolute isolation might be devoid of significance, aggregate an importance, that sometimes reverses the whole current of a nation's affairs. The real value of an individual life can only be accurately estimated when its accidental combinations, as related to an entirety, are taken into account. The fortuitous complications of social environment, that are effected by forces operating without the limits of human knowledge, give potentiality to an individual life, rather than any singular thing differentiating it from the masses.

Treasuer Lubbock has filled a principal place in the political structure of the State of Texas, and for this reason, what to him might have been lost in an unwritten biography, is claimed by the State as an essential part of its history. The length of his public service, and its diversified relations in office, have given satisfactory proof of his unswerving integrity. No citizen of Texas can boast a larger share of public confidence than he.

Treasurer Lubbock is a South Carolinian, having been born there in the year 1815, on the sixteenth day of October. Early in life he embarked in the mercantile line of business. At the inexperienced age of nineteen, he became a citizen of New Orleans, and two years subsequently, committed his fortunes with those of the Republic of Texas.

His first public service was in the office of assistant clerk of the House of Representatives at Houston, in the year 1837, and at the succeeding session of Congress, was promoted to the desk of the Chief Clerk. By appointment of President Houston, he filled the office of Comptroller. While discharging faithfully the duties of his office, he was made Adjutant of the Bonnell Command, organized for the defense of the western frontier. His fidelity in public affairs insured for him a continuous succession of official positions. He was elected District Court Clerk in 1841, and served until 1857, when he tendered his resignation to accept the high office of Lieutenant-Governor, to which he was elected on the democratic ticket in 1857, having been nominated at the Waco Convention; and in 1861, he was chosen Governor of the State.

He entered the Southern army on the day he ceased to be Governor; took position as Lieutenant-Colonel in the Adjutant-General's Department, and served with General Magruder; was subsequently assigned to General Green, and still later on, to John A. Whorton. From this position he was selected by President Jeff. Davis as a member of his staff, with the rank of colonel, and was with the Confederate leader at the time of his capture, remaining in Fort Donaldson till the close of the year 1865.

After the war between the States, Treasurer Lubbock made his home in Galveston. In 1878, he was first elected State Treasurer, and has held the office by regular re-election ever since. By the last election, in November, 1886, his work was re-indorsed, and he holds this responsible and trusted office for another term.

The trend of Governor Lubbock's education has been entirely directed to business and practical life. His conservative views of public economy have inspired the confidence of the people by whom he has been so continuously honored. The friend and patron of literature, he has left its pursuit to the natural aptitudes found in others, and has bent all his mighty energies toward the practical varieties of life. As evidence of this, the whole structure of his success has been built on this corner-stone. His proficiency, as a student of human nature, his accurate prophecies from predicates present and undeniable, and his ready acumen in the discernment of probable results, describe, in a measure, the intellectual outlines of this patriot and honored Treasurer of the State of Texas.

He is now more than seventy years of age, yet possessing the vigor and buoyancy of young manhood. The contour of his person is fashioned after an approved model, but in physique, he belongs to the Liliputian race of great men. His movements are quick, and betoken the ready determinations of purpose that have made his life distinguishable. Fluent and graceful in speech, and possessing the elements of true politeness and gentility, the masses are drawn to him, in answer to his extraordinary manifestation of the social instincts. His private character is in perfect harmony with his public record—so that both have been duly impressed upon the state-life of this great commonwealth. Entering the State in 1836, with but little else than the indomitable determination to win, and the assured friendship of the goddess of fortune, the hero of this sketch is an example of the possibilities that are attainable to the few.

JAMES STEPHEN HOGG.

ATTORNEY-GENERAL.

THE lineal descent of the adipose Attorney-General is Scotch-Irish. His mother was a member of the McMath family, an honorable kindred of Scotland, who, at an early period of American history, had their representatives in the New World. His father was of Irish extraction. The Hogg family first established themselves in Virginia, and subsequently spread through the Carolinas to Georgia. In the year 1839, the father of Judge Hogg immigrated to Nacogdoches, Texas, and with his young wife, whom he had married in Tuscaloosa county, Alabama, became established in the citizenship of the country. James Stephen was born on the twenty-fourth of March, 1851, at Rusk, Cherokee county, Texas; and enjoyed, in his infancy, the competency his provident parents had gathered. He was left an orphan at the age of twelve. During the war between the States, his mother died in Texas, and his father at Corinth, Mississippi, at the head of the brigade afterwards known as the Ector Brigade. The demise of General Hogg and his wife, broke the bond of the family, and, the property all swept away, young Hogg entered the struggle of life single-handed, having only, as his capital, the inexperience and incompetency of the age of fifteen. For a while he did manual labor as an honest means of a livelihood. His education was not finished at the end of a college curriculum, but has been a life-long work—not by the process of absorption from centers of learning, while reclining on the lap of affluence, but by methods of toil and economy, that acquire and heroically win. In the school at Rusk, he obtained his first educational aids, and, like President Cleveland, Secretary Bayard, Speaker Carlisle and others, he has reached the ends of true education, by dint of energy, that tunnels the granite mountains of difficulty rather than construct the highway over level valleys and even plains. In this he is truly a self-made man. As a means of practical education, he entered the compositor's office before he had reached his majority, and served as the printer's devil. From this first office in the "Art Preservative," he carved his way to the editorial tripod. He established, and run successfully, for a while, the *Longview News*; subsequently removed to Quitman, Wood county, Texas, under the head of *Quitman News*.

His legal education, like his literary, has been coined from the crucible of privation and assiduity. He read law four years, while residing at the towns of Tyler, Longview and Quitman, in the midst of the other duties that multiplied upon him. He entered the bar in 1874, and after four years of successful and lucrative practice, at the earnest and persistent request of the presiding judge and his associate attorneys, he became a candidate for county attorney of Wood county. His election was without opposition. He served one term in this office at a financial sacrifice to himself. Succeeding this service, he was elected district attorney of the Seventh judicial district, which position he held for four years. Judge Hogg was married to Miss Sallie Stinson, of Wood county, in 1875; and, starting without inherited wealth, they have been successful in accumulating a competency. His successes—and they have crowned every endeavor—have not been the accidents of a favored personage, on whom fortune has lavished her gifts; he has carved every step, and chiseled every niche of the structure of honor on which he now stands. His recent election to be the legal counsel and guardian of the great State of Texas, is sufficient proof of his legal ability and trusted integrity.

In physique, the Attorney-General presents a commanding personal appearance; six feet and two inches high, having a tendency to an obese developement, that may sometime prove inconvenient; his average weight is 285 pounds avoirdupois. Forensic combat in the prosecution of the criminal and in the defense of the innocent, has not steeled his warm and generous nature. He possesses a high degree of personal magnetism, and, displaying a courtly affability toward guests and company, makes admirers and friends without number. Being yet in his thirty-sixth year, he has not attained to the full manhood of his intellectual strength, nor unlocked the magazine of prowess, that may further win.

WILBURN HILL KING.

ADJUTANT-GENERAL.

IT does not always follow that military genius is inseparable from curtness of expression and abruptness of manner. General King, who possesses the former, is pleasant in address, and practices, by nature, an urbanity of manners that classes him as a polished gentleman in the social circle. Possessing strong volitional force and an inexorable purpose, to take hold is, with him, to accomplish. He does not possess those social idiosyncracies which drive men from him, but, on the contrary, is a friend to be prized and a foe to be dreaded. He is above the average, physically; has a dark complexion, black hair and eyes, and a countenance that indicates peacefulness of mind as he entertains his friends, but would arm itself with fierceness at the first sound of conflict. He was born in Crawford county, Georgia, June 10, 1839, and in 1856 came to Texas, remaining only a short time. He, however, returned to this State in the spring of 1861, and located in Cass county. In the beginning of the war between the States, he enlisted in the service of the Confederacy, and was elected Major of the Eighteenth Texas Infantry, commanded by Colonel W. B. Ochiltree.

His courage and ability as an officer so distinguished him that he soon rose to the rank of Brigadier-General. Although he did not recieve his commission as such, he, for most of the time, commanded the famous Walker's Division. After the cessation of hostilities, he studied law and began practice in Cass county, Texas. In 1873 he removed to Jefferson, Texas, and pursued his profession at that place with remarkable success. Having removed to Sulphur Springs, Hopkins county, in 1774, he was subsequently elected mayor of that city. He was a member of the Texas Legislature that convened in 1879, and soon became a leader in the House. To fill the vacancy, occasioned by the death of Adjutant-General Jones, General King was appointed by Governor Roberts in July, of 1881. This office he held under reappointment of Governor Ireland, and has recently received reappointment by Governor Ross. His skill in the management of the military affairs of the State has been warmly commended. Lawlessness has been greatly suppressed through his efforts as Adjutant-General, and the desperado has not found in Texas a land free to his occupancy. The positive character of General King is to be admired.

General King was married in New Orleans, to Miss Lucy

Furman, in the early part of the year 1867, who died about one year later. The General has no living children. Mrs. King was the daughter of Dr. Sam Furman, a practicing physician of Kentucky, and grand-daughter of Rev. Dr. Sam Furman, President of the Baptist University in South Carolina.

RICHARD MOORE HALL.

COMMISSIONER OF THE GENERAL LAND OFFICE.

IN the person of Commissioner of the General Land Office, North Carolina has made her contribution to one of the most important departments of the government of Texas. Beyond the Appalachian Highlands, in the midst of the romantic hills that have remained unchanged since the British soldiery marched over them, in revolutionary times, the new Commissioner was born, on the seventeenth of November, in the year 1851, in Iredell county, in that venerable State.

He is the son of the late Dr. James K. Hall, a distinguished physician of Greensboro, North Carolina. Mr. Hall was educated at a famous old Quaker college, at New Garden, in Guilford county, where the battle of Guilford Court House was fought, in the Revolutionary War, under command of General Greene.

A knowledge of the Quaker system is only needed to know how thorough their work of education is.

Possessed of a good intellect, with a decided taste for mathematics, Mr. Hall chose civil engineering as his profession.

Having immigrated to Texas in 1872, he has spent fully one-third of his life in this State. He served as county surveyor of Grayson county, for a term of three years. from 1875 to 1877, inclusive.

R. M. HALL.

He was happily married in 1880, to Miss Bettie Hughes, of Jefferson, Texas, and for some time past, has been living in Williamson county, engaged in farming and stockraising.

The Commissioner is in the very prime of young manhood, and would be classed as a man above the average in stature, and of florid complexion. He is a pleasant gentleman, not inclined to be obtrusive, but possessing a mind of his own when necessary to decide.

OSCAR HENRY COOPER.

SUPERINTENDENT PUBLIC INSTRUCTION.

LITERATURE crowns her votaries. In the lines of genealogy, where the pursuit of the learned professions, has been prominent, the maintenance of a high order of talent, follows by necessary physiological law, an illustration of this truth is afforded in the case of the subject of this sketch.

Dr. William H. Cooper, the father of Oscar Henry, was, by birth, a Mississippian. He came to Panola county, Texas, in 1849, and throughout Eastern Texas, was distinguished for his learning and skill as a physician and his fine literary attainments.

The Superintendent of Public Instruction was born in the county of Panola, Texas, about five miles from Carthage, on the twenty-second of November, 1852. Maternally, he is closely related to the Rosser family of Virginia. General T. L. Rosser of Virginia, who was educated at West Point as a Texas student, and who was a distinguished cavalry officer in the army of Virginia during the war between the States, is, by consanguinity, an uncle of Mr. Cooper.

Private tutors gave young Cooper his first instructions and training, which preparatory course he concluded at the college at Marshall, Texas. He entered Yale, and after taking the regular course, graduated in the year 1872. As an important part of his educational advantages he visited

Europe and spent a year in the University of Berlin, Germany, returning to America in September, 1885.

The life-work of Mr. Cooper has been that of an educator; he is enthusiastic in the cause of education, and a lover of philology. He has taught successfully in various schools of reputation and prominence, including Henderson Male and Female College, Sam Houston Normal Institute, and three years in Yale, his *alma mater.* At the time of his election to be the head of the mighty educational interests of Texas, he was principal of the Houston High School.

The project of the Sam Houston Normal Institute, as an elementary factor in the educational system of the State, embodying the proposition of the $6000 annual donation from the Peabody Fund, was submitted and argued before the State authorities by Mr. Cooper, under appointment of the State Teachers' Association. He was the prime mover in hastening the establishment of the University. In the *International Review*, the first article appeared, arguing the feasibility of hastening the organization of the University of Texas. This article bore the signature of Oscar H. Cooper. The joint committee of the House and Senate requested his aid in the preparation of a University Bill, which was given, and the present law is, with slight modifications, the result of his labors.

Prof. Cooper is choice in his language; possesses an intellect given to plan, device, enterprise, and is not abashed at great difficulties of accomplishment. He is a Texan, but not a narrow provincialist. He could not be said to excel as an orator, yet, his lectures display real culture, and his colloquial talents are of a high order. Like his predecessor in office, he is small in stature, and unlike him, the tendency of his complexion is blonde.

Prof. Cooper was married in Marshall, Texas, on the twenty-fourth of November, 1886, to Miss Mary B. Stewart, grand-daughter of Dr. James H. Starr, of Marshall, Texas, who was, at one time, a member of President Lamar's cabinet.

L. L. FOSTER.

State Officers.

L. L. FOSTER.

COMMISSIONER OF INSURANCE, STATISTICS AND HISTORY.

THERE is no better illustration of the oft-quoted expression that, "in this country every plow-boy is a candidate for the presidency," than in the life of L. L. Foster, Commisioner of Insurance Statistics and History, under Governor Ross' administration.

Eighteen years ago, in the eighteenth year of his age, L. L. Foster, left Cumming, Forsyth county, Georgia, near where he was born, to seek fortune and fame in the West, and arrived at Horn Hill, Limestone county, Texas, December 12, without a cent in his pocket, or a friend to aid him, but with that indomitable energy characteristic of the man, he began work at whatever his hands found to do, picking cotton, cultivating the soil, laying brick and stone, for four years. This, however, was merely a means to the end. Young Foster was animated by an ambition that had its secret source in the knowledge of his own powers—a laudable ambition to become a "man among men" in the higher walks of life, and to lead, not follow, at the command of another. The difficulties before him were great, but with that superior confidence that belongs alone to the pioneer in thought, he wedged his way through obstructing forces, and ever encouraged by vicissitudes, he pressed on to the mark of the high calling he had chosen for his career. With the money earned at manual labor, he entered Waco University, diligently and eagerly inquiring the path to the arcana of learning. It goes without saying, that he stood high in all of his classes.

In November, 1873, he removed to Groesbeck, and in 1876 began the publication of the *Limestone New Era*. Thoroughly imbued with the principles of the Democratic party, the *New Era* became a power for good in the hands of a man whose partizanship sprang from patriotism. The

New Era gradually, but surely, gained the respect and confidence of the people of Limestone county, and in time, its influence extended beyond county lines and throughout Central Texas.

In 1880, the people of Limestone county elected Mr. Foster to represent them in the Seventeenth Legislature, and in 1882, he was chosen to represent the Sixty-second District, composed of the counties of Limestone, Falls and McLennan, in the Eighteenth Legislature. With the experience gained in the Seventeenth Legislature, and a close study of parliamentary law, Mr. Fostor, at once took position as one of the leaders of the House. Great questions arose for solution upon which political economy and precedent were silent, and the determination of which required versatility of mind and originality of thought far above the average. In the discussion of these questions, Mr. Foster made a State-wide reputation as a debator and parliamentarian, which resulted in his election as Speaker of the House of the Nineteenth Legislature. He was the youngest man ever elected to that office in this State, and on that account it may be considered a special honor to him. His administration of the office was fair and impartial; and such was the confidence in the justice and correctness of his decisions on all questions arising in the course of legislation, that no appeal was taken from any decision rendered during the session.

Mr. Foster is a particular friend of Governor Ross, and used his extensive influence to secure his nomination and election. He is a forcible speaker, and possesses a style of oratory at once persuasive and convincing. His appointment to the office of Commissioner has met with the hearty approval of the press of the State with which he has long been connected, and was received with gratification by the people throughout the State.

Mr. Foster is yet a young man, with many advantages over his condition eighteen years ago, when he first arrived in Texas. By his industry and prudence, he has acquired

a competency, and is surrounded by friends who delight to honor him.

He is about six feet tall, straight and slight in person, with a finely chisled face, the lower part of which is hidden by a thick, black beard, worn at a moderate length. He has a commanding presence and address, and is graceful and dignified in manner. He is now in the prime of life, and gives promise of many more years of usefulness to his friends and the State of his adoption.

FRANK RAINEY

SUPERINTENDENT OF THE INSTITUTE FOR THE BLIND.

THE subject of this sketch is a native of Alabama. He was born in 1840, received an honorable degree in Franklin College, and graduated in the medical department of the University, of Louisiana, 1860. Removing to Texas, in 1861, he entered the office of Dr. F. L. Merriwether, for the practice of medicine in Houston county. The civil war having commenced, he entered as a private in Captain Tucker's company, Randall's regiment. He was early detailed for medical service, and put in charge of the sick at Shreveport, Louisiana. Soon after his return to his command, he was taken ill, and for a time retired. It was several months before he could resume military duty. He was transferred to the cavalry command under Sibley's brigade, and soon after received his commission as assistant surgeon in the cavalry service. He was with General Green's command in all the Arkansas and Louisiana engagements. Most honorable mention is made of his professional attainments in the History of Green's Brigade. After the close of the war, he resumed the practice of medicine in Houston county. He entered political life, and was a representative in the Twelfth, Thirteenth and Fourteenth Legislatures. Retiring from legislative duties, he was appointed by Governor Coke, Superintendent of the State Institute for the blind, in May, 1874. He has exhibited most marked ability, from that date to the present, in the managment of that institution, receiving reappointment by successive administrations. It is not only prosperous, but is a great honor to the State of Texas. The number restored to sight-or else had their vision improved, and the success in instructing the blind in various useful manual employments have wrought out for the superintendent, a most honorable record. He is genial, humane and philanthropic, has educated himself up to the highest qualifications for the position, and has the affection of the inmates and the admiration of the public. He has been efficient and faithful, and has distinguished himself in every chosen or assigned position in life.

He is a true type of a southern gentleman, of a physique well proportioned and symmetrical, black hair and eyes, and a fair complexion. As a member of society, he is pleasant and entertaining, as a scholar he is broad and comprehensive; and as a physian and surgeon, he is philanthropic and kind. Fearless as a soldier, he may yet be deeply touched by human suffering. As a legislator, he was wise and discriminating; and as a successful superintendent of instruction for the unfortunate blind, his continuance in office under the changes of so many administrations is all the testimonial required.

JOHN SPEARS DORSET.

SUPERINTENDENT OF THE ASYLUM FOR THE INSANE.

AT an early period in the Colonial history of America, the Dorset family became established in Virginia, as an offshoot of English parentage. Thomas B. Dorset and Annie Dorset, *nee* Miss Annie Spears, were the parents of the subject of this sketch. Mr. Dorset was a farmer of the true Virgina type, and gave to his sons the healthful freedom of rural life, and open-air exercise during the formative period of their lives. The family were honored and respected citizens of Powhattan county, Virginia, where John S. Dorset was born on the twenty-fifth of August, 1833. At Tomahawk, Chesterfield county, of that State, he received an academic education, which laid broad the foundations of a useful and honorable life. At both Philadelphia and New York, he attended a thorough course of lectures in the medical schools—graduating with high honors. In the war between the States, he had a varied, adventurous and perilous experience. He served as a private—as Second Lieutenant, both of infantry and cavalry—was assistant surgeon with Dr. Bell Gibson, in General Hospital No. 1, in the City of Richmond—was wounded in June, 1863—twice a prisoner, and concluded his military services, proper, with General Early in his daring campaigns in Virginia and Maryland. Under order of Judah P. Benjamin, Dr. Dorset visted England, returning to Washington City on that memorable night of the assassination of President Lincoln. After his escape from the Libby Prison on the seventeenth day of May, 1865, he went to New York and received an appointment as Physician and Surgeon on the steamer Mariposa, by Captain Allan McLane, President of the North Atlantic Steam Ship Company, who also was brother-in-law of General Joseph E. Johnston. On the sixteenth of June, 1870, Dr. Dorset was married to Miss Martha Bird Moore, daughter of Henry

State Officers.

Carter Moore, Esq., of North Garden, Albemarle county, Virginia. He and his bride immediately came to Texas, and settled in Bonham. Fannin county. Under appointment of county authorities, Dr. Dorset has filled the office of Physician and Surgeon to the poor of the county. He received the onorous and vastly responsible appointment as Superintendent of the State Asylum for the Insane under Governor L. S. Ross. His administration began on the fifth of February, 1887. He is a member of the Methodist Episcopal Church South. As a scholar, he is profound, and especially learned in all that department of knowledge that is relevant to his favorite profession. He has won a reputation as a physician and surgeon that justly gives him a place not inferior to the ablest men of his profession. He is of tall and symmetrical figure, and has a vivacious and graceful movement. His head is large, having a massive forehead, covered with soft black hair, that grows thin, almost to baldness, on the crown. He has a fair complexion, and a large black eye. He converses readily, and manifests a commendable degree of modesty. He was born to rule, but his imperial nature is dominated by an unrestrained philanthropy. To him order is law, and system is the equivalent of accomplishment, but his generous nature tempers his authority, and mingles mercy in judgment. He would be recognized anywhere as a man of mark. His manners are easy and gracious, and even a stranger would not feel repelled from his presence.

W. A. KENDALL.

WILLIAM ADDISON KENDALL.

SUPERINTENDENT OF THE INSTITUTION FOR THE DEAF AND DUMB.

THE Superintendent of the Institute for the Deaf and Dumb, is a Virginian, born in Tazewell county, August 6, 1830. His parents were Allen and Elizabeth Kendall, who removed to Kentucky while William Addison was quite young. In that State he received his education, and at the age of twenty-three years, was married to Miss Mary C. Daily, daughter of Dr. Hiram Daily, of West Liberty, Morgan county. Mr. Kendall came to Texas with his family in 1858, and settled in Denton county, where he has since resided. Early in the conflict, he entered the southern army under the command of General John H. Morgan. He was captured in the raid into Ohio, while commanding Company A, Third Kentucky Cavalry, and was one of six hundred officers held for retaliation. In 1865 he returned to his home in Texas. His second marriage was to Mrs. J. V. Wear, in 1871. His occupation has been farming, in which he has been successful. For a portion of his time, he has also been engaged in the land agency business. Major Kendall's public life began by his election to the Eleventh Legislature of the State of Texas. He was subsequently elected to the Nineteenth Legislature.

Under appointment of Governor Ross, he took charge of the Institute for the Deaf and Dumb, on February 1, 1887, which responsible position he now holds. As a citizen, Major Kendall has been loyal and true; as a soldier, trusted and reliable; as a legislator, wise and influential, and as a friend, faithful and trustworthy. His figure physically, is well ordered, being six feet in stature, and weighing one hundred and sixty-five pounds. His eyes are blue, complexion fair, movement quick, and he converses readily and without hesitation. His physiognomy indicates a fine degree of intelligence, while he possesses a happy equilibrium between the ability of planning and that of executing. Urbane in manners, and socially attractive, his friendships are readily made, numerous and of an ardent and enduring type.

THOMAS J. GOREE.

SUPERINTENDENT OF STATE PENITENTIARIES.

THE Superintendent of the Penitentiaries of the State of Texas, is an Alabamian. He was born in Perry county of that State, on the fourteenth of November, 1835. He is, by adoption, a Texan, since the close of the year 1850. He began his education at Howard College, Marion, Alabama, and concluded it in graduation, both in literature and law, from Baylor Univerity, Independence, Texas, in the year 1856. Captain Goree read law under Colonel W. P. Rogers, and in firm with his preceptor and Judge James Willie, entered into practice in the City of Houston, Texas, prior to the war between the States. He resumed his professional business, in firm with Senator L. A. Abercrombie, in Huntsville, Texas, in 1873. He had never served in any official capacity, except as justice of the peace, until his appointment by Governor Coke as one of the directors of the Huntsville Penitentiary, in which capacity he served until his appointment by Governor Hubbard as Superintendent of the Penitentiary, at Huntsville, in the year 1877. He has been successively appointed to this responsible position by Governors Roberts, Ireland and Ross; his appointment under so many successive administrations being an approved testimonial of his efficiency. In the spring of 1861, he went to Virginia, in company with Colonels Frank Terry and Thomas Lubbock, and with them served as a scout for the Command of General G. T. Beauregard. On the eighteenth of July, 1861, he was appointed aid-de-camp on the staff of

THOS. J. GOREE.

General James Longstreet, which position he held during the entire war. He parcipated in nearly all the great battles of the Virginia campaign; viz: Manassas, Williamsburg, Seven Pines, Seven Days Before Richmond, Sharpsburg, Fredricksburg, Gettysburg, The Wilderness, Appomatox, in fact covering the whole march of the active corps of Gen. Longstreet to the close of the war. He was a citizen of Walker county at the time of his first appointment in charge of the State Penitentiary, and now resides at Huntsville. the county seat of that county, in the house—at one time occupied by General Sam Houston. He was married to Miss Eliza T. Nolley, formerly of Mississippi, June 25, 1868, and has a family of three children. He is a Democrat in politics, a member of the Missionary Baptist church, a Mason and a Knight of Honor. He is of florid complexion, and of dignified manners, possessing the marks that by nature and education give him distinction. He might not be said to be socially magnetic, neither is he repulsive, but possesses strong purpose and solidity of character that give a growing intensity to friendship. He has fine executive ability, and bears, into society and business life, the air of natural dignity that commands respect. In physique, he is an average specimen of the American gentleman—compact, rotund, of good figure, and a smoothly shaven face.

WILLIAM P. HARDEMAN.

SUPERINTENDENT OF PUBLIC BUILDINGS AND GROUNDS.

THE prominent chapter in the history of the life of General Hardeman is his record as a soldier. While his secular occupation has been that of the farmer, to which he was brought up, the salient fact of his long and eventful career has been his military service. He came to Texas in 1835 as a soldier, and when the Alamo massacre was pending, and the appeal of Travis was published, with the conditions that there would be neither retreat nor surrender, young Hardeman, with others, answered the call, but too late to prevent the slaughter. He served under Deaf Smith in 1837, and in following years, in various campaigns against the Indians. In 1846, he served also in the war with Mexico, under Colonel Hays. His service in the war between the States, was in the Trans-Mississippi Department of the Southern army. He entered at the beginning as a captain, and came home at the close, having the title of Brigadier-General. His public service has been limited to that of a member of the Secession Convention, and an appointment under Governor Ross to the Superintendency of Public Buildings and Grounds. He was educated at Nashville University, Tennessee, but did not complete his course. He has been three times married, his present wife being Mrs. Mary Campbell, *nee* Miss Mary Collins, to whom he was married in February, 1874. He is a Royal Arch Mason. General Hardeman is of Irish descent, born in Williamson county, Tennessee, on November 4, 1816, six feet high, weighs one hundred and forty pounds avoirdupois, has dark auburn hair, now turned gray, a fair complexion, blue eyés, and belongs to that class of old Texans whose warm hearts and ardent friendship have not been frozen out by the new order of things.

HENRY MARCUS HOLMES.

EXECUTIVE SECRETARY.

THE Private Secretary of Governor Ross, is an American by adoption and naturalization, and an Englishman by nativity. Judge Holmes was born in England on the ninth of December, 1836, and landed in Texas, October 25, 1850. He is a lawyer by profession, being educated partly in Europe, and partly in America. Mr. Holmes was in the United States army at the beginning of the war between the States, and participated in the engagement at Val Verde, New Mexico, and thereafter at the battle of Fredericksburg, and continued in the regular cavalry brigade till the third day of the battle of the Wilderness, where he was taken prisoner. Regaining his liberty by exchange of prisoners in August, 1864, he remained in the army until the surrender of General Lee. Soon after Mr. Holmes landed in America, friendless, penniless, a foreigner, and a youthful invalid, he became the *protege* of Captain and Mrs. Ross, the father and mother of the Governor incumbent, which fact accounts for both gratitude and intimacy. His wife was Miss Lucia Sheldon, of Rhode Island, to whom he was married in 1865. His religious proclivities are with the Episcopal church. He has filled the office of justice of the peace and county judge, is affable and obliging in his manners, has a keen blue eye, and a physical development according to the best classes of the English type.

STEPHEN HEARD DARDEN.

CHIEF CLERK OF THE COMPTROLLER'S OFFICE.

AS a resident, a citizen and public officer, Colonel Darden is distinctively an old Texan. His entrance into Texas was as a volunteer soldier from the State of Mississippi, under Captain David M. Fulton, in the year 1836. In 1841, he became permanently established as a citizen of Texas. He is of English-Irish descent, and a native of Mississippi. He was raised as a farmer's boy, and was educated in the common schools of the country, and at Cumberland College, Kentucky, where he completed his course, except the languages. He served as an officer in the war between the States, being noted for his gallantry and reliability. His last service was the command of a regiment on the coast of Texas. His political history embraces service in the legislative halls of the State, a Congressman to the Confederate Congress, Comptroller of the State of Texas for three terms. Superintendent of Public Buildings and Grounds. and, under Mr. McCall's administration as Comptroller, has received the appointment of Chief Clerk. His connection with the civil departments dates, perhaps, farther back than that of any man now living, having served as a clerk in the office of the Comptroller under the Provisional Government of the Republic of Texas in September, 1836. He is physically tall and well proportioned. The movement of his mind is not quick, but meditative and profound. He studies for causes. He is fair-minded and has a keen sense of justice. He is pleasant in his manners, and possesses an obliging disposition, that insures for him the friendship of the masses.

JOHN T. DICKINSON.

SECRETARY OF THE CAPITOL BUILDING COMMISSIONERS.

JOHN T. DICKINSON, Secretary of the Capitol Building Commissioners, also Clerk of the Capitol Board and Penitentiary Board, was born in the City of Houston, June 18, 1858, where his family have lived for the past fifty years. He attended school while a boy in England and Scotland. From the age of thirteen to sixteen he was employed in the general freight and passenger department of Houston and Texas Central Railway. at Houston. He then went to college in Virginia, taking the degree of Bachelor of Law, at the University of Virginia, when he was twenty-one years of age, having graduated in several of the academic schools of that institution, and being for some time editor of the *University Magazine*. He then returned to Houston, Texas, secured his license to practice law, but soon engaged in the newspaper business. In January, 1881, coming to Austin, he was elected Journal Clerk of the Seventeenth Legislature. In the summer of 1881 he was selected by a committee of the citizens of Austin, to make a canvass of the State, visiting forty towns, in behalf of the City of Austin for the location of the State University, which was decided by a popular vote at a special election on September 6, 1881. He again served as Journal Clerk at the called session of the Seventeenth Legislature, in May, 1882, and, when that body created the office of Secretary of the Capitol Building Commissioners, he was, on the tenth of May, 1882, appointed to the position by the five heads of State Departments constituting the State Capitol Board. Since his appointment in May, 1882, Mr. Dickinson has, under both Governors Roberts and Ireland, acted as clerk of various State boards, of which they were President, keeping all papers and accounts and making the reports of these boards to the Legislature, in addition to his regular duties under the law as Secretary of the Capitol Building Commissioners and as Clerk of the Capitol and the Penitentiary Boards.

R. L. WALKER.

SUPERINTENDENT OF CONSTRUCTION OF STATE CAPITOL.

GENERAL R. L. WALKER, Superintendent of Construction of the new State Capitol building, was born in Albemarle county, Virginia, May 29, 1828. He graduated at the Virginia Military Institute at Lexington, and engaged in engineering and railroad pursuits until the outbreak of the civil war, when he enlisted in the Confederate service as captain of artillery, being promoted in that service, until at the close of the war he was General commanding the Third Corps of Artillery of the army of Northern Virginia. After the war, General Walker resumed the pursuit of railway engineering and superintendence of railroads, and while thus engaged, and also in superintending the construction of public works in Richmond, Virginia, he was called by the State Capital Board to superintend the construction of the new State Capitol of Texas, and assumed the duties of this position February 10, 1884.

M. H. McLAURIN.

CAPITOL BUILDING COMMISSIONER.

MR. M. H. McLAURIN, one of the Capitol Building Commissioners, was born in Sumter, Sumter county, South Carolina, March 26, 1849, where he was engaged in engineering. He came to Austin, Texas, June 8, 1882, where he followed his profession as an engineer. He was soon afterwards appointed as superintendent to reconstruct the Temporary Capitol building, and to finish the construction of the State sewer. He was then appointed by Governor Ireland to superintend the erection of the North Texas Insane Asylum, at Terrell, which being completed under his superintendence, he was shortly afterwards, on the seventh of April, 1885, appointed by the State Capitol Board as one of the Capitol Building Commissioners.

JOSEPH LEE.

CAPITOL BUILDING COMMISSIONER.

JUDGE JOSEPH LEE, one of the Capitol Building Commissioners, was born near Hamilton, Butler county, Ohio, on the fourteenth of April, 1810, and came to Texas in Feruary, 1840, stopping a short time at Houston, and then coming to Austin, where he has since resided. He is a Texas veteran, and during his long career in Texas, has been identified with a great many of the principal events that have occurred in the State, from its earliest history to the present time, and has filled with fidelity and ability several official positions of honor and trust.

UNITED STATES SENATORS.

RICHARD COKE.

FEW men are more generally known in the United States than the subject of this notice. He was, by his manhood and elements of mind and heart, specially fitted for the responsible positions he has been called upon to fill.

He is a native of Virginia, and was born at Williamsburg, March 13, 1829. William and Mary College was his *alma mater*. Graduating with honor at the age of twenty, he took his first degree in law at the age of twenty-one. Soon after doing so, moving to the State of Texas, he opened a law office in Waco, where he still resides, and continued in the active practice of law, except when called to other public service. As a young man, he was characterized by habits of soberness, energy and industry. His integrity and ability very early gave him an honorable standing in his profession, and marked success attended him.

His nativity, association and education directed his political alliance, consequently he early enlisted in the service of the Southern Confederacy. He served honorably as a soldier. After the close of the war, his legal ability was in demand. In 1865 he was appointed District Judge. He presided with much ability. His superior attainments as a judge of law led to his early promotion as a Justice of the Supreme Court. The United States military usurpation led to his arbitrary removal, as his incumbency could not be expected to add to the tyranny of "reconstruction." His ability and justice, while on the bench at this trying epoch in the State's history, so impressed itself on the public mind as to lead to his successful entrance upon high civil trusts.

In the memorable session of the Thirteenth Legislature he took high rank among the many able and patriotic men of that body. At that session important amendments to the Constitution were passed. Then followed the organization of the Democratic party, and the formulating of a platform of principles, which was adopted at a State Convention in Austin in 1873. This Convention expressed its preferences for standard-bearers by nominating Judge Coke for Governor, and R. B. Hubbard for Lieutenant-Governor. They were elected by about 50,000 majority. This will of the people of Texas was sought to be defeated by the military government under Governor Davis, and through the Supreme Court of this revolutionary government, proceedings were instituted and a decision reached declaring the election null and void. and Governor Davis issued his order prohibiting the assemblage of the Fourteenth Legislature and reconvening the defunct Thirteenth. The latter, with the Davis so-called administration, occupied the lower floor of the capitol, and Governor Coke and the former occupied the upper floor. Governor Davis appealed to Grant, President of the United

States, who sent him soldiers to enforce the unconstitutional rule.

The Fourteenth Legislature elect counted the vote for Governor and Lieutenant-Governor, and put the machinery of State government in motion, peacefully ignoring the Davis administration. Governor Coke refused every proposition of compromise, and even seeming recognition of the Davis faction, and held a firm hold upon his constitutional rights and power.

General Grant, to his honor, upon learning the facts, said that it was an iniquitous conspiracy against constitutional authority, as expressed by a majority of freemen, and refused further interference. This was the death-knell to the Davis power. In this the prudence and wisdom of Governor Coke stood forth with majestic power, by averting civil war.

A writer in the *Texian*, thus epitomizes the sequences of the Davis collapse of power: "Everything was left in chaos; the State liabilities were unknown; evidences of indebtedness were multiplying continually; taxes were in many cases uncollected; the State credit was at a low ebb, and government warrants were hawked on the streets and sold at a heavy discount."

The Chief Executive was equal to the the position and exigencies of the crisis. His sound judgment, legal acumen and financial ability suggested plans, the execution of which led to successful financial results. His firmness in these matters of State had to combat even legislative opposition of no small proportions. He exercised his executive power with prudence, boldness and independence, till finally his measures triumphed to his honor and the augmenting of his political influence and power. He had the wisdom and forethought to know and teach that all the then existing evils could not be corrected short of calling a constitutional convention under the laws then existing. Through that convention, which was called into being, are we indebted for the present State Constitution and its prosperous workings. A general election was at once ordered, and resulted in the re-election of Coke and Hubbard by 100,000 majority and the adoption of the Constitution by nearly the same vote.

The State of Texas needed his services in the Congress of the United States. In 1876, he was elected to the United States Senate.

At the expiration of his first term, he was re-elected to a second term to Congress. So acceptable is his course in Congress, and such his great influence as a Senator, the indications are that he will be his own successor for a number of terms to come. Upon the great leading questions of the day he holds, and aids to enforce, true Democratic principles. He is an honored leader from a national standpoint.

JOHN H. REAGAN.

THE highest type of American citizenship is not aboriginal. The discovery of the New World was a universal bid for the best talent and divinest energy among the nations of the earth. As a result, learning, science, industry, invention and statesmanship, have kept pace with the vanguards of modern civilization elsewhere. Real genius is often obscured for want of opportunity. Distinction is im-

Members of Congress from Texas.

possible to all who merit it. It is often accidental—rarely ever misapplied. Senator Reagan has won distinction—he has merited it; it has not been to him accidental. He is, by lineal descent, of Irish ancestry; he was born in Sevier county, Tennessee, on the eighth of day of October, 1818. He began his education at the academy at Sevierville, in his native county, and afterwards concluded his course at the Southwestern Seminary, in that State.

Judge Regan's career through life has touched the experiences of the farmer, the jurist and the statesman. He began his public life as a deputy surveyor in Nacogdoches and Houston land districts—serving from the winter of 1839, four years consecutively. In 1842, he was elected justice of the peace and captain of a military company. In the following year he commanded a company ordered out to suppress the war between the moderators and regulators in Shelby county. His next publicservice was in the office of Probate Judge, in 1846, at which time he was also made colonel of the malitia of Henderson county. He served as a member of the Second Legislature of the State of Texas, being elected in 1847. He was chosen District Judge of the Ninth Judicial District in 1852. In 1856, he resigned his judgship,and was subsequently re-elected. His Congressional career began with the Thirty-fifth Congress of the United States, his election taking place in 1857. He was also a member of the Thirty-sixth Congress. In 1861, he was elected by the Secession Convention, of which he was a member, to the Provisional Congress of the Confederacy. In March, 1861, under the Provisional Government of the Confederate States, President Jeff. Davis appointed Judge Reagan Postmaster-General. When the Constitutional Government was organized, he was continued in this office by appointment in February, 1862. The additional duties of Acting Secretary of the Treasury were assigned to him by appointment in 1865. After the surrender of General Lee, Judge Reagan returned to his home in Texas, and in 1874 was returned by his constituency to membership in the United States Congress. Serving in the Forty-fourth Congress, he has been successively re-elected to the Forty-fifth, Forty-sixth, Forty-seventh, Forty-eighth, Forty-ninth and the Fiftieth. The Twentieth Legislature of the State of Texas added, perhaps, the last laurel that it is reasonable to expect will adorn his brow. He was elected to the high office of United States Senator. His service in Congress has been attended with remarkable success. The Interstate Commerce Bill originated with Judge Reagan, and, it is believed, owes its passage to his indefatigable labors. His position in the United States Senate will not be a shame and a reproach to his State. He is a member of the Methodist Episcopal Church South, and also a Mason. having membership as high as the Commandery. His wife was Miss Hollie F. Taylor, daughter of John F. Taylor, Esq., of Anderson county, Texas. He is a man of remarkable physical constitution, and needs only to be seen, to command the respect, and even the veneration, of the masses. Long and continued service in the interest of his State has not only given to him a vast store of knowledge, but has broadened his statesmanship into national fame. He is one of the best orators of his day, and the peer of his associates in the legislative halls of the nation.

MEMBERS OF CONGRESS.

CHARLES STEWART.

CHARLES STEWART, of Houston, was born at Memphis, Tennessee, May 30, 1836; is by profession a lawyer; was elected to the Forty-eighth Congress, and was re-elected to the Forty-ninth Congress, as a Democrat, receiving 24,145 votes against 15 votes scattering. Re-elected. He represents the First District, composed of the counties of Angelina, Brazos, Chambers, Grimes, Hardin, Harris. Jasper, Jefferson, Liberty, Madison, Montgomery, Newton, Orange, Polk, San Jacinto, Trinity, Tyler, Walker, and Waller.

Mr. Stewart is an able and successful member of the Texas bar, and in his political career has met the expectations of his admiring friends.

Members of Congress from Texas.

C. B. KILGORE.

THIS distinguished gentleman, who is now Congressman elect from the Third Congressional District of the State of Texas, composed of the counties of Camp, Gregg, Harrison, Hunt, Panola, Rains, Rusk, Shelby, Smith, Upshur, Van Zandt, and Wood, is a native of Newnan, Georgia, born on the twentieth of February, 1835.

His father immigrated to Texas in 1846, while the subject of this notice was but a lad. Mr. Kilgore received his education at Henderson, in Rusk county, Texas. By profession, he is a lawyer. Having a natural aptitude to the study and practice of the law, his success was noticeable and marked from the beginning. He has shared largely in the confidence of the public, and is a strong and influential practitioner at the bar. Mr. Kilgore entered the war between the States, under General Sterling Price and General Van Dorn, and remained with them until after the battle of Elk Horn. He then went into the Cis-Mississippi Department, and under General Kirby Smith, participated in the famous Kentucky campaign. Perryville, Murfreesboro, Jackson, the fall of Vicksburg, Chickamauga—at which place he received a severe wound—were among the principal battles in which he was engaged. He rose in military rank to that of captain and was also adjutant-general of Ector's brigade. His political career began by election to the office of justice of the peace in 1869. In 1875, he was a member of the Constitutional Convention. In the year 1880, he was a Democratic elector on the Presidential ticket of Hancock and English. He was elected by a handsome majority to the Senate of the Nineteenth Legislature of the State of Texas, and was made president pro tem., which office he held for two years, ending January 11, 1887. He was also chairman of the Committee on Constitutional Amendments. Having received the nomination for Congress, by the Democratic convention of September, 1886, he

Members of Congress from Texas.

resigned his place in the State Senate, leaving two years of his term unexpired. At the November election of 1886, he received a majority of 9,336 votes—his term of office as Congressman beginning on the fourth of March, 1887. Judge Kilgore is a member of the Presbyterian Church (old school), belongs to the Masonic fraternity, and is also a Knight of Honor. In 1858, he was married to Miss Fanny Barnett, daughter of Major Slade Barnett, of Rusk county, Texas, and has a family of seven children, six of whom are daughters. He possesses by nature a rich endowment of the elements of personal popularity, and has won in the political fortunes of the State an enviable share. Successful in the law, attractive in public oratory, broad in comprehension of the needs of the people, and trusted by his constituents, his advance in statesmanship has been proportionably manifested as he has been promoted in office.

DAVID B. CULBERSON.

DAVID B. CULBERSON, re-elected from the Fourth District, composed of the following counties, to-wit: Bowie, Cass, Delta, Fannin, Franklin, Hopkins, Lamar, Marion, Morris, Red River and Titus, was born in Troup county, Georgia, September 29, 1830; was educated at Brownwood, LaGrange, Georgia; studied law under Chief Justice Chilton, of Alabama; removed to Texas in 1856, and was elected a member of the Legislature of that State in 1859; entered the Confederate Army as a private, and was promoted to the rank of colonel of the Eighteenth Texas Infantry; was assigned to duty, in 1864, as Adjutant-General, with the rank of colonel, of the State of Texas; was elected to the State Legislature in 1864; was elected to the Forty-fourth, Forty-fifth, Forty-sixth, Forty-seventh and Forty-eighth Congresses, and was re-elected to the Forty-ninth Congress, as a Democrat, receiving 23,165 votes against no opposition. Re-elected from the Fourth District.

Few men are more richly endowed by nature than the eloquent Congressman from the Fourth District in Texas. Education and a long and varied experince in public life, have added largely to the store of his knowledge, and qualified him to be a leader of the people. His reputation has grown with the years of his public life, and his thorough knowledge of the wants of the State inspire an implicit confidence in him. Successive re-election to the high and trusted office he now holds is the people's testimonial of his worth. His congressional career has attracted public attention in and out of his own State, giving to him a national reputation as well as an approval by his constituents.

WILLIAM H. CRAIN.

WILLIAM H. CRAIN, re-elected from the Seventh District, composed of the counties of Aransas, Bee, Brazoria, Calhoun, Cameron, Dimmit, De Witt, Duval, Encinal, Fort Bend, Frio, Galveston, Goliad, Hidalgo, Jackson, La Salle, Matagorda, Maverick, McMullen, Nueces, Refugio, San Patricio, Starr, Victoria, Webb, Wharton, Zapata, and Zavala, of Cureo, Texas, was born at Galveston, Texas, November 25, 1848; graduated at Saint Francis Xavier's

College, New York City, July 1, 1867, and received the degree of A. M. several years afterwards; studied law in the office of Stockdale & Proctor, Indianola, and was admitted to practice in February, 1871; has practiced law since that time; was elected a State Senator on the Democratic ticket in February, 1876; was elected as the Democratic candidate for district attorney of the Twenty-third Judicial District of Texas, in November, 1872; and was elected to the Forty-ninth Congress as a Democrat, receiving 15,471 votes, against 9,586 votes for R. B. Renfro, Republican, and 1,032 votes for Richard Nelson, colored, Republican.

The youthful Texan, who is making himself distinguished in Congress from the Seventh District of Texas, is furnished with a thor•ugh collegiate drill. This advantage has not been bankrupted in dishonor. As a lawyer in the regular practice, he was the peer of the chiefest. Both his management and tactics in conducting his cases gave him a high place in the esteem of the people, and his eloquent pleadings at the bar made him a favorite. He ranks with the first orators of the State. His ability and personal popularity give him victory over opposition that may take shape and make active resistance in his district. His hold upon the people is strong, and his record, as a Congressman, has given it intensity. He is esteemed as one of the foremost Statesmen of Texas.

Members of Congress from Texas.

ROGER Q. MILLS.

ROGER Q. MILLS, of Corsicana, was elected to the Forty-third, Forty-fourth, Forty-fifth, Forty-sixth, Forty-seventh and Forty-eighth Congresses, and was re-elected to the Forty-ninth Congress as a Democrat, receiving 22,333 votes against 9,049 votes for Osterhout, Republican. Re-elected from the Ninth District, composed of Bell, Burleson, Falls, Limestone, McLennan, Milam, Navarro, and Washington counties. Mr. Mills is an average specimen of Southern manhood. In stature, bodily development and natural physique, he is a man of model type. In intellect he ranks with the great men of his State, and of the country. His mental habitudes are analytical. Logical in every part of his speeches, his conclusions are well-nigh irrefutable. Long experience in national politics has familiarized him with all the living, current questions of the day, and made him a master in debate. His popularity throughout the State is an honor accorded to but few. In his Congressional district, he is first as the choice of the people. He is fearless in expressing what he believes to be right, and is true to convictions and the best lights he has at a given time. In Congress, he is recognized as a man of marked ability and among the best representatives from the South.

Members of Congress from Texas.

SAMUEL W. T. LANHAM.

SAMUEL W. T. LANHAM, of Weatherford, was born in Spartanburg District, South Carolina, July 4, 1846; received only a common-school education; entered the Confederate Army (Third South Carolina Regiment) when a boy; removed to Texas in 1866; studied law, and was admitted to practice in 1869; was district attorney of the Thirteenth District of Texas; was democratic elector of the Third Congressional District of Texas in 1880; was elected to the Forty-eighth Congress and was re-elected to the Forty-ninth Congress as a Democrat, receiving 29,738 votes against 184 for Saylor, Republican. Re-elected from the Eleventh District, composed of the counties of Andrews, Armstrong, Bailey, Borden, Briscoe, Brown, Callahan, Carson, Castro, Childress, Cochran, Collingsworth, Comanche, Coryell, Cottle, Crosby, Dallam, Dawson, Deaf Smith, Dickens, Donley, Eastland, El Paso, Erath, Fisher, Floyd, Gaines, Garza, Gray, Greer, Hale, Hall, Hamilton, Hansford, Hardeman, Hartley, Haskell, Hemphill, Hockley, Hood, Howard, Hutchinson, Jack, Jones, Kent, King, Knox, Lamb, Lipscomb, Lubbock, Lynn, Martin, Midland, Mitch-

Members of Congress from Texas.

ell, Moore, Motley, Nolan, Ochiltree, Oldham, Palo Pinto, Parker, Parmer, Pecos, Porter, Presidio, Randall, Reeves, Roberts, Scurry, Shackelford, Sherman, Somervilie, Stephens, Stonewall, Swisher, Taylor, Terry, Tom Green, Throckmorton, Val Verde, Wheeler, Yoakum, and Young—83 counties.

An Empire of territory is embraced in Mr. Lanham's district. About half of the eighty-three counties in his district are unorganized, any two of which cover an area equal to an average State. Mr. Lanham deserves great credit for his successful struggle against stubborn difficulties. He is self-educated, and is now an untiring student. For a time, he taught school as a stepping-stone to the practice of the law. In his profession, he has been eminently successful. Not only as a judge of law, is he eminent, but as a pleader and advocate at the bar, he is well nigh resistless. His eloquence is impassioned, his words well chosen, and his elocution almost faultless. He is small in physical stature, of rotund bodily contour, and of a restful movement. Genial in the most commendable degree, he both entertains his friends in pleasing conversation, and is himself entertained by them. He has shown, in his Congressional course, the same indomitable purpose to excel that has so saliently marked his entire history. But few men have labored harder, done more, and risen in the esteem of the nation faster, during the same length of time at the beginning of Congressional service, than has this cultivated gentleman. Mr. Lanham is nature's child, under the dominating influence of education and an unconquerable ambition to excel.

JOSEPH D. SAYERS.

JOSEPH D. SAYERS, of Bastrop, was born at Grenada, Mississippi, September 23, 1841; removed with his father to Bastrop, Texas, in 1851; was educated at the Bastrop Military Institute; entered the Confederate Army in 1861 and served continuously until April, 1865; when the war terminated, taught school and at the same time studied law at Bastrop, Texas; was admitted to the bar in 1866, and became a partner of Hon. George W. Jones; served as a member of the State Senate in the session of 1873; was chairman of the Democratic State Executive Committee during the years 1875-1878; was Lieutenant-Governor of Texas in 1879 and 1880; and was elected to the Forty-ninth Congress as a Democrat, receiving 21,523 votes against 12,253 votes for John B. Rector, Independent. Re-elected. He represents the Tenth District, composed of the counties of Bandera, Bastrop, Bexar, Blanco, Burnet, Coleman, Comal, Concho, Crockett, Edwards, Gillespie, Kendall, Kerr, Kimball, Kinney, Lampasas, Llano, McCulloch, Mason, Medina, Menard, Runnels, San Saba, Travis, Uvalde and Williamson.

For fifteen years past, Mr. Sayers has been a prominent

figure in the politics of the State of Texas. He is recognized as a profound thinker and an adept in political economy. His service as State Senator in the year 1873 brought him prominently before the leading men of the State, while his reputation as a lawyer extended far beyond the limits of the bar he was accustomed to attend. The relation between himself and his constituency is not cold and official, but vital and ardent. His popularity is attested by the very complimentary vote he received from his district, and the tokens of recognition received in return from him. He is a fine, logical speaker and strong in polemical discussion. In Congress he is not a mere figure, but a member whose influence is felt. He is too broad to be sectional in his record, and too true to his State to see her interests slaughtered without a manly resistance.

STATE SENATORS.

LEONARD ANDERSON ABERCROMBIE.

BROADLY educated and of profound legal acquirements, Senator Abercrombie at once took an enviable place in the legislative halls of the State of Texas. He was elected State Senator in November, 1886, and his entrance into the arena of polemical and parliamentary war has made a favorable impression as to his present skill and previous preparation. He was a member of the following committees, viz: Judiciary Committee No. 1, Education, Finance, and others.

He has been successful in the practice of his profession, and has won laurels as a Texas legislator. He is fifty-one years of age, a native of Alabama, and has been thirty-one years in the State of Texas. He is not impulsive nor impatient, but gives evidence of real refinement, is a fine speaker, close reasoner, and a safe legislator.

WILLIAM ALLEN.

KENTUCKY contributes to the Twentieth Legislature of the State of Texas a model specimen of American manhood, physically, morally, and intellectually, in the person of her gifted son. Honorable William Allen.

Senator Allen was born in Barren county, Kentucky, March 18, 1835. He begun his education in his native State, and has gone through the college curriculum. He has been an educator; he is now engaged in farming and stock raising. In literature this distinguished gentleman has taken a reputable part. He is author of "Five Years in the West," and of "The South no Dishonored Realm," in

MS., besides being a contributor to some of the ablest periodicals of the country.

Since the year 1860 he has been a minister of the gospel, a member of the Methodist Episcopal Church South, filling the positions of Trustee of Southwestern University, delegate to several Annual Conferences, to the General Conference of 1882, and other important places. He is also a member of the Masonic fraternity. After two years service as a soldier under General Dick Taylor, in the war between the States, in which he fairly vindicated his Jeffersonian Democracy, Mr. Allen was given a chaplaincy in the army. His first appearance in political life was as Senator from the Seventeenth Senatorial District, composed of Collin county and Denton, to which position he was elected by a majority of 1050 votes. He was chairman of the Committee on Agricultural Affairs, and served as a member on others of importance. He married Miss Abbie, the accomplished daughter of Dr. R. B. Mayes, of Collin county, Texas. Senator Allen has made a fine reputation as a wise legislator, and commands the respect of the Senate. Having the elements of a worthy character, his social attractions are strong, and his influence like the silent forces which operate so mightly in nature.

C. K. BELL.

C. K. BELL was born in Chattanooga, Tennessee, on the eighth of April, 1853, and came to Texas in 1871. He established himself in Belton, Bell county, where he remained till 1874, and during that year, removed to Hamilton, where he now resides. Senator Bell obtained license to practice law in 1874, and by his studious habits and discrete management of the cases under his charge, soon won recognition as a talented rising young lawyer in the west. He was elected district attorney of the Thirtieth judicial district, which gave him an enlarged field for the encouragement of his aspirations and the proof of his abilities. In 1884, he was elected State Senator from the Twenty-third senatorial district, composed of Bell, Coryell, Lampasas and Hamilton counties. He served in the Nineteenth Legislature as chairman of the Committees on General Land Office and Engrossed Bills, and as a member of other important committees. In the Twentieth Legislature, he at once took a prominent place, and was held to be a brilliant star in the political constellation of the West. He is thoroughly educated, and gentlemanly in his parliamentary and social intercourse. Senator Bell is a member of the Episcopal Church, and also of the fraternity of Ancient, Free and Accepted Masons. He was educated at Sewanee, at the University of the South, and has had, in his professional service, the advantage of thorough culture.

ROBERT HENRY BURNEY.

SENATOR BURNEY'S ancestry runs back into English citizenship. In the early settlement of America, this family made its appearance in Virginia and North Carolina, and subsequently in Tennessee. In McNary county, of that State, on the twenty-second of October, 1854, Robert Henry was born. In 1856, his father, Judge H. M. Burney, immigrated to Kerr county, Texas, where he still lives, having served as one of the first judges of the county. Senator Burney is the eldest of nine brothers composing the filial part of the household. Brought to Texas when he was an infant, he was primarily educated in this State. He was a student at Southwestern University, Georgetown, Texas, where in 1876 he was recognized as leading the mathematical class, having won a gold medal as a testimonial, and at the commencement of the following year, bore off the palm of oratory. In 1878 he took the degree of A. B., and the following year received the degree of Bachelor of Laws at the Vanderbilt University, Nashville, Tennessee. He joined the State Rangers under Captain Neal Caldwell in the spring of 1874, and appropriated the earnings of this service to his education. The hardship of ranger life on the frontier brought him into actual sympathy with the out-post structure of Texas society and the frontier people. Professionally he is a lawyer, at one time partner with Judge T. P. Hughs, of Georgetown, Texas, and now a prominent member of the bar at Kerrville, where he resides. His district (the Twenty-eighth Senatorial) is composed of sixteen counties, embracing an area of over 63,000 square miles. As a senator in the Twentieth Legislature of the State of Texas, he makes his *debut* in the political arena of the State by a popular majority of over 11,000 votes. He is chairman of the Committee on Public Printing, and a member of Judiciary No. 2, Educational and Internal Improvements, and five others, and for his promptness and urbanity of manners in general committee work, has received compliments from his fellow members. On the thirtieth day of September, 1879, he was married to Miss Mattie Prather of Palestine, Texas, and has a family of two children. He is of slender figure physically, weighing on an average one hundred and forty-five pounds, and being six feet in stature. He has a fiery hazel eye and is of fair countenance. As an orator, he is vehement in speech and logical and concise in diction and argument. He is fortunately endowed by nature with psychic affinities, which make his friendship ardent, and his influence over his fellow men controlling. He is true to his convictions of right, but not inflexible to the counsel of his friends. To the suavity of manners which is nature's gift, has been super-added the polish of classical drill, giving him advantages that may well be coveted. The pang of ingratitude he is incapable of inflicting, and is open-hearted and frank in rewarding the aid that has in any way contributed to his welfare.

He is a close student, an inveterate worker and prompt in attendance at the sessions of the Senate.

Though young in legislative circles, he has grown rapidly in the confidence and appreciation of his constituents and fellow-members, and deservedly occupies a foremost place in the Senate.

He is always well informed on every subject of importance before the Senate, and takes an avowed position with a determined purpose.

W. T. ARMISTEAD.

W. T. ARMISTEAD was born in Georgia on the twenty-fifth day of October, 1848. In 1864, he enlisted in the Confederate Army as a private, and participated in the engagements around Atlanta; was wounded at the battle of Jonesboro, Georgia, and was made a prisoner at Girard, Alabama, in the closing days of the war. He had been promoted to a captaincy before his capture. He graduated at the University of Georgia in 1871, and immediately moved to Douglassville, Cass county, Texas, where he taught school, and thence removed to Jefferson, Texas, in 1872, where he still resides, and there began the practice of law in 1873. He has been a delegate to every State Convention since 1874; was elected representative from the Seventeenth District to the Eighteenth Legislature, and re-elected to the Nineteenth with an increased majority. He was elected Senator to the Twentieth Legislature, from the Fourth District, over the Honorable D. T. Hearne, by nearly five thousand majority. He is a successful lawyer and an active, earnest and conscientious legislator. He is a Knight Templar Mason, a member of the Baptist Church, the Legion of Honor, and the Ancient Order of United Workmen.

W. T. ARMISTEAD.

State Senators.

WILLIAM HENRY BURGES.

THE Senator from Guadalupe, Hon. W. H. Burges, is a native of Tennessee; born in Madison county, January 8, 1838, and was chiefly educated in his native State. He has been in Texas thirty-two years. His legal education was acquired at the Law Department of the University of the State of Louisiana. He is a lawyer, and has been successful in securing a large and lucrative practice.

At the time that Judge John Ireland was elected the Chief Magistrate of the State of Texas, Mr. Burges was a member of the law firm of Ireland & Burges, of Seguin, Texas.

During the war between the States he rendered four years' service as a soldier in the famous Hood's Brigade, partipated in most of the engagements led by that officer, and was seriously wounded in the battle of Sharpsburg.

Mr. Burges began public life as county attorney of Guadalupe county, and served with credit to himself and the people. Afterward he was elected district attorney. In 1876 he was a Democratic elector on the presidential ticket in the State of Texas. He was also a member of the Boundary Commission, having in charge the investigation and establishment of the Greer county lines. He has been twice State Senator—his first service having been rendered in the Seventeenth Legislature of the State of Texas. He was elected to the Twentieth Legislature as Senator from the Twenty-fifth district in November, 1886, by a majority of 4951 votes. He has maintained a consistent and rising course in his legislative work, and manifests a deep concern in the great measures brought before the Senate. His district is composed of Hays, Guadalupe, Blanco, Kendall, Comal, Caldwell and Llano counties.

He is chairman of the Committee on Public Debt, and a member of the most important Senate committees. He is not tall, having a tendency to obesity. His hair is black, and his eyes black and piercing, though not large. He is pleasant in his manners, and enjoys the society of his friends. He knows how to be obliging, and how to say "no." He is above the average as a lawyer; a fine speaker, close investigator, an ardent friend, and possesses a good investment of will force. He enjoys a growing reputation as a legislator. He has been three times married—has a family of five children, and is a member of A. F. and A. M.

JAMES HENRY CALHOUN.

THE Calhoun family have a history inseparably interwoven with that of the whole country. More especially has the South learned to appreciate its worth and recognize its value in the mighty current of our great civilization. Under a plain physiological law, operating in heredity, any distinctive characteristics of a family, whether for good or evil, may be expected to appear under favorable conditions along the line of the history of that family. Senator Calhoun is an illustration in point. He is a Georgian, from Troupe county, in that State, born on the seventeenth of January, 1849. His education is collegiate. He graduated from Homer College, at Homer, Louisiana, in 1870. In the following year he moved to Texas, stopping for two years at the city of Waco. While residing there he read law under General Tom Harrison, and was licensed to practice on the eighth day of August, 1873. The following September he settled in Eastland county, and subsequently established himself at Eastland, the county seat, where he now resides. For a while after his admission to the bar, he engaged in the land business, and has proved himself to be an able and successful lawyer. His public life began by his election to the office of county judge of Eastland county. Subsequently he served two terms as district attorney of the Twelfth judicial district. In November of 1884, Judge Calhoun was elected State Senator from the Twenty-ninth

Senatorial district, by a majority of over 5000 votes. His district is composed of twenty-three counties, embracing an area of more than 20,000 square miles. He at once took a prominent place in the Senate of the Nineteenth Legislature, and served as chairman of the committee to investigate the Comptroller's and Treasurer's offices, and as a member of other prominent committees. In the Twentieth Legislature he is chairman of the Committee on Land Office, and also of the special committee for the Relief of the Drouth Sufferers. To him, more than any one else, is the credit due for the $100,000 appropriation to relieve the sufferers in the drouth stricken counties.

As an attorney, he has had a general practice—not having confined himself, from inclination or necessity, to any special branch of the profession. His finely cultured mind and extensive experience and observation, give him a high rank as a State Senator. As an orator, he is impassioned. He speaks with naturalness and ease, and often rises into strains of fiery eloquence, that takes full possession of his auditors. He is a member of the Methodist Episcopal Church, South; also of the Masonic fraternity, and of the Independent Order of Odd Fellows. On January 1, 1882, at Eastland, Texas, he was married to Miss Jennie Conner, and has a family of two children. Senator Calhoun is an average specimen of American manhood. He is five feet ten inches in stature, and turns the scales at 170 pounds. He has a vigilant blue eye that kindles into brilliancy in his happiest moments of public speaking. His hair is black, while his beard is a light brown. He has a florid complexion, and a forehead that is its own witness of indwelling intelligence. While Judge Calhoun is true to his honest convictions of right, he is ready to hear the arguments of those who differ from him. He is a true friend and a generous foe—a lover of the pure and good, and can be touched with a feeling of human suffering.

State Senators.

JOHN LAFAYETTE CAMP, JR.

JOHN LAFAYETTE CAMP, Jr., Senator from the Sixth Senatorial district, is a native of Gilmer, Upshur county, Texas; born September 23, 1855. He attained his manhood and still resides at the place of his nativity. His education was obtained at Trinity University, Tehuacana, Texas, and at the Military Institute at Austin. He entered the legal profession in his native town, and has evinced a high order of talent. In 1884 he was elected to the State Senate without opposition. In the Nineteenth Legislature he was chairman of the Committee on Privileges and Elections, besides serving as a member on several other important committees. In the Twentieth Legislature he was chairman of the Committee on State Affairs and also on Rules. He is one of the youngest and most brilliant of the members of the upper House. He is of small figure, dark blue eyes, black hair, and a complexion of a dark tendency. He is of modest mein and converses freely. He occupies a front place in the young Democracy of the State, and shows great promise for the future.

JNO. M. CLAIBORNE.

JNO. M. CLAIBORNE, a member of the Senate of Texas from the Tenth Senatorial district, composed of the counties of Galveston, Brazoria and Matagorda, was born in the State of Tennessee, February 27, 1839, came to Texas with his father, Colonel Phil. Claiborne, in the early part of the year 1846 and settled in Bastrop county, and was educated at the Bastrop Military Institute and at Baylor University, Independence, Texas. He read law with his father, with a view of practicing the profession, but abandoned the idea to go into commerce and farming, in both of

Yours truly
Jno M. Claiborne

State Senators.

which he is now engaged. He served as clerk in the Comptroller's Office in 1860 and 1861; was both district and county clerk of Bastrop county since the war; was chairman of the State Democratic Executive Committee for two years; was Aide-de-Camp on the staff of Governor Roberts for four years, and Major-General of the Texas Volunteer Guards for three years.

In 1861, at the breaking out of the late war between the States, he left the city of Austin as a private in company D, Terry's Texas Rangers, and was, in 1863, appointed adjutant of the regiment. In July, 1864, he was detached and placed in the secret service department by General John B. Hood, who, on December 14, 1864, promoted him for gallantry in front of Nashville, and recommended him to the War Department for an adutant-generalcy of division with the rank of colonel. He participated in every battle fought by the Army of Tennessee, except while wounded, and bore the last order ever delivered to the lamented Claiborn, General Claiborn having been killed while the order was being delivered, at the battle of Franklin, Tennessee, at 9:50 at night. He received three dangerous and two slight wounds, and lost in action, killed under him, four horses, had two wounded, two being killed in the one engagement at Farmington, Tennessee, 1864, thus speaking louder than words for his gallantry in battle. Yet, with one exception, he has had no personal difficulty since the close of the war.

General Claiborne's popularity is sustained by the overwhelming majority he received over all four of his competitors in his recent election, although from a district Republican by some 450 majority.

He is chairman of one, if not the most, important Senate committees, that of Commerce and Manufactures, and is second on Military Affairs.

General Claiborne is one of the straightest Democrats in the State, and is entirely in accord with the principles of the party.

General Claiborne married Miss Sue M. Phillips, of Kentucky, in 1865. They have three children, two sons, R. Sidney and Tom Jack, and one daughter, Hattie Overton.

General Claiborne has a taste for political and military life, and has manifested the peculiar ability of a successful one. He has a striking and attractive appearance, genial manners, and a *bonus socius* that admits him readily to the people, of whatever occupation or class. He is a man of great general intelligence, and an easy and fluent public speaker.

He is in the prime of life, well known throughout the State, and has the best possibilities ahead of him, and, fortunately for him, he has the laudable ambition and enterprise to take advantage of all his splendid endowments, and is destined to make a conspicuous figure in the political and military history of Texas. His term of office is for four years.

General Claiborne's platform is, that the people are capable of self-government, and that this is "a government of the people, for the people; equal and exact justice: equal privileges to all: exclusive privileges to none."

WILLIAM WALLACE DAVIS.

W. W. DAVIS was born in Houston county, on the fifteenth of March, 1831. His education received only its rudiments in the schools of the county, near his native place. Like all true education, his has been a lifetime work. He is both a farmer and a merchant, and may be said to represent those honorable vocations of our civilization in the Twentieth Legislature of the State of Texas. Senator Davis was a soldier in the late civil war of 1861-5, participating in the battles of Mansfield and Pleasant Hill, Louisiana, and others less sanguinary, elsewhere. He first appears in the political history of the State as a member of the House of Representatives, Fourteenth Legislature of the State of Texas. He was elected Senator from the Eighth Senatorial district by a majority of some 8000 votes. During the Twentieth Legislature he served as chairman of the Committee on Retrenchment and Reform. He is a member of the Methodist Episcopal Church, South, and also of the Masonic fraternity.

Senator Davis is a safe legislator. He is not obtrusive, but solid. There is no lightness in what proceeds from him as a citizen, legislator or member of society. He possesses great moderation, and his manners are easy and natural.

WILLIAM LEVI DOUGLASS.

W. L. DOUGLASS, the subject of this notice, is a Mississippian, born in the year 1853. Senator Douglass came to Texas soon after the close of the war between the States, with the purpose of practicing his chosen profession. He was a member of the House of Representatives in the Seventeenth and also the Eighteenth Legislature of the State of Texas. In 1884 he was elected to the State Senate from the First Senatorial district. In the Nineteenth Legislature he was chairman of the Committee on Military Affairs. In the Twentieth Legislature he served as chairman of the Committee on Public Health, with prominent membership on others. His re-election to legislative honors and service is a well merited endorsement by his constituents.

State Senators.

ELBRIDGE GEARY DOUGLASS.

AMONG the new Senators appearing for the first time in the Twentieth Legislature of the State of Texas, is the Honorable E. G. Douglass, of Grayson county. Mr. Douglass is a farmer, with broad and liberal views of the needs of the people, thoroughly acquainted with the lines of business and trade, and of the necessary legislation required to promote prosperity. He is a native of Missouri, is forty-two years of age, and has been in Texas twenty-eight years. He was prompt and attentive to the business of the Senate, and has fairly and favorably won the confidence and esteem of his co-legislators. He is not especially demonstrative in making speeches, but serves the interests of his constituents more particularly in what he does and how he votes. He is tall and well proportioned in figure, and of good address. He is a member of the following committees, viz: Finance, Penitentiaries, Military Affairs, and chairman of the Committee on Privileges and Elections.

LOUIS NAPOLEON FRANK.

L. N. FRANK, the subject of this brief notice, is a lawyer by profession, and resides at Stephensville, Erath county, Texas. By his fidelity, fine talent and personal popularity in his professional relations to the people, he won in the race for State Senator in the fall of 1886, and is a new and rising member of the Twentieth Legislature of the State of Texas. He is a native of the State of Louisiana, is thirty-seven years of age, and has been in this State thirteen years. Though modest and unobtrusive, he is nevertheless noticeable for the judicious part he takes in legislation. Serving on several important committees, he is also chairman of the Committee on Penitentiaries. He is of average stature and physical developement, having a rather dark complexion, black hair and large hazel eye. He is of a solid character and urbane in his social relations. He attends to the business entrusted to him conscienciously.

SCOTT FIELD.

THE physical appearance of the subject of this sketch tends fairly to the Liliputian type. He is in stature and weight below the average. Though small, he is not frail. Vivacity, and what to the average man would be haste, are natural characteristics of his way. Of dark complexion, dark auburn hair and dark blue eyes, full beard, well trimmed, he is the very impersonation of vigilance. Senator Field is a native of Mississippi, thirty-nine years old, having been a resident of Texas fourteen years. He is a lawyer by profession, thoroughly educated, and enjoys the highest degree of confidence and esteem accorded by the people. No man in the profession visiting the bar in Robertson and adjoining counties is more respected for his ability and noble character than Judge Field. His politeness and refinement show his thorough culture, which supervenes upon the natural gentleman. His first public service is in the office of State Senator in the Twentieth Legislature of the State of Texas. He has fastened himself upon the confidence of his co-legislators. He never retrogrades. The longer he is known, the more he is appreciated. He will contribute honor to the Senate, and when he retires, he will be more admired by that intelligent body than when he came to it. He is chairman of the Committee on Treasurer's and Comptroller's Offices. He is a good judge of law and has had fine success in his profession. Not obtrusive, he is inclined to be reticent, but when the proper time comes for him to be heard, he has something to say, and knows how to say it.

CALEB JACKSON GARRISON.

C. J. GARRISON was born in Carroll county, Georgia, May 31, 1828. In 1851 he immigrated to Texas, and stopped for two years at Caledonia, then established himself at Henderson, Rusk county, where he has since continued to live. In the war between the States he was a member of company K, Fourteenth Texas Infantry, Ector's Brigade, Army of Tennessee. Senator Garrison is a lawyer by profession, having been admitted to the bar in 1855. He has also engaged in farming out of natural fondness for agricultural pursuits. His public life begun as assistant clerk of the Senate, and the following session was elected engrossing clerk. In the same year (1855), he began the practice of law. In 1856 he was elected clerk of Rusk county. He was a member of the House of Representatives in the Fifteenth, the Sixteenth and the Eighteenth Legislatures of the State of Texas. In 1884, he was chosen State Senator from the Second Senatorial district. In the Nineteenth Legislature he was chairman of the Committee on Insurance, Statistics and History. In the Twentieth Legislature he was chairman of the Committee on Penitentiaries, and during his entire legislative career has given efficient aid to various important committees. He is a member of the Methodist Episcopal Church, South, and of Ancient, Free and Accepted Masons. He is a gentleman of liberal education and solid character. His age, experience in public affairs, and knowledge of the wants of the people give him great consideration and respect among his co-legislators. He is above the average in stature, spare, black hair, dark blue eyes, and has a pleasant, sedate countenance.

G. W. GLASSCOCK.

GEORGE WASHINGTON GLASSCOCK.

G. W. GLASSCOCK, from the Twenty-Fourth Senatorial district, is a native of Travis county, Texas, and born in the month of January, 1846. He left his native county less than ten years ago and settled at Georgetown, the county seat of Williamson county. He is a lawyer by profession, and has had a good degree of success and gained recognition for his talent at the bar. He served during the war between the States in Colonel Duff's regiment, Twenty-third Texas Cavalry. In public service he has been county attorney, county judge, and State Senator. In the Nineteenth Legislature he was chairman of the Committee on Public Grounds and Buildings, and also served as a member of other important committees. He is, in the Twentieth Legislature, chairman of the Committee on Education, besides serving on other committees as a member. His legislative record is a voluminous as well as a good one, having introduced or assisted in the passage of many important bills. The following are a few of the most important, selected from a long list, to-wit: "An act to better enable cities and incorporated towns to utilize their convict labor;" "An amendment to the road law, simplifying it and relieving it of its cumbersome machinery under precinct overseers and jury of view, by putting it under one overseer and the commissioners' court;" "An amendment to the fence law;" "An act to prevent limitation to adverse possession of streets in towns and cities;" "An act in certain cases to authorize the extension of time for the filing of statements of fact;" "An act to regulate architecture;" "An act to regulate pharmacy;" "An act to provide for the revison of the civil and criminal code;" "An act to provide for the payment of jury commissioners for services rendered;" "An act to give pasture owners a lien on stock grazed therein;" "An act to more correctly define the Sunday law;" and "An act to make it a penal offense to officiate in the ceremonies of illegal marriages, or to fail to return marriage licenses within a specified time."

Senator Glasscock is a member of the Missionary Baptist Church, is an Odd Fellow, and a Knight Templar Mason. He is a matter-of-fact man. He does not deal in speculation so much as statistics; facts of reality go further with him than figures of rhetoric. He is a stout man, of very decided character, of florid complexion and gentlemanly manners. As a financier he has justly merited distinction, while no man shares in a higher degree the confidence of his constituents for reliability and trustworthiness. In politics, as in business, he is a man of his word. As county judge of of Williamson county he was immensely popular and became much loved by the people. In the Senate, he is recognized as a tower of strength, and his views and opinions carry with them a controling weight.

Judge Glasscock was married to Miss J. H. Boatner, of Anderson county, Texas, in March, 1865. He has accumulated a good fortune, and resides in Georgetown, Texas.

ALEXANDER WHITE GREGG.

OF an amiable and generous turn of mind, this distinguished gentleman and Senator holds justly and meritoriously a high place in the Twentieth Legislature of the State of Texas. Nature gave to him the qualifications that are ordained to social friendships, and education has prepared a way to distinction. He is of average height and stoutly built physique—has a pleasant countenance, lit up by a glowing, genial soul. His complexion is fair, his hair black and eyes a light hazel. He moves gracefully and converses freely. He enjoys society and is not in the least degree misanthropic. Senator Gregg is a native Texan, thirty-two years of age, and resides at Palestine, Texas.

He graduated at Bristol, Tenn., and attended the law department of the University of Virginia. At the bar in Eastern Texas he has won a prominent place, and was elected State Senator as his first public office, at the November election in 1886. Besides service on other important committees, he was chairman of the Committee on Internal Improvements.

RICHARD HENRY HARRISON.

THE young Senator from the Twenty-second Senatorial District, embracing McLennan and Falls counties, was born in Monroe county, Mississippi, on the eighth day of September, 1857. He is the son of General James E. Harrison, a gallant soldier of the South. In 1858 the family removed to Waco, Texas, and when young Harrison was sixteen years of age, he was left to his own resources by the death of his father. By dint of earnest endeavor and rigid economy, he educated himself and graduated from the law department of Cumberland University, Lebanon, Tennessee, having distinguished himself for his assiduity, thoroughness and rapid progress.

Senator Harrison served for a short time as a deputy sheriff of McLennan county, and for about one year ending in 1878, in a battalion of the frontier military organizations. His professional career began in 1881, when he grew rapidly into prominence by reason of his legal acumen and fine oratory. He was elected State Senator by a majority of 2500 over W. R. Reagan, Esq., brother of Hon. John H. Reagan, United States Senator elect. During the Nineteenth Legislature he was chairman of the Committee on Counties and County Boundaries. His legislative work was, distinctively, the introduction of the bill to prohibit corporations from acquiring and holding lands in the State for speculative purposes; also the bill to restore the Greer county lands that have, as he and others maintained, been illegally patented. In the Twentieth Legislature he was made chairman of the Committee on Private Land Claims, and maintains his high standing among his co-legislators. He is a member of the Missionary Baptists, and of the order of the Knights of Pythias. Of medium height and fair countenance.

TEMPLE HOUSTON.

ACCORDING to this gentleman's own admissions, his life contains no fit material for a biography.

JOHN JONES JARVIS.

TARRANT, Wise, Parker and Jack counties compose the Twentieth Senatorial district, represented in the Twentieth Legislature of the State of Texas by Hon. J. J. Jarvis, of Fort Worth, Texas. Major Jarvis is a North Carolinian, born in the year 1832, and has been in Texas for thirty years. He received his education in his native State and in Tennessee. By profession, he is a lawyer, and is highly esteemed by all who know him, for his sterling integrity and moral worth. Prior to his election as State Senator, which took place in November, 1886, by a majority of about 1100 votes, he had served respectively in the offices of district attorney and county judge. He entered the war between the States at the beginning—served in the Trans-Mississippi Department as private, adjutant and major. His wife, to whom he was married in 1866, was Miss Ida Van Zandt, daughter of Hon. Isaac Van Zandt, minister from the Republic of Texas at Washington. Major Jarvis

HERMANN KNITTEL.

is tall, slender, and has a fair and pleasing countenance. He is a member of the Christian Church, and as a citizen, lawyer, business man and Senator sustains an enviable reputation. He served on the following Senate committees of the Twentieth Legislature, being chairman of Finance and a member of Judiciary No. 1; Private Land Claims, Internal Improvements, Education and Engrossed Bills.

HERMANN KNITTEL.

WITH one exception, the only foreign born member in the Senate of the Twentieth Legislature is Senator Knittel, who was born in Silesia, Prussia, on December 4, 1835. He came to America and settled in Washington county, Texas, in 1852. He is a respected and honored citizen of Burton, of that county. He distinguished himself as a brave soldier in the war between the States, serving as a second lieutenant of Waul's Texas Legion. He was elected Senator from the Twelfth Senatorial district in 1884, and has acquitted himself as a discreet and safe legislator. In the Nineteenth Legislature, he was chairman of the Committee on Retrenchment and Reform, and served as chairman of the Committee on Contingent Expenses in the Twentieth Legislature. He is a member of the Lutheran Church, and a Mason. Senator Knittel is a good specimen of Prussian gentility, has light hair and fair complexion, of pleasing manners, and shows a high degree of intelligence.

JONATHAN LANE.

SENATOR LANE was born in Texas, October 15, 1854. He was educated in Fayette county, and for a man of his age, has attained proficiency in his chosen profession, the law. He is a prominent member of the bar at LaGrange. He was elected State Senator from the Thirteenth district, composed of Fayatte, Bastrop and Lee counties, at the November election in 1886, by a majority of 3378, a high and deserved compliment paid to his talent, and promise for the future. He is an efficient committeeman on the committees as follows: Judiciary No. 1, Private Land Claims, Military Affairs, and others, besides being chairman of the Committee on Insurance, Statistics and History. He is of small figure and quick motion, and shows a good degree culture. He is an earnest, logical, forcible speaker, and possesses rare qualities which draw men to him. His popularity among his constituents and co-legislators has real, substantial ground. His wife was Miss Alma Harrison, who, with one little girl, constitutes his family. He is a Royal Arch Mason and a Knight or Honor. At twenty years of age he began merchandising, and had been a practitioner at the bar five years before his election to the Twentieth Legislature.

HENRY D. McDONALD.

THE subject of this sketch is of fair complexion, black hair and eyes. His speech is quick and his movement restless almost to impatience. He is affable, and of a tall, erect figure. He is a native of Texas, being thirty-six years of age. He was educated in Texas, at McKenzie College. His education is of a practical and useful character. He read law in 1872, and has been a successful barrister, favor-

W. H. POPE.

ably known in North Texas. His first public office is as State Senator, to which he was elected in November, 1886. He has done good work in the Senate, and serves as chairman of the Committee on Judicial Districts, besides having membership on other committees. He resides at Paris, Texas.

FRANCIS EDWARD MACMANUS.

SENATOR MACMANUS is a native of Ireland, is fifty-five years old, and has been in Texas thirty-one years. He is a lawyer by profession, and resides at Corpus Christi, Texas.

WILLIAM HENRY POPE.

IMMEDIATELY prior to the war between the States, the Pope family emigrated from Wilkes county, Georgia, and settled at Marshall, Texas. At this time William Henry was a boy of twelve summers. He was thoroughly educated at the University of Virginia and admitted to the bar at Marshall in 1868. He served as county attorney, and had won for himself high honors as district attorney, when he was elected State Senator from the Third Senatorial district in 1879, in 1884 re-elected, and without opposition in both instances. He served during his legislative career as chairman of several of the most important Senate committees. In the Twentieth Legislature he served as chairman of the Committee on Public Lands, and was a member of several of the most important committees of the Senate. He was also appointed by Governor Ireland commissioner to represent Texas for the collection of claims for the frontier protection.

Early in his boyhood, Senator Pope gave evidence of great

promise. His bright intelligence has increased with multiplying years, and the opening flower of young life is now yielding the harvest of intellectual excellence. As a lawyer, he ranks with the leaders of the profession in Eastern Texas, and as a legislator, he may have equals, but few if any superiors. Gallant as a soldier, which he demonstrated in his daring, being associated with Terry's scouts and Wharton's cavalry in the war of 1861–5, and as a citizen true and loyal, he has earned and now receives the confidence and esteem of his entire constituency. He is small in stature, and of a vivacious movement. With jet black hair, a dark countenance, a black, flashing eye, he gives the strongest external evidence of inflexible purpose. By his keen piercing eye, he is an accurate reader of human nature, and is fearless in speaking as he thinks. He excels in the gift of the orator, and in his happiest efforts is more impassioned than ornate, more real than imaginative. He has fine social qualities, but makes confidents of men only after strict trial and due examination.

ELDRED JAMES SIMKINS.

THE distinguished gentleman of whom this is a sketch was born in Edgefield District, South Carolina, October 13, A. D. 1839, educated at Beaufort, South Carolina, and graduated in the class of 1859, at South Carolina College. He volunteered in the Hampton Legion at the beginning of the war between the States, and in 1862 was appointed in the regular artillery service, and served during the rest of the war in Fort Sumpter and other posts around Charleston. His home in Beaufort, South Carolina, and all the property of the family in the island around the town, were confiscated under the act of Congress passed in 1862, and he moved to Florida and began the practice of law in

State Senators.

1867, with his brother, under the firm name of Simkins & Simkins, at Monticello, Florida. He was elected chairman of the Democratic Executive Committee of the county, and held that position until his removal to Texas in 1871. He settled in Corsicana, in this State, and engaged in the practice of his profession with his brother, under the same firm name. In 1872, he was elected district attorney of the Thirtieth judicial district, and held that position for four years. In 1882 he was appointed University Regent. In 1884 he was a member of the National Democratic Convention. In 1886 he was elected State Senator by a majority of more than 2800 votes, from the Fifteenth Senatorial district, composed of Navarro, Limestone and Freestone counties. Mr. Simkins was known in Florida, as he is in Texas, as a zealous Democrat. In 1869 and 1870 he was editor of a Democratic journal, and on removal to Texas edited a Democratic paper until his election as district attorney. He served also as chairman of the Democratic party in his county from 1872 to 1876. Mr. Simkins is a member of the Episcopal Church, a mason—Master of his lodge, and member of the Grand Lodge. He was married to Miss Eliza Trescott, of Beaufort, South Carolina, and has a family of five living children.

As a Senator, he is distinguished, being chairman of the Committee on Federal Relations, and a member of others. He is free in conversation, and urbane in his manners. In physique he is tall, and of symmetrical figure, light complexion, and commanding presence.

SAMUEL DAVID STINSON.

AS an orator, Senator Stinson is vehement and impetuous, his strains often rising to the elevation of true eloquence. In argument he does not disdain the tactics of the skillful polemic in the free use of sarcasm and irony. As a lawyer, he has attained to a high degree of eminence for one so young in years. His legislative record has been approved by his friends, and has effectually disarmed the criticism of those who differ from him. He began public life by service as county attorney of Hunt county, in 1880. In 1884, he was elected State Senator from the Fifth Senatorial district, receiving over 10,000 votes, being elected without opposition. In the Nineteenth Legislature, he was chairman of the Committee on Private Land Claims, and a valuable member of several other committees. He is, in the Twentieth Legislature, chairman of the Committee on Public Buildings and Grounds, rendering service also as a menber of other standing committees. He has been pronounced in favor of the education of the masses by the public free school system, and has accordingly introduced and favored measures to this end. He has taken the initiative to do away with secret sessions of the Senate, called executive sessions, by introducing in the Twentieth Legislature a joint resolution to that effect. He is a member of the Independent Order of Odd Fellows. Senator Stinson is, physically, a gentleman of the prevailing American type, in stature five feet ten inches, and weighs one hundred and fifty pounds. He is of ruddy countenance and fair complexion, and possesses a blue eye that flashes in brilliancy during heated discussion. His hair is light in color and falls carelessly over a brow that is the external covering of indwelling intelligence. He has a leisurely movement and all the politeness of true culture. He possesses that mysterious psychic condition that draws even the stranger to him, which is one of the secrets of his popularity. He is a Texan, born in Hunt county, April

S. D. STINSON.

11, 1852, lived at Gilmer thirteen years, and since that time he has been a resident of Greenville. He is thoroughly educated, and graduated from the law school of Trinity University. He entered his profession in the year 1878.

J. O. TERRELL.

AMONG the most brilliant young men in the Twentieth Legislature of the State of Texas, is Senator Terrell, from the Sixteenth Senatorial district. As an orator, he is earnest and forcible, and often rises to flights of true eloquence. He is tall and slender in physical figure, having light hair and blue eyes. His countenance is fair, but possesses distinctive outlines of a commander. His movement is positive and his determinations unalterable. He is pleasant, gentlemanly and urbane. He possesses a self-equipoise that is not disturbed by environments or conditions. Senator Terrell was born in Kaufman county, Texas, April 6, 1856. He was educated at Trinity University, Limestone county, Texas. At the age of twenty-one he was admitted to the bar, and soon became prominent for the merit he disclosed and the success which attended his professional career. He was elected State Senator in 1884, and in the Nineteenth Legislature was chairman of the Committee on Commerce and Manufactures. He was the chairman of Judiciary Committee No. 1 in the Twentieth Legislature. He is a member of the Methodist Episcopal Church, South, and carries with him in his social relations an elevating influence.

State Senators.

SAMUEL CROCKETT UPSHAW.

THIS able Senator and lawyer is a resident of Hillsboro, Hill county, Texas. He has been in Texas thirty-six years, having entered the State at the age of ten years—his present age is forty-six. He is native of Arkansas. In the practice of the law he has been successful, and as a speaker he is logical and convincing. He takes great pains in his speeches to give every argument its full force, and introduce his proofs in the most advantageous order. He has taken an honorable and respected place in the Twentieth Legislature as a discrete and safe Senator. He is of medium size and symmetrical figure, sparkling blue eye, and shows a degree of social urbanity and intellectual strength that makes him noticeable in the midst of his associates. He is a member of various important committees, and chairman of the Committee on Roads and Bridges.

JOHN WOODS.

SENATOR WOODS is an Alabamian, and thirty-nine years of age. He came to Texas in 1853. In November, 1884, was elected Senator from the Eleventh Senatorial district, composed of Colorado, Wharton, Gonzales and Lavaca counties. He appeared first in the upper House in the Nineteenth Legislature of the State of Texas. Previous to his election as Senator, he had served a term of three years as district attorney of Lavaca county, and was a member of the House of Representatives in the Eighteenth Legislature, both the regular and called sessions. In the Nineteenth Legislature, Senator Woods introduced Senate bill No. 8, which finally became a law. The law forbids the sale of lands to corporations for purposes of speculation, and has been accepted with great favor. He also evinced a commendable degree of foresight and political sagacity in the introduction of the bill to establish a reformatory and house of correction for youthful criminals. The bill passed the Senate, but failed to become a law. The movement was only previous, as Senator Woods was in advance of the opposition, for such an institution is demanded. He has been put on record as an earnest and able advocate of public highways throughout the State. This too, so commendable in itself, was only a little in advance of time.

Senator Woods is logical, but not vehement. He reasons, considers, weighs, but does not aim to carry his points by storm. He is a lawyer and banker, and is well qualified to take care of the interests of his constituents. He is tall, symmetrical and has a sedate bearing in the circles where he moves. His physiognomy indicates consecutive thought and analytical consideration of every proposition brought before him. He is respected by his co-legislators, and held in high esteem. He makes no fiery speeches, and uses more the figures of arithmetic than those of rhetoric. Among his constituents he is respected and honored for his integrity. His course has been so uniform, and generally approved, that he has the friendship of all and the enmity of none. He enjoys good health, and is so steady in the habits of his living, that, throughout his career as a legislator, he has never missed roll-call nor an appointment for a committee meeting. This praiseworthy virtue has awarded to him the soubriquet of "Punctuality." Senator Woods was married to Miss Mary E. Ricinger, of Fayette county, and has two children. He is a Mason and an Odd Fellow. He was educated in Texas, and is a gentleman of fine intelligence and manners.

State Senators.

WILLIAM H. WOODWARD.

SENATOR W. H. WOODWARD was born August 30, 1817, in Todd county, Kentucky, and was educated in the "Old Field Schools" of that State, with an academic course. He engaged at maturity in farming, but soon abandoned that for the law. He studied law in Nashville, Tennessee, and commenced the practice in that city in 1849.

In 1852 he removed to Indianola, Texas, where he engaged in the practice of his profession. He remained at Indianola until that town was swept away by the cyclone of August 20, 1886, when he removed to Port Lavaca, where he now resides and continues the practice of law. He has served as county judge and United States commissioner. He represented the counties of Calhoun, Jackson, Aransas, Refugio, Victoria, DeWitt, Bee, Goliad, Live Oak, San Patricio, Wilson, Karnes and Atascosa, composing the Twenty-fourth Senatorial district, in the Senate of the Twentieth Legislature. He served as chairman of the Committe on Military Affairs. His experience in the field gave him many advantages on that important committee.

When the civil war commenced, he entered the army and was appointed brigadier-general of State troops and assigned to duty with the Twenty-fourth brigade, which operated on the coast of Texas, principally about Matagorda bay. General Woodward was detailed in 1863 by General Magruder to proceed to Louisiana on an important special mission.

General Woodward is a man of fine personal appearance, about six feet tall, straight as an arrow, and weighing about two hundred pounds, and made a conspicuous officer on the field. His features are of that large caste that evidences the highest order of intelligence. His forehead is high, eye bright, mouth large, composing a face of chaste intellectual strength. His face is a true reflex of the mind and soul of the man. His mind is comprehensive and cultivated, and

W. H. WOODWARD.

State Senators.

he is fully impressed with that broad sympathy for his kind that in such a great degree distinguishes men as representatives of the highest type of American citizenship. As a speaker and debater, General Woodward is fluent, logical and concise, quick to catch the full scope of debate, ready to sift the truth and establish it by argument. His manners are genial and his conversational powers so agreeable that his influence as a man and Senator is very great.

It goes without saying that such a man is a Democrat of the old school, with a full knowledge and understanding of all the delicate relations of the different departments of government. His popularity is evidenced by the fact that only fourteen votes were polled against him in the senatorial race.

General Woodward married Miss Penelope R. Woodward, of Christian county, Kentucky, and has three children living, one daughter and two sons.

OFFICERS OF THE SENATE.

CHAPLAIN.

THE office of Chaplain is one of the most important of all the offices of the Legislative department of our country. From the organization of the government down to the present time, both branches of the American Congress have had a chaplain. Every State in the Union has a chaplain in each branch. The army and navy have their chaplains in every regiment of soldiers and every fleet of ships. Some of most prominent and eloquent of American divines have filled these positions.

The office of Chaplain is based upon the idea that ours is a *Christian government*, which fact is embodied in our *Constitution* and found in our *Bill of Rights*. Mr. Jefferson said every Christian government should have men of character, piety and ability to fill this office.

RICHMOND KELLY SMOOT.

REV. RICHMOND KELLEY SMOOT, LL. D., was born in Huntingdon, West Tennessee, March 15, 1836. He graduated at Hanover College, Indiana, August 6, 1856, studied divinity at Danville, Kentucky, and graduated in theology in May, 1859; was licensed to preach by the Presbytery of Western District, in Tennessee. His first charge was at Bowling Green, Kentucky. He was ordained and installed pastor of the Presbyterian Church, in that city, on May 20, 1860, and remained there until November, 1876, when he took charge of the Presbyterian Church in Austin, Texas, which pastoral charge he still holds. His first appearance in a General Assembly was in St. Louis, in 1866; then again in Mobile, in 1869; in Little Rock, in 1873; Columbus,

Officers of the Senate.

Mississippi, in 1874; Savannah, Georgia, in 1876; Atlanta, in 1882; Lexington, Kentucky, in 1883; Augusta, Georgia, in 1886.

In 1873, he was chosen reading clerk of the General Assembly, and also chosen by that assembly, with Dr. B. M. Palmer, Dr. Wm. Brown, and Dr. Jos. R. Wilson, to visit New York and negotiate with the Dutch Church for co-operative union. In 1875, Dr. Smoot published a work on "Parliamentary Principles," in their application to the courts of the church, which has had a wide circulation, and come into general use in the Southern Presbyterian Church. The title of Doctor of Divinity was conferred on Dr. Smoot in 1875, by the Presbyterian University, at Clarksville, Tennessee. In 1882, he was chosen Moderator of the General Assembly, at Atlanta, Georgia, the highest office in the Presbyterian Church. In 1884, he, in conjunction with Rev. Dr. R. L. Dabney, opened a theological school in Austin for the training of young men for the ministry, with an especial view to the work in Texas.

He was first elected Chaplain of the Senate of the Seventeenth Legislature of Texas, at the called session in April, 1882, and was re-elected to the Eighteenth, the Nineteenth and the Twentieth.

Dr. Smoot is five feet six inches high, weighs 182 pounds, has blue eyes, fair complexion, light hair, and is in the vigor of his manhood; preaches entirely without notes, being an off-hand speaker.

Officers of the Senate.

WILLIAM NEAL RAMEY.

IT may be affirmed of Colonel Ramey that he is a natural gentleman. In clerical work, in the cause of education, in the editorial sanctum, and in the broad field of literature generally, he had his delight, and the trend of his life has been in this direction. In 1857 he made his appearance in Texas—living in Harrison county five years, and subsequently in Shelby county fifteen years, and then removing to the city of Austin, Travis county; he has remained there ever since. At the age of sixteen he taught school as a means to higher education. In this he was successful. In the war between the States he rose from private to adjutant-general, and made a noble record as a soldier, true and brave. He has been justice of the peace, Superintendent Public Grounds and Buildings, and was a member of the Constitutional Convention of 1875. He was elected Secretary of the Senate in the Seventeenth Legislature, was elected again in the Nineteenth, and also re-elected in the Twentieth. He has made an able and efficient officer, and like as in other services rendered, he has the praise of the people. He was born in Rutherford county, Tennessee, on the fourth of July, in the year 1835. He is a member of the Masonic fraternity, and has been an earnest advocate of temperance all his life, and gives to his advocacy a consistent exemplification in his life. He is a man of fine intellect, warm heart and generous impulses, is much respected and regarded as among the best class of citizens.

RUFUS GREEN CHILDRESS.

THE polite Calendar Clerk of the Senate, Judge Childress, was born in Marshall county, Alabama, in October, 1838. He came to Texas in childhood, in the spring of 1845, under the care of his parents, and became established in Rusk county till the breaking out of the war, in 1861. What education in the schools he could obtain, he got in Rusk county. He was raised on the farm and was used to the out-door exercise and labors which have led to a healthy manhood.

He entered the war between the States from the beginning and continued to the close, serving most of the time in the Army of Tennessee. For two years he was a member of the special scout of General L. S. Ross, and was a favorite of that gallant commander. After the war he remained for a time in Mississippi, but returning to Bosque county, Texas, in 1870, he has remained there ever since. He served as a deputy sheriff of Rusk county before the war, and as a citizen of Bosque county, has been honored by political preferment. Four years as a justice of the peace and six years as county judge, show how much he has been held in popular favor.

In the year 1866, he was married to Miss Mary A. Taggart, of Holmes county, Mississippi, and has a family of seven children. He is a zealous Mason and a popular citizen; is five feet nine inches high, weighs 170 pounds, has a blue eye, and converses fluently and pleasantly. He has made an efficient Calendar Clerk of the Senate of the Twentieth Legislature; is a true gentleman, and reliable.

Officers of the Senate.

W. T. BREWER.

THIS reputable gentleman is a native of Memphis, Tennessee, born on the twenty-second of February, 1836. He came to Texas in 1844, and was a citizen of Fannin county for three years after he arrived in the State. He has since been a resident of Rusk county. He was second lieutenant of company E, Locke's regiment of the Tenth Texas cavalry in the late war, and participated in the battles of Mansfield, of Pleasant Hill, and others. He was sheriff of Rusk county from 1879 to 1884, and was regarded as one of the best officers of that portion of the State. He was elected Sergeant-at-Arms of the Nineteenth Legislature, and was esteemed highly for his gentlemanly bearing and fidelity in office. In the Twentieth Legislature he was elected Assistant Doorkeeper, and before the session closed was promoted to the principal office of Sergeant-of-Arms. A more efficient officer, trustworthy in responsibility, and decorus in the enforcement of rules, will not readily be found. He is a farmer, and has executive ability, not of that rigid character which is devoid of politeness, but rather efficient through a due proportion of exactness and kindness. Mr. Brewer is a member of the Methodist Episcopal Church, South, and of the order of Ancient, Free and Accepted Masons. He is also a Knight of Honor.

GEO. C. PENDLETON.

REPRESENTATIVES.

GEORGE CASITY PENDLETON.

SPEAKER OF THE HOUSE.

THE absence of the elements of endurance from the person of the Speaker of the House of Representatives has a cause. The hardships of army life at so youthful an age as seventeen years, have left an irremediable effect. By nature, he never possessed that remarkable constitutional vigor that could resist the encroachments of bodily ill.

He entered the war between the States early in the struggle, and remained in the field to the close. His service was rendered altogether in the Trans-Mississippi department, being a member of Colonel B. W. Watson's regiment—the Nineteenth Texas Cavalry. He distinguished himself in commendable fidelity and trustworthiness, which one so young could scarcely be expected to exhibit, being exposed to the peculiar temptations of the soldier's life.

Speaker Pendleton's education began in the common schools, laying only the foundations of a broad, self-taught attainment, which is both the product and accumulation of a well-ordered life. The ambition of his early life was to enter the legal profession. Returning from his adventures in the war of 1861-5, he entered the college at Waxahachie, Texas, intending to graduate in the practice of law, but his health failed him, and he was forced to desist.

For ten years, consecutively, he was a commercial traveler. To this active, migratory order of life, he is probably indebted for the restoration of his health.

In 1870 he was happily married to Miss Helen Embree, daughter of Elisha Embree, Esq., of Bell county, Texas. Since his marriage, Mr. Pendleton has been engaged in rural merchandising, agriculture and stock-raising. The measure of success that has followed his endeavors has given him the prestige of the foremost citizens of his county.

His political career began with his election to represent Bell county in the Eighteenth Legislature of the State of Texas. He was re-elected to the Nineteenth, and being returned to the Twentieth Legislature, was chosen the Speaker of the House without opposition. His record as a legislator has been pronouncedly approved by his constituency at home, by their unbroken support; and himself, by his co-legislators of the Twentieth Legislature, by their awarding to him the first honors of the House.

Speaker Pendleton was born on the twenty-third of April, 1845, in Coffee county, Tennessee. Mrs. Sarah Pendleton, mother of George C., was the daughter of General William Smartt, a hero of the war of 1812. The entire family came to Texas in the year 1857, and settled in Ellis county, George C. being only twelve years of age.

He is of delicate physique, weighs one hundred and fifty pounds avoirdupois, and is five feet eleven inches in stature. His complexion is dark, eyes blue, and his facial outline indicative of keen discernment. He is reflective, cautious, seeks the counsel of his friends, and is devoid of those angular phases of character which pierce unyielding forces and unify opposition. Firm in his decisions, respectful in his attention to others, and courteous in his negations, he wins to hold, and holds that he may further win.

Representatives.

FRANK P. ALEXANDER.

FRANK P. ALEXANDER, Representative in the Twentieth Legislature from the Twenty-fifth district, composed of Hunt county, was born in Pickens, South Carolina, September 1, 1853, and came to Texas in 1870, locating then at Jefferson, Marion county. In 1872 he became identified with the press of that city, as one of the editors and proprietors of the Daily Jefferson Democrat, he being then in the twentieth year of his age, and remained there until 1874. In 1876 he located permanently at Greenville, the county seat of Hunt county, assuming editorial control of the Greenville Independent, and in 1879 established the Greenville Herald, which soon became, and is still, one of the leading journals of that section; but Mr. Alexander served his connection with it about three years ago, and is now engaged in the insurance business. As an editor, Mr. Alexander had clearly and forcibly indicated his position on all the leading questions of State policy, and his course as a member of the Nineteenth and Twentieth Legislatures has proven the earnestness and sincerity of his convictions, as he has here given organic form to the ideas and principles so ably advocated by him in the newspapers.

The leading measure proposed by Mr. Alexander in the Nineteenth and again in the present Legislature, was a bill to create a State railway commission, prohibit discriminations, pooling and other abuses, and regulate freight and passenger traffic. The first bill introduced by him in the Twentieth Legislature was to prevent legislative, judicial and executive officers from accepting or using free railroad passes, and he scored a victory early in the session by securing its passage through the House. He framed and introduced other important bills too numerous to mention in this connection.

The policy proposed by Mr. Alexander on these and other matters goes to the root of evils that the wisest men in the State believe to be important to the well being and prosperity of the citizens of this State. He is yet young and has before him a broad and bright field of usefulness, and the gratification of his ambition, which is to contribute to the material, mental and moral elevation of his fellow-citizens. Such an ambition is laudable, and such an emulation worthy of example to the rising youth of the land. He has demonstrated what a young man, without any advantages of fortune or influence, may do in obtaining the respect of his people and gratitude throughout the State, for a wise and beneficial political economy, introduced and accomplished by a persistent pressing before the people, in the newspapers and Legislature of the State. Mr. Alexander served in the Eighteenth and the Twentieth Legislatures as chairman of the Committee on Insurance and Statistics, and is second in place on Internal Improvements and Finance committee, as also that of Printing. On all of these committees Mr. Alexander gave assiduous and intelligent attention throughout the session to the business in hand, and has left his distinctive mark upon the legislation of the State and the organic law thereof. All measures of reform, of a practical kind, received Mr. Alexander's ready and hearty support.

JOHN CHAMBERS SPRIGG BAIRD.

JOHN C. S. BAIRD was born November 28, 1846, in Kaufman county, Texas. When about three years old his parents moved to Navarro county, Texas, where he was educated. At sixteen years of age he joined company E of the Twelfth Texas cavalry, and served in the army of the Trans-Mississippi Department, and charged with the lines of gray on many a hard fought field. In victory and defeat, he remained true to the flag whose broad folds had so often floated "o'er the purple tide of war."

On the sixth day of February, 1870, he was married to Miss Bettie Street, and has now a family consisting of seven children, four boys and three girls. He is a member of the Knight Templars, Odd Fellowsand Farmers' Alliance.

He is a Democrat who has labored for the success of his party in season and out, a profound thinker, and was one of the most influential members of the Twentieth Legislature. He was a member of the following House committees: Constitutional Amendments, Educational Affairs, Privileges and Elections, Counties and County Boundaries, and a member of the joint committee to investigate the Comptroller's Office, and for services rendered on this latter committee received the personal compliments of Governor Ross.

Mr. Baird is an ordained elder in the Methodist Episcopal Church, South, and in addition to his labors in the House of Representatives, entertained the congregation at Tenth street Methodist Church, and other congregations in Austin. He is of course a temperance man, but holds peculiar views on the prohibition question. He claims that it is neither a political nor a temperance measure, but simply a police regulation, and should be dealt with as such by the Legislature and the people.

His introduction into politics was not a matter of his own solicitation, but some of his friends being aware of the fact that he contemplated retiring from the pastorate, in order that he might make better provision for his family, and knowing his strength as a debater, and withal his devotion to the Democratic party, urged him to accept the nomination, which he did, and it is admitted that the success of the Democratic party in the Seventy-seventh district was due to his personal popularity and his power as a platform orator.

In physical structure he is tall and spare, having a dark complexion, black hair and a brilliant hazel eye. He has a basso voice, strong and full, and as an orator excels. In polemics, he is a knight of untarnished plume; strong and comprehensive in argument, his mightiest feats are performed in his dextrous use of the disputant's most destructive weapons, viz: ridicule, irony, sarcasm and ready repartee. It is noticeable that he has in some instances turned the tide of legislation, by making a feint upon the weakest point of a pending bill. He has taken a prominent place in the esteem of the House. He is outspoken and independent. In social nature he is happily constituted, and is obliging and true to his friends.

H. A. P. BASSETT.

H. A. P. BASSETT was born in Grimes county, Texas, March 14, 1857. In early childhood he was entirely debarred from the culture and refinement that tend to make a man of intellectual attainments. He enjoyed his first school days in the year 1867, amid great disadvantages, in the town of Anderson, the county seat of Grimes county. His father and mother being very poor, and tillers of the soil, a great many of his days that would have been devoted to study were spent in labor on the farm. In the year 1875 he attended Straight University, of New Orleans, Louisiana. In the fall of 1879 he went to Fisk University, Nashville, Tennessee, where he remained for three years. On the second day of September, 1886, he was married to Miss Cordelia Foster. On the second day of November, of the same year, he was elected from the county of his birth, being the Fifty-second Representative district, to the Twentieth Legislature of the State. He is a member of the Missionary Baptist Church, and has great faith in the teachings of the Bible.

C. I. BATTLE.

C. I. BATTLE, Democratic member of the House of Representatives of the Twentieth Legislature from the Sixty-sixth Representative district, composed of the counties of Galveston, Matagorda and Wharton, was born January 12, 1842, in Wilkes county, Georgia, and was educated in Washington and Mount Zion, Georgia, Baylor University, Texas, and the University of Virginia. He is a farmer, and served as justice of the peace in Wharton county. Mr. Battle was a soldier in the late civil war, serving in the Army of Northern Virginia from its organization until its surrender at Appomattox Court House. He was never wounded or sick, and never absent from the army on but one occasion, when he had a furlough of thirty days; a soldier could have no better record.

Mr. Battle married Mrs. Anne M. Sanford, but has no children. He belongs to the Baptist Church, the Masonic fraternity, and the Oriental Order of the Palm and Shell.

He was devoted to a strict performance of his duty in all the responsibilities of life, and whether as a soldier or the servant of the people in the halls of legislation, he is ever at his post, watchful, alert and vigilant.

GEORGE WYTHE BAYLOR.

G. W. BAYLOR was born at Fort Gibson, in the Cherokee Nation, on August 24, 1832. His father was Dr. John Walker Baylor, eldest son of Judge Walker Baylor, of Bourbon county, Kentucky, whose wife was Miss Jane Bledsoe, a sister of Honorable Jesse Bledsoe, of Kentucky, celebrated in his day as the peer of Henry Clay, Webster or Calhoun as an orator.

His mother was Miss Sophia Maria Weidner, of Baltimore, Maryland, her father being Henreich Weidner, of Hessen Cassel, Germany, and her mother being Marie Chartelle, of an old Hugenot family.

Born in a fort, under the old flag, all his earliest associations are connected with garrison life, and familiar sounds are the calls of the bugle and the sound of reville by drum and fife.

Representatives.

His father moved at an early day from Bourbon county, Kentucky, to Fort Gibson, with his family, going down from Louisville to the mouth of the Arkansas river on a keel boat, and this boat was dragged by the soldiers up the river to Fort Gibson. His mother took along a lot of fruit trees, roses and plants, probably the first ever carried out there.

His father dying when he was only four years old, his mother, then on Second Creek, Mississippi, back of Natchez, went to Pine Bluff, Arkansas; then to Little Rock, and finally to Fort Gibson again. In December, 1845, he came to Texas; stopped at Ross Prairie, Fayette county, and went to school for awhile to Professor Halsey at Rutersville, and afterwards was sent by his uncle, Judge R. E. B. Baylor, to Baylor University, at Independence, Texas, then under the control of Dr. Henry Graves.

He went from school to San Antonio, and, lured by the golden dreams of the New Eldorado, left there March, 1854, for California, five months being required to make the trip. He remained in California five years, and, althoguh brought out by the Democratic party in 1859 for the Legislature, he preferred to come back to Texas. Returning to San Antonio in May, 1859, he left for Parker county.

In 1860 he commanded a company of rangers in what was known as the Buffalo Hunt, but the Indians gave them a wide berth, only three or four Indians being killed. There were some 300 men in this expedition, some of the members of the Twentieth Legislature having also served in this campaign.

The war breaking out, he joined Captain Hamner's company at Weatherford, March 17, 1861, and was elected first lieutenant, the company being attached to Colonel John S. Ford's regiment of cavalry.

General Albert Sidney Johnston subsequently gave him the appointment of aide-de-camp. Colonel Baylor followed this great chieftain to Shiloh, and held his head in his dying moments.

After the close of the war he lived in Galveston, Dallas and San Antonio, and 1879 was sent out as junior lieutenant of company C, Texas Rangers, to El Paso, by Governor Roberts. His first fight with the Apaches was on the seventh of October, three weeks after he got to his post.

Colonel Baylor's next campaign was in the Candelaria mountains, Mexico, where he went to attack old Victorio, who had killed thirty Mexicans from Carizal. His attention was afterwards given to suppressing fence-cutting, and having been placed in command of the Texas Rangers, with rank of major, made a raid on an organized band in Nolan county, arrested nine, and the practice has been quite unpopular since.

He was elected both from real merit, and as a reward for the great services he has rendered the State. He is tall and of a spare figure, courageous as a soldier, and was a prominent member in the House.

C. C. BELL.

CAPTAIN W. W. BELL, father of C. C. Bell, the affable Representative from Denton county, removed from Natchez, Mississippi, in 1836, to Old Nashville, Texas, on the banks of the Brazos, near where the magnificent iron bridge of the International and Great Northern Railway now spans that river. It was at this place the Hon. C. C. Bell was born, on the twelfth of October, 1840. In 1842 the family removed to Old Warren, on the banks of Red River, then the county seat of Fannin county. The family consisted of seven children, of whom the subject of this sketch is the youngest. He was raised on a farm, and although ambitious to acquire a collegiate education, the obstacles thickened till the war between the States hopelessly overhrew his purpose. After attending Mound Prairie Insti-

Representatives.

tute in Anderson county, he went to McKinzie College, under that noblest of old-time educators in Texas, Dr. J. W. P. McKinzie. At the breaking out of the war the whole tenor of his life was changed. A practical sense of duty called him to leave the fond pursuit of learning and to take up the equipments of war. He was a good soldier, and escaped with his life and its endowments, but nothing else. In young manhood he sought the hand of Miss Inge, of Kentucky, and after marriage opened the Denton High School, at Denton, Texas, in 1867, continuing in this line of life for three years. He has been engaged in the out-door pursuits of the farm since that time, on account of delicate health and a fondness for the business. He is regarded as a successful man in his business engagements, and a financier of no ordinary ability. The caste of his intellect is reflective. He thinks profoundly, and has a just view of the interests of the people. As a legislator he is vigilant, faithful and full of discrimination. In the halls of the Legislature he is calm and conservative. He has enlarged views of the current demands of legislation, and is sound in his judgment. He was a member of the Nineteenth Legislature, and also of the Twentieth, representing the Thirty-second district. In the Nineteenth Legislature he was a member of the committees on Finance, Revenue and Taxation, Incidental Expenses, and also on Military Affairs. He has ever gained by experience, and in the Twentieth serves on committees of like importance to safe legislation. He is an exemplary member of the Methodist Episcopal Church, South, holding official relationship, a faithful Sunday-school worker, and full of good deeds. His speeches are clear and logical. He is not afraid to be heard, nor does he cringe before the mightiest. His place in the Legislature is high on the roll of distiguished members.

ROBERT VALENTINE BELL.

ROBERT VALENTINE BELL, that accomplished lawyer and gentleman who represented the Thirty-first Representative district of the counties of Cook and Grayson in the House of Representatives of the Twentieth Legislature of Texas, born August 2, 1846, in Rhea county, Tennessee. He received a primary education in the schools of his native county, but completed his studies, literary and law, at Lebanon, Tennessee, from which school he was graduated in 1872, and removed the following year to Texas, arriving and settling at Gainesville, Cook county, on the sixteenth of May, 1873. His ability and sterling worth were soon appreciated, and he was elected by the people respectively county and district attorney of Cook county. His popularity and standing is further evidenced in that he was elected to the Twentieth Legislature by a majority of 2350 votes, and although it was his first session in any legislative body, he was made chairman of the Committee on Privileges and Elections, and also held the second place on the Committee of the Judiciary No. 1. He also served on the Committees of Insurance, Statistics and History, and County Government and Finance, upon all of which committees Mr. Bell proved to be a most efficient and useful member, and has left the marks of his fine practical sense on the legislation of the State. He is a man of fine presence, an easy and impressive speaker, and gentle manner. It goes without saying that Mr. Bell is a Democrat. He is also a member of the Cumberland Presbyterian Church; he belongs to the orders of the Knights of Pythias, Knights of Honor, and Knights and Ladies of Honor. Mr. Bell married Miss Callie Peery, of Texas. They have two daughters. Mr. Bell, by his ability, integrity, and close attention to business, has obtained a fine practice in his section, and is destined to rise higher in the "stock of trade" of the Democracy of Texas, and an ornament to his profession.

Representatives.

JAMES M. BIARD.

JAMES M. BIARD was born in Limestone county, Alabama, October 24, 1834. He dwelt in the place of his nativity until eleven years of age, and then moved to Lamar county, arriving there in the year of 1846, where he has since resided, and there received his education. He is a minister of the gospel and a farmer. The kindly seasons and unrelenting energy have enabled him to accumulate a competency. He was elected from the Twentieth Representative district without opposition. The people who sent him here have known him from his boyhood, and their cordial support is an earnest of his worth as a citizen and a sterling Democrat.

He is a member of the Knights of Honor and Farmers' Alliance lodges.

Mr. Biard is now in his fifty-second year, and has never

been sued or sued a man in a court of justice. He is a man of a high order of mind, disciplined and powerful in its logical analysis. He is a fine speaker and stood in the front ranks of the House. The future lies before him a laurel grove, and he has only to weave the wreath that crowns the brow of successful merit with his own hands. The citizens of Lamar county have a bold and fearless representative in Mr. Biard.

He was a member of the committees on State Affairs, State Asylums, Penitentiaries, Agricultural Affairs and Constitutional Amendments. His ministerial life has been one of success.

THOMAS A. BLAIR.

THOMAS A. BLAIR was born in Victoria county, Texas, August 6, 1840. He represented Nueces, San Patricio, Bee, Live Oak, McMullen and LaSalle, constituting the Eighty-fifth Representative district, in the Twentieth Legislature, as a member of the House, and served on the following committees, to-wit: Judiciary No. 2, Finance, and Committee to Examine Comptroller's and Treasurer's offices.

Mr. Blair married Miss Mattie Platt, of Louisiana, and has one son. He is a man of mind and purpose of life, and is compact and direct to the point, both as a lawyer and a law-maker. With a large and tall person, he at once commands the attention and respect of any audience. While he is a politician to the extent of an earnest interest in the political affairs of his State, he takes a greater interest in the material advancement of the great State of Texas generally, and his immediate district specially.

Mr. Blair served in the Confederate army under Colonel Buchel, First Texas Cavalry, as second lieutenant of company B, and participated in the battles of Mansfield and Pleasant Hill, Louisiana, and all others on Red River.

THOS. A. BLAIR.

He is a practicing lawyer and served as county attorney of Refugio county, in 1876. He was educated at Aranama College, Goliad, Texas, and completed his studies of law in 1874, when he obtained a license and at once entered into the practice.

JOSEPH HENRY BOOTHE.

THE lineal descent of Joseph Henry Boothe, Representative from Gonzales county, is English—his progenitors having immigrated to the New World in the Colonial age. Mr. Boothe's parents now live in Wake county, North Carolina, where he was born on the twentieth of November, 1851. He was educated at the Ruffin-Badger Institute, in Chatham, county of that State, from which institution of learning he graduated in literature and law in the year 1871. He came to Texas thirteen years ago, unaccompanied by relative or friend, and entered business life as a teacher, in which profession he continued for six years, and until failing health drove him to out-door and more exposed life. For seven years he has been engaged in farming and stock-raising, and appears in the Twentieth Legislature of Texas, from the Ninetieth Representative district, in the class of the agriculturist. Mr. Boothe is a Democrat in politics, and was elected to represent his county by a majority of 749 votes. He is a member of four several standing committees, viz: Educational Affairs, Contingent Expenses, Public Lands and Land Office, and Penitentiaries. He was married to Miss Jimmie Lea, granddaughter of the late Judge Pryor Lea, of Goliad, Texas, in October, 1879, and has a family of three little boys. He is five feet eleven inches in height and of average weight, of dark complexion, and feeble natural constitution. His manners are easy and pleasant. He is firm in the maintenance of what he believes to be right, but is not of an obtrusive disposition.

Representatives.

JAMES NATHAN BROWNING.

AT an early period in the history of the State of Arkansas, William F. Browning and his wife, Mary L. Browning, whose maiden name was Burke, entered that State and became established in the agricultural pursuits of the country. They belonged to the class of well-to-do, respectable and humble people. Mrs. Browning, though herself possessing but an ordinary education, was apt to teach, and inspired her son, James Nathan, with an indomitable ambition to excel, and imparted to him an insatiable thirst for knowledge. He is a remarkable example of a self-taught and broadly educated gentleman. It is a noteworthy fact, that less than eight months describes the whole time of his attendance at school, perforce of irremediable conditions, substituting therefor self-instruction and the auxiliaries that came within the grasp of an ingenious energy. He was raised on a farm and used to manual labor. His father having died when James Nathan was only four years old, the natural guide and shield of his youth was denied him. He was born in Clark county, in the State of Arkansas, on the thirteenth day of March, 1850, and at the age of sixteen years came to Cook county, Texas. In the following year he went to Stephens county, where he engaged in the cattle raising business. In 1875 he began the study of law, for which, from a child, he had possessed a growing ambition, under the preceptorship of C. K. Stribling, Esq., at Fort Griffin, in Shakelford county. In October of the following year he was licensed, and immediately began a successful career as a western lawyer. In 1881 he went to the Panhandle and now resides at Mobeetic, Wheeler county, Texas. He begun his public career as a justice of the peace; subsequently he served two years as county attorney of Shackelford county. By appointment of Governor Roberts he served as district attorney of the judicial district embracing the Panhandle counties, which office

J. N. BROWNING.

Representatives.

however, he resigned after one year's service. In his candidacy for election to membership in the Eighteenth Legislature of the State of Texas he had two honorable opponents, but was elected by a very creditable majority of one-third over both of them. He has since been elected to the Nineteenth and also to the Twentieth Legislature without opposition, and in both of these sessions, to meet existing emergencies, has been chosen to the office of Speaker pro tem. by acclamation. In the Eighteenth Legislature and also in the Nineteenth, he was chairman of the Committee on Stock and Stock Raising. He is now the efficient chairman of Judiciary Committee No. 1, in the Twentieth Legislature. The number of his district is the Forty-third, the largest in the world, embracing 67,000 square miles, divided into sixty-seven counties, forty-five of which are unorganized, the remainder, twenty-two, being organized. Representative Browning has been twice married. His first wife was Miss Caroline E. Beckham. His second marriage was to Miss Virginia I. Bozeman, of Fort Griffin, Texas, on the ninth of March, 1879. He has five living children. He is a member of the Methodist Episcopal Church, South, and of the fraternity of Ancient, Free and Accepted Masons. As a Mason, his proficiency and standing have won for him a third term of service as District Deputy Grand Master. The personal appearance of Judge Browning would command recognition anywhere. In stature he stands above the floor six feet and nearly two inches, weighing two hundred and six pounds avoirdupois. He has a full blue eye that reposes meditatively as he sits in his seat or moves in social ease among his friends, but dances and flashes in polemical discussion. He has a plethoric facial development, and a complexion having a florid tendency. His hair is black, and his movements are of graceful ease, which nature has bestowed rather than the angular stiffness of military drill. The bent of his mind and the trend of his nature have inclined him to civil, rather than criminal practice in his profession. With a strong tenor voice, to which nature and self-culture have fixed a musical scale of modulation, his mode of address has a charm as well as the substance of discourse. The principal measures he has introduced have been on the great land interests of the State. He is well known to be an advocate of progress, to oppose the lease law, and to favor the sale of lands to actual settlers in small quantities. The influence Judge Browning wields in the House, and his popularity among his constituency, are not matters of surprise to any one who knows him well. He is a true son of nature, to whom self-culture has appointed the lordship of an American citizen according to the genius of our free institutions.

FELIX GRUNDY BRANSFORD.

FELIX GRUNDY BRADSFORD, from the Forty-fourth Representative district, composed of Clay and Montague counties, was born on the fifth of September, 1828, in Barren county, Kentucky, and was educated at Glasco, Kentucky, and Richmond, Missouri. He combines the occupation of a farmer with the practice of the profession of law. He served as a notary public for eight years. At the commencement of the war Mr. Bransford was a citizen of Missouri, and enlisted in the Missouri State Guards, and served with them during the first campaign under General Price, when he, with the Guards, were mustered into the Confederate States army. He participated, with General Parsons' brigade, in the battles of Carthage, Wilson's Creek, Siege of Lexington, Missouri; Fort Scott, Kansas; Prairie Grove, Elkhorn, Cross Hollows and Helena, Arkansas. He is a member of the Methodist Church, South, and the Masonic fraternity. He married Miss S. A. Scott. They have three boys and three girls.

Representatives.

AMOS WILSON BUCHANAN.

THE subject of this sketch is thirty years of age, having been born in DeSoto parish, Louisiana, March 23, 1857. In his boyhood, at the age of nine years, he left Louisiana under the charge of the family, who cast their fortunes with the great State of Texas. Mr. Buchanan received his education chiefly from the the public schools of Brazos county, where he now resides, and which county he represents in the Twentieth Legislature. By occupation he is a farmer, and is an influential member of the order of the Patrons of Husbandry. He was elected from the Fiftieth Representative district, embracing Brazos county, by a majority of 650 votes, and is an active member of the following committees, viz: Penitentiaries, Public Printing, State Affairs, Federal Affairs and Military Affairs. He was married to Miss Anna Peters, of Brazos county, and has a family of three children. Mr. Buchanan is in politics a Democrat, in religion a Missionary Baptist, and is a good talker on the floor of the House. He is scarcely of average size, having a preponderance towards a florid complexion and sanguine temperament. He cares more for the substance of what he says, than the manner in which it is said. He is a good specimen of the young Democracy of the State; progressive, but not daring; desirous of thrift, but would take no risks to attain it.

A. G. CAMP.

DR. A. G. CAMP, the subject of this brief sketch, was a member of the Eighteenth, Nineteenth and Twentieth Legislatures of Texas, in the House of Representatives. He was born in Jefferson county, Kentucky, in 1827, and educated in Louisville, where he graduated in medicine from the University of Louisville in 1856, and for one year served as resident physician in the Louisville Marine Hospital. He then removed to Saint Joseph, Missouri, where he engaged in the practice of his profession, and continued to do so until the war between the States. Dr. Camp was an outspoken Southern man and a Democrat, and none but those who lived in the border States, entertaining Southern sympathies, can appreciate the persecution and heroic endurance suffered by them.

Although there was a large majority of the citizens of Saint Joseph of Southern sympathies, that city was early occupied by Colonel Curtis' Iowa regiment, which gave protection and license to the Red Republican German population to wreak their vengeance on Southerners. Unawed by the bayonets of the Iowa soldiers, and the vindictiveness of the "Home Guard," composed of German turners, Dr. Camp refused to be silenced by either threats or assaults, and literally fought his way from the city to his home in the immediate suburbs every day.

The Southern element of the city soon left for the field, and Dr. Camp returned to his old home near Louisville, Kentucky. He immediately organized a company of boys, all that was left in his neighborhood of Southern men, and used them to protect trains conveying contraband of war to the Conefederate camp of General Johnston, at Bowling Green. The Federal lines closing about him and his devoted followers, he repaired to Bowling Green and reported for duty to General Johnston, who assigned him to duty as surgeon at the Market Street Hospital, at Nashville, Tennessee.

DR. A. G. CAMP.

He was ordered thence on the same duty to Atlanta, thence to Corinth, and finally to Ringgold, Georgia, where he was appointed on a board of examiners, composed of the eminent surgeons, Drs. Stout, Saunders, Pimm and himself, upon which he served to the close of the war.

He then returned to Saint Joseph, Missouri, and endured the same kind of persecution until 1870, when he removed to Groesbeeck, Texas, and engaged in the practice of his profession, at the same time opening a drug store.

Dr. Camp soon exhibited a Kentuckian's fondness for politics, and acquiring popularity by his social traits and sound sense, the people of Limestone county sent him successively to the Seventeenth, Eighteenth, Nineteenth and Twentieth Legislatures. His characteristic is watchfulness. No job escapes his vigilant eye, and no measure against the interests of the people can pass the Legislature after the scathing rebuke administered by the member from Limestone. No man in the House is so much feared by jobbers and lobbyists as Dr. Camp. Always in his place, and always informed upon every measure proposed, he stands as a sentinel on the watch-towers, and his fellow-members have so much confidence in him that a measure opposed by him has small chance of success.

It goes without saying that he is a "red-hot" Democrat, and for the last two sessions has served as chairman of the important Committee on Assylums.

With a vigorous mind and large experience, he brings to bear upon his duties an assiduity that knows no fatigue or defeat, and he stands with a State reputation as one of the most solid and influential law-makers of the State of Texas.

In 1865 Dr. Camp married Miss Juliet Jane, of Brandon, Mississippi. They have had five children, only two of whom are living; two daughters.

Representatives.

S. J. CHAPMAN.

THIS distinguished gentleman who represented the Thirty-sixth district (Johnson county), was born in Taladega county, Alabama, June 16, 1833. During the civil war he served in Texas State troops on the frontier and was assigned to the quartermaster's department, where he served from 1862 to 1865.

Mr. Chapman is a member of A. F. and A. M. lodge, Farmers' Alliance and the Grange, and while a member of no church, is an earnest believer in future rewards and punishments. He has been twice married. His first wife was a Miss Susan J. Strahan, who died in 1881. In 1882 he married his present wife, who was a Miss Elizabeth S. Harris, of Georgia. He is the father of six children, four boys and two girls.

His property was squandered and scattered and the Indians came in and stole all that he had in the way of wealth, and left him where he commenced in the world, except a wife and three children to support. But not to be outdone by adversity, he gathered up his wife and children and moved to Johnson county, in May, 1866, and resolved to quit stock raising and go to farming.

When he moved to Johnson county he had no money, and bought the first eighty acres of land he owned in that county on credit, and settled on it and improved it with his own hands, and made the money on the place to pay for it; and by hard labor, honesty and economy, has added to his wealth one thousand acres of land, second to none in Texas, has it well improved, and from almost nothing in 1866, he has accumulated the handsome sum of $25,000 in twenty years.

The subject of this sketch was raised by poor parents on the farm, and had but few educational facilities—only what he could pick up at short intervals at a common country school—but being a great lover of books and of a studious mind, he has made himself a fair English scholar. He is now a Representative by almost the unanimous voice of his people. Honesty has been his motto all his life, coupled with fervency and zeal. He has lived on the frontier of the State fourteen years in Cook and Denton counties. Assisted by his neighbors, he has chased many marauding bands of Indians, who had stolen property and murdered and carried off women and children.

Though not a member of the church, he is a strict pattern of morality, a Sabbath school worker, and a temperate man; a lover of God and country, always endeavoring to obey the laws of both.

He is a Jeffersonian Democrat, and was elected to the Twentieth Legislature by a majority of 2764 votes. He was a member of the following committees: Roads and Bridges, Stock and Stock Raising, Statistics and Health.

While not a man anxious to make a display, he was considered one of the ablest thinkers in the body of which he was a member. In the committee room and on the floor, he was listened to with respectful attention, and seldom failed to convince his hearers.

In the election of Mr. Chapman, Johnson county selected one who is a worthy representative of her intelligence and refinement.

CHARLES M. CHRISTENBERRY.

C. M. CHRISTENBERRY, Representative from the Thirty-eighth district, (Hill county), was born in Perry county, Alabama, July 14, 1854. He was educated partially in Alabama, but principally at Trinity University, Limestone county, Texas. Mr. Christenberry is the architect of his own fortune. Leaving his native State without means, he first came to Smith county, Texas, a mere boy, where he remained one year, farming. He then went to Bell county, where he farmed four years, then went to Trinity University, where he studied one year, not, however, consecutively, having to teach school to defray his expenses. He left Trinity and taught school for a time, and meanwhile read law. He then went to Waco and devoted all his time to the study of his profession in the office of Anderson Flint, where he remained for six years. He was licensed in the fall of the same year, when he went to Hubbard City, Hill county, and commenced the practice of his profession, and by the same indomitable energy that animated his youthful efforts he has succeeded in drawing around him a respectable and lucrative clientage.

He is a Democrat, never in his life having scratched a name on the Democratic ticket, and was elected over both of his opponents, both members of former Legislatures, by a majority of 502. He is unmarried.

Mr. Christenberry has a large and imposing frame, a

bright face, pleasant manners, and is destined to make his mark on the jurisprudence and legislative affairs of his adopted State, to whose general interest and prosperity he is devoted. He was a member of the following House committees: Judiciary No. 2, Federal Relations, and Counties and County Boundaries.

J. B. CONE.

MR. CONE represents an honored class of Texas citizens. He is a man of vast experience and an extended fund of knowledge. He was born in Georgia, on the tenth day of March, 1825. His education took the course so many of the noble youths of his day were compelled to take. He received what instruction he could in the little log school house. But in the view that life itself is a course of education, he has gone on till his attainments are of a creditable order. He is a farmer, and in this pursuit has had a good degree of success. For a good portion of the time of the late war, Mr. Cone served with Colonel J. E. McCord, and also with Colonel Stephen H. Darden. He was a good soldier, and trustworthy. He began his political life when elected to represent the Eighty-second district, composed of Karnes, Wilson and Atascosa counties. His wife was a Miss Walker, and his family consists of seven children. He is a Mason and a Knight of Labor. In his views of life he is cosmopolitan, and seeks to be in harmony with nature. With his age, he carries forward a noble purpose to look after the best things. He is not demonstrative in the House of Representatives, but faithful to all the interests and duties of his office. Being rather quiet, he has come forward more from a sense of duty than to win glory. His constituents will be pleased to note the consistency of his record, as they have seen in him a fit man to voice their interests in the Twentieth Legislature.

G. C. CLEGG.

THE Representative from Trinity county, Honorable G. C. Clegg, was born in Florida on the twelfth day of October, 1858. He came to Texas in 1872, and stopped in Harris county till 1876, when he removed to Trinity county, where he now resides.

Mr. Clegg is well educated, and a man of fine intelligence. He received his education at the Waco University, and at the Agricultural and Mechanical College of Texas, at Bryan. He is a lawyer, not having yet reached the prime of his life, nor of his professional career. His talents, as a rising member of the bar, are recognized, and he has not only acquired a good practice, but has also won the confidence of the voters of his district. He is held in esteem as a staunch Democrat, and, as such, was elected in November, 1886, to a seat in the Twentieth Legislature by a majority of about 1800 votes. His district is the Fifty-fourth, composed of Trinity, Waller, Harris and Montgomery counties. In 1880, he was married to Miss Jennie Barnes, daughter of J. P. Barnes, Esq., of Trinity county, and has a family of four children. Mr. Clegg is a member of the Ancient, Free and Accepted Masons. In the capacity of legislator, he has shown wisdom and fidelity and has been watchful of all the great interests passing under legislative review. His work in committee room and in the sessions of the House has made for him a record of which neither he nor his constituents will be ashamed.

JAMES CLARK.

JAMES CLARK, from the Eighteenth Representative district, composed of Red River county, was born March 19, 1838, in Red River county, Texas, and educated in that county by the Rev. John Anderson, Master of Arts. Mr.

JAMES CLARK.

Clark is a farmer in his native county, and one of the most respectable and intelligent of that class of citizens. His education under the Rev. John Anderson was very thorough, and combining with that a native shrewdness and comprehensive intellect, he soon assumed a high position in the House, and acquired an influence over his fellow-members. His popularity in his county is evidenced by the fact that he was elected without opposition. He served on the following committees, to-wit: Judiciary No. 1, Public Lands and Land Office, Agriculture, and Contingent Expenses. Upon all of these committees Mr. Clark was considered one of the most important and efficient members; bringing to bear, as he did, upon every question his practical sound sense and disinterested patrotism, his opinions and his motives were fully trusted.

Mr. Clark is a Democrat, basing his politics upon a thorough examination and understanding of the organic principles of the government.

Mr. Clark, in the beginning of the war between the States, served as an orderly until the battle of Oak Hills. After that he served as captain of company B, Crump's Battalion; then as captain of company I, Twenty-ninth Texas Cavalry, Colonel Charles DeMorse. When General W. R. Scurry received his appointment as Brigadier-General, he offered, and Captain Clark accepted, the appointment of aid-de-camp on his staff. He served in that capacity until General Scurry was killed at Jenkins Ferry; he then served with his successor, General Richard Waterhouse, until the close of the war, as aid de-camp.

Has been twice married, the first time to Miss M. B. Anderson, daughter of Rev. John Anderson, by whom he had four children, two daughters and two sons; second time to Miss M. M. Gaffrey, by whom he had three children, two living, one girl and one boy.

He is still faithful to the church of his fathers, the Catholic, and he is as broad in his religious and humenitarian views as the spirit of progress demands.

The Twentieth Legislature was the first in which Mr. Clark served, but he left his mark on the laws of his State, and if his tastes are political, will yet figure prominently in the affairs of the State.

JOHN H. CLARK.

THE gentleman of whom this is a brief biographical sketch is a Mississippian, born in Holmes county, of that State. In 1866, he came to Paris, Texas, and was educated in the schools of that place. Mr. Clark is, by profession, a lawyer, having been admitted to the bar of North Texas, in 1876. He engaged in, and continued a successful practice, in Paris, Texas, until the year 1883. During this year, he removed to Uvalde, Texas, where he now lives, and pursues his profession in honor, and with a fine degree of success. He was elected in the November election of 1886 to a seat in the Twentieth Legislature, from the Eighty-first Representative district, composed of seven large counties. He is a member of Judiciary Committee No. 2, Public Lands and Land Office, and others. Successful as a lawyer, he is not less distinguished as a legislator. He is a man of thorough devotion to what he believes to be the best interests of the people. His wife was Miss Rucker, of Paris, whom he had the great misfortune to lose, by death, in the city of Austin, while at his post of legislative duty.

JOHN THOMAS CURRY.

IN 1879, a trio of Kentuckians, to-wit, James Q. Chenoweth, T. M. Hunt and J. T. Curry, who had been schoolboys together, came to North Texas, and settled in that fertile portion of the State, each of whom has been, at some time,

JOHN H. CLARK.

Representatives.

a legislator of the State of Texas. Mr. Curry, who is a resident of Van Zandt county, and represents the Twenty-sixth district, was born at Harrodsburg, Kentucky, October 28, 1837. He was mainly educated in the common schools of the country, attending one year, however, at the Asbury University, Greencastle, Indiana. He is a farmer, and appears in public life for the first time as a member of the Twentieth Legislature, to which he was elected in November, 1886, receiving 1886 votes out of 2500 votes cast. He served as a member of the Committee on Finance, Revenue and Taxation, and others. Mr. Curry has a family of seven children. His wife was Miss Lizzie A. McBroyer, of Lawrenceburg, Kentucky. He is a member of the Methodist Episcopal Church, South, a Mason, and belongs to the Farmers' Alliance. He has broad and liberal views of the questions demanding the action of the Legislature. He is a solid man, of an exemplary life, intelligent, and acting according to the matured convictions of his mind. He has the confidence of his co-legislators, and is held in high esteem as a man of integrity. He is not especially given to speechmaking, but is prompt in all the duties of his position. He is pleasant, and capable of ardent friendships; tall, of florid complexion, light colored hair, and is a fine specimen of polite manhood.

TOM C. DAVIS.

TOM C. DAVIS, Representative in the Twentieth Legislature from the Fifteenth district, Harrison, Rusk, Panola, Shelby, San Augustine and Sabine counties, was born in Shelby county, Texas, August 4, 1850.

From 1876 to 1878, he filled the office of county attorney, and from 1878 to 1880, served as county surveyor for Shelby county. He is a Democrat, a member of the Ancient, Free and Accepted Masons and the Knights of Honor.

He is a member of the following important committees: Judiciary No. 2, Finance, Land and Land Office, and Roads, Bridges and Ferries.

JONATHAN JACKSON DAVIS.

THERE is variety in the pursuits of the Representative from the Fifty-fifth district. He is a farmer, having followed this honorable business from the days of his boyhood. He is also a minister of the gospel, in the ordained ministry of the Missionary Baptist Church. Mr. Davis is a native of Benton county, Alabama, born on the sixteenth of February, 1833. His father removed to Mississippi when Mr. Davis was but a child, and in that State he was educated. He came to Texas in the latter part of the year 1865, and stopped till the year following in Robertson county, when he removed to Falls and became permanently settled. He was a soldier in the war between the States, serving as lieutenant in company D, of Thirtieth Regiment, Mississippi Infantry. He took part in that memorable campaign from Kentucky, through Tennessee to the South, being engaged at the battle of Perryville, Murfreesboro, Keenasaw Mountain, and others; was severely wounded in the engagement on the right at Atlanta a few days before the evacuation by the Confederate forces.

Mr. Davis was elected to a seat in the Twentieth Legislature of the State of Texas, in November, 1886, and has acquitted himself well. He is a member of the Committee on Revenue and Taxation and others. Mr. Davis has proved himself a good legislator, and has a just and impartial view of the matters of legislation. He is tall, of dark complexion and affable in his manners.

NELSON P. DOLEN.

NELSON P. DOLEN was born in Sullivan county, Tennessee, March 26. 1832, and was educated at Pactolus Seminary. By education, he is a physician, but has not practiced the profession, engaging rather in farming and stockraising. He represents the Ninety-second Legislative district in the Twentieth Legislature, composed of the county of Harris. His politics are Democratic. He served in the Missouri State Guard, and afterward in the Confederate army, and participated in the battle at Lexington, and other engagements, also doing much secret service, incurring imminent risk, that was of great benefit to the generals commanding the Confederate armies.

His first wife was Miss Sallie McMinn, of Tennessee; his present wife was Miss Mary Gillette, by whom he has had ten children, eight now living—six girls and two boys.

Mr. Dolen's characteristic is readiness and adaptability to his environvents and happenings, at any and all times equal to any emergency that may befall him. With a strong mind, and direct in purpose, and energetic in performance, it follows that he is an eminently useful citizen, and a valuable member of the law makers of the State. His appreciation of the resources, and the ultimate development of Texas, makes him enthusiastic on behalf of the greatness and glory of Texas, to which he is attached with the warmest and most patriotic pride. As in all the affairs of life with him, he readily caught the genius of legislation, and threw all his mind and trained energy into the accomplishment of the purposes for which his constituents sent him to Austin. He served on the following House committees: Chairman of the Committee on the Revision of Rules, and a member of Internal Improvements, State Asylums, and Stock and Stock Raising.

J. L. ELLISON.

J. L. ELLISON, from the Ninety-first district, composed of the counties of Hays, Guadalupe and Caldwell, was born August 31, 1837, in Mississippi, but his parents immigrated to Texas in his youth, and he was educated in Caldwell county, Texas. He is a farmer, and married Miss Martha W. Martindale August 23, 1866. They have seven children, three sons and four daughters.

Mr. Ellison joined the Confederate army in 1861, and served in Texas and Louisiana during the war in the Thirty-second Regiment, Texas Cavalry. He was in the Red River campaign against the Union General, Banks, and participated in the battles of Blair's Landing, Yellow Bayou, or Norwood Farm, and others, and was wounded on Rapides Bayou, near Alexandria, Louisiana, in April, 1864. He is a member of the Baptist Church, and a strong party man in behalf of a Democratic nomination.

Mr. Ellison is a man of shrewd sense, a good judge of men and measures, social and agreeable in his manners and habits, and acquired, in a short time, considerable influence with his colleagues.

T. A. FULLER.

REPRESENTATIVE T. A. FULLER was born in Fannin county, Texas, January 20, 1859, and was educated at the Aricultural and Mechanical College of Texas. He is, by profession, a lawyer, and gives promise of success. He was a member of the following important committees: Judiciary No. 2, Judicial Districts, Military Affairs, Public Lands and Land Office, Willis Investigation Committee, and Committee to Visit State Schools.

H. M. GARWOOD.

HIRAM M. GARWOOD.

HIRAM M. GARWOOD, member of the House from the Seventy-fourth Legislative district, Bastrop county, was born in Bastrop county, Texas, January 11, 1864, and is the youngest member of the Twentieth Legislature. He obtained a very thorough English and classical education at the "University of the South," Sewanee, Tennessee, and studied his profession, the law, in the office and under the tutorship of the Honorable Joseph D. Sayers, in his native place. Mr. Garwood is thoroughly indoctrinated in the principles of the Democratic party, and takes a conservative and comprehensive view of the State and Federal governments. He is of medium height, but slight and compact in person. He has a chaste and intellectual face, denoting at the same time purpose and determination. His manners are easy and graceful, and his presence, for one so young, decidedly impressive. His educational training has been rigid and full, and he brings to bear on all questions an analytical and strong mind. There is no young man in the State who gives greater hope of success in his profession and the broad arena of politics than this young member of the House.

Mr. Garwood is unmarried, a member of the Episcopal Church, a Mason, and a member of the Greek Letter College Society. His popularity is evidenced by a majority over his opponent of 1746 votes in his native county of Bastrop. His position in the House advanced in influence, and recognition of his talents and good judgment was not withheld. He was appointed to membership on Judiciary Committee No. 1, and also on the Committee on Constitutional Amendments. As a special trust, he was made a member of the special committee to whom all the educational bills of the House were referred. His record as a legislator, like his reputation as a gentleman, is commendable and discreet.

M. V. GARNER.

HONORABLE M. V. GARNER, the subject of this brief sketch, is a native of Morgan county, Alabama, born September 30, 1839. He was educated in the common schools of his native State. He has consistently pursued agriculture as the business of his life. He was a good soldier in the late civil war in the United States, serving in the Eleventh Arkansas Infantry; was captured at Island No. 10, and having escaped from prison, rejoined the army, Second Arkansas Regiment, and was elected second lieutenant. His Church relations are with the Missionary Baptist. He is also a member of the Ancient, Free and Accepted Masons.

Mr. Garner was married to Mrs. S. A. Hays, of Robertson county, in the year 1865. Four children, two of each sex, constitute his family.

He was elected in November, 1886, to the Twentieth Legislature by a majority of 936 votes. His district is the Forty-eighth Representative. He is not an obtrusive man in official affairs, but follows his convictions, founded on the best information he has at the time.

ABEL SKENNEL GILL.

ABEL SKENNEL GILL, the subject of this biographical sketch, made his appearance first in Texas, as a citizen of Rusk county, in the fall of 1858. After the close of the war between the States, in the year 1867, he became a citizen of Navarro county, where he now resides. He is a native of Calhoun county, Alabama, where he was born on the twelfth day of February, 1835. He received an academic education at Oxford, Alabama, and has since continued to advance by experience and the ordinary processes of mental improvement, until he is a representative man in intelligence among the citizens of the State. He is a farmer, and was elected from that class of useful and honorable citizens a member of the Twentieth Legislature by a majority of 619 votes. His is the Sixtieth Representative district. Colonel Miller, of the Corsicana Observer, and other distinguished citizens of Navarro county, disputed the honors with Mr. Gill in the convention which gave him the nomination in July, 1886. He belonged to Company G, of the Eighteenth Texas Infantry, and in the Trans-Mississippi Department of the Confederate army. He is a member of the Methodist Episcopal Church, South, of the Masonic fraternity, and also of the Farmers' Alliance. On the fifteenth day of September, 1855, he was married to Miss R. E. Neighbours, and has a family of four children. He has a strong preponderance to a blond complexion, hair that in his young manhood was of a dark auburn, and a light blue eye. He is above the average in stature, being six feet two inches in height, and weighs one hundred and ninety-five pounds. He is not demonstrative, but advances to a question in debate with a purpose that is invincible. Not being professionally trained to oratory, he gives evidence in his speeches of natural gifts of an enviable order. He would not crowd himself into leadership, nor meanly scheme to defeat an opponent, but having won distinction, he would disdain to abuse confidence.

J. L. GILLELAND.

J. L. GILLELAND, from the Fourth district, composed of Angelina and Nacogdoches counties, was born in Angelina county, Texas, July 15, 1840, and educated in the common schools of the county. He is a farmer in his native county, and has served there as county commissioner and justice of the peace. He belonged to the committees on Privileges and Elections, Agriculture, and Revenue and Taxation. Politically, he is a Democrat, and served as a Confederate soldier in Company F, Thirteenth Texas dismounted cavalry, commanded by Colonel John Burnett, in the Trans-Mississippi Department. During the war, he suffered with dropsy, and was at home on furlough on that account at the time that the army to which his regiment was attached encountered the severe engagements of Mansfield and others. He was a member of the Methodist Episcopal Church. He married Miss Sarah M. Porter on the seventh of April, 1864, by whom he has had seven children—five daughters and two sons. He was attentive to his duties as a member of the Legislature, always at his place, and watchful of the interests of his constituents.

CARL GOETH.

CARL GOETH was born March 7, 1835, in Wetzlar, one of the former imperial free-towns of Germany, now a part of the Rhenan province of Prussia. After a course in the public school, he entered the Royal College of his native town, where he studied classics and mathematics, his grandfather, Ernest Franke, being one of the professors. At the age of sixteen, he learned the trade of compositor, emigrated with his parents to the United States in 1852, and landed in Galveston July 4, from where the family started with an old-fashioned ox-team towards Austin county, and bought there a farm in cultivation, with all the stock, on the identical spot where now the small town of New Ulm is situated.

Here the young man worked at the farm and helped to reap the first year's crop in the fall of the same year, ten bales of cotton and fifteen hundred bushels of corn. Three

CARL GOETH.

years afterwards, his only sister having married a saddle-maker, young Goeth connected himself with his brother-in-law in the then quite profitable business. After having learned the trade, he traveled and worked as saddle-maker in different parts of the United States, and when five years in the country, he became a citizen of the United States in Ohio, in the year 1857, when he cast his first vote for Governor Payne, the Democratic candidate for Governor of that State.

Returning to Texas, he started his own business in New Ulm, and married Miss Ottilie, daughter of Adolphus Fuchs (Fox), professor of music, a gentleman well known among the early settlers, having immigrated in 1845, first settling at Cat Springs, Austin county, and eight years afterwards in the southern part of Burnet county, near Marble Falls, becoming the first sheep raiser in that part of the State.

At the beginning of the civil war, Carl Goeth also moved into Burnet county to leave his wife and child under the protection of her parents, while he himself had to serve the State in the quartermaster's department in Austin, under Major James McKinney, as saddle-maker. During the Indian raids, he was detailed to join the scouting party near his family's home, but still making saddles for the government.

At one of the Indian raids, when a neighbor and his wife were killed by the savages, and a white boy while fishing at the creek captured, all of Mr. Goeth's horses were stolen; but in the neighborhood of Fort Mason the Indians were attacked, some killed, the rest routed, and the white boy and forty horses recovered.

After the close of the war, Mr. Goeth moved to Cypress Mill, Blanco county, his present domicil, where he engaged in the sheep business with his brother-in-law, Adolphus Varnhagen, grand-nephew of Varnhagen von Ense, and a practical sheep man. He was successful, like many others, and is at present the owner of a fine homestead and splendid range in one of the most beautiful valleys of our State, chiefly occupied in the wool business, having large herds of fine merinos, interbred with the famous Rambouilet stock.

Mr. Goeth's family consists, besides his wife, of five boys and two girls; the oldest girl is married to John Wenmohs, a neighboring sheep-raiser; and his eldest son to Julia, daughter of the well-known hardware dealer, Walter Tips, of Austin. The younger children are at home, helping hands to their parents.

In 1867, General Reynolds offered Mr. Goeth the assessor and collectorship for Blanco, but the latter declined, as an appointment to office by the military authorities was at the time quite unpopular, but since, after the State had been re-admitted to the Union, Mr. Goeth held at various times different offices, such as school trustee, justice of the peace, county commissioner, etc.

At the Democratic district convention, previous to the election of 1886, he was nominated for the office of Representative for the Eighty-ninth district, composed of the counties of Blanco, Comal and Gillespie, and elected by a vote of 2585 against 174 cast for the Independent Republican candidate.

ANDREW CARROLL GRAVES.

THE Sixty-third Representative district is composed of Coryell and Hamilton counties, and is represented in the Twentieth Legislature in the person Honorable A. C. Graves. Mr. Graves' majority in the last election was 276 votes. He was a member of the Constitutional Convention of 1875. His education is academic, having been primarily obtained in the common schools. His secular business has been that of surveying; he has also been a farmer through the greater part of his life. For twenty years, he has been a regular minister in the Missionary Baptist Church. Owing to delicate health, he served but a short time in the war between the States. He was born in Wilson county, Tennessee, on the tenth of January, 1831, and on the twenty-third of November, 1852, in the place of his nativity, was married to Miss Eveline Bennett. He has a family of nine children, is a Mason, and a member of the Farmers' Alliance. He is tall, spare, and of frail constitution. He makes a good soldier in polemical warfare, when the attack crowds him, but never sallies out to bring on an engagement.

G. S. HULING.

G. S. HULING, a member of the House of Representatives of the Twentieth Legislature, from the Forty-second district, composed of the counties of Collin and Denton, was born at ——— in February, 1845, and educated at West Point. By occupation he is a farmer, a member of the Democratic party, the Farmers' Alliance, and the Masonic fraternity.

Mr. Huling served, in the Confederate army, and was attached to the army of Northern Virginia, commanded by General R. E. Lee, and participated in the battles of Sharpsburg, or Antietam, Cold Harbor, Seven Pines, Garnett's Farm, and Chickamauga.

He is a member of the Baptist Church. He has been married twice, first to Miss C. A. Ticewell, of Harris county, Georgia. His second wife was Miss Mary G. Marble, by whom he has two children. Mr. Huling is a Democrat, and made a safe and conservative member of the Twentieth Legislature.

S. H. HARGIS.

S. H. HARGIS, from the Thirtieth Representative district, was born in Nacogdoches county, Republic of Texas, August 8, 1842, and was educated in various places in Georgia and Alabama, principally in the latter State. He is a farmer on Red River, Walnut Bend, Cooke county. He has served for two years prior to the last general election, as public weigher in Cooke county. In the Twentieth Legislature, he was a member of the following important committees, to-wit: Penitentiary, Judiciary No. 1, and Engrossed Bills. He has been a resident of Cooke county for fifteen years. During the late civil war, he served in Colonel McIntosh's regiment of Mounted Rifles; volunteered fourth day of July, 1861, in Benton county, Arkansas, in Company G, of the aforesaid regiment. He served variously under Generals McCulloch, Beauregard, Bragg, Johnston and Hood, and was engaged in many hard fought battles, and was wounded three times, but fought to the last ditch, and finally surrendered to overwhelming numbers. He married Miss Nancy C. Price. They have ten children, equally divided in sexes. Mr. Hargis was a laborious and consciencious member of the Legislature, doing his full duty to his constituents, and to his State.

NAT. M. HARRISON.

AT Athens, in Limestone county, Alabama, on the twelfth day of May, 1849, Mr. Harrison was born. He came to Texas in 1856, and has been a resident of Upshur county ever since. He was educated in that county under Professor M. H. Looney. He is professionally a druggist and dealer in medicines. By appointment, he served as tax collector of

Upshur county in 1876 and 1877. In 1878, he was elected by the people and served two years. At the expiration of his term of service as collector, he was elected county clerk, and subsequently twice re-elected, serving thus three terms in the office of county clerk. Mr. Harrison was elected to a seat in the Twentieth Legislature from the Eleventh Representative district, by a majority of 550 votes over two opposing candidates. He is appreciated as a legislator, having been appointed as a committeeman on the committees on State Affairs, Revenue and Taxation, and other important ones. His vindication of what he believes to be for the best interest of the people cannot be questioned. He has given proof as to the clearness of his convictions, and of the firmness with which he maintains them. He is a man of intelligence, not inclined to demonstration so much as accuracy. He has fine business talent, and has had opportunities through official services to become well educated in public affairs. He would not discard a matter because it is small, but would consider its relation to a whole and its effect upon a compound. He has been quite successful in the former trusts he has held in maintaining the confidence of the people, and bids fair in his office as legislator to be not less so.

He was married to Miss Lizzie Chadick, of Upshur county, and has a family of two boys. He is a Mason and a Knight of Honor. He has the social attractions which insure popularity, and is withal full of genuine politeness.

EPHROISE C. HEATH.

MR. HEATH was born November 4, 1850, in Kaufman, now Rockwall county, Texas. He was reared and educated in his native town, and still resides there. In 1881 he was united in matrimony to Miss Ida A. Collins, to whom he is devotedly attached, and who has been the guiding star and sweet inspiration of his life. To them two children have been born—a son and a daughter.

Mr. Heath is a man of learning, of and a thoughtful, vigorous and philosophical mind, which is stored with information, useful and varied, and he handled his forces in the Twentieth Legislature in a manner that showed him fully equal to the requirements of parliamentary warfare. During the course of his useful and eventful life, he has filled many positions of trust; was county judge of Rockwall county from November, 1882, to November, 1886. In that position he found a fair field for the exercise of his abilities, and made a bold, active, efficient and popular officer. When elected, he found the county of Rockwall badly in debt, with a rate of county tax at fifty-five cents. At the close of his term the rate of county taxation had been reduced to twenty-five cents, the county out of debt, and a cash balance on hand. The men among whom he grew to manhood, and who were thoroughly acquainted with his intellectual and other qualities, seemed to have delighted to honor him, as evidenced by a majority of 3831 votes, received in the counties of Dallas, Tarrant and Rockwall, composing the Thirty-fifth district, over his competitor for Representative to the Twentieth Legislature. He was chairman of the Committee on Roads and Bridges, and a member of several other committees.

He is competent to fill absolutely the highest position to which the people of Texas can raise one of the native born sons of the Lone Star State, for he is a man of the highest talents, most unimpeachable honesty, bold and fearless in his support of men and measures, and a christian gentleman. He is a Mason, Good Templar, and a member of the Methodist Episcopal Church, South.

G. P. HUMPHREY.

G. P. HUMPHREY was born in Marion county, Alabama, the twenty-first of March, 1827; moved to the Creek Nation, Alabama, in 1832, thence to Mississippi in 1835, thence to California in 1849, thence to Texas in 1855, and settled at Prairie Lea, Caldwell county, and in 1859 moved to his present home in Lavaca county, which is the Sixty-ninth Representative district, and which he represented in the Twentieth Legislature with honor to himself and his constituency. He is a Democrat, and served on the following committees, to-wit: Commerce and Manufactures, Agriculture, Roads, Bridges and Ferries, and others. In the late war, he served as paymaster of the Confederate Cattle Company. He is a member of the order of Masons; married Miss Mary Ann Prellian, of Mississippi, and they have eleven children, ten of whom are boys.

Mr. Humphrey is a farmer and stock-raiser, and is identified with the agricultural interests of the country. As a legislator, he was conservative, careful and attentive to his duties, and had, in all his efforts, the co-operation and confidence of his fellow-members.

THOMAS MEMUCAN HUNT.

IN December, 1856, the Representative from the Seventy-second district, made his entrance into Texas, and settled in Washington county, and has been in Texas ever since. Mr. Hunt is a native of Danville, Kentucky, born on the twenty-fourth of April, 1839. His education was obtained at the schools of Harrodsburg, Kentucky, and at Center College, Danville, Kentucky. Being a successful merchant, he may be said to represent that worthy class of Texas citizens in the Twentieth Legislature. He volunteered in the Southern army in March, 1862, serving in the Trans-Mississippi department. His last service was rendered as inspector-general on the staff of General Richard Waterhouse, of the famous Walker Division of Texas Volunteer Infantry. His public service began in 1870 as clerk of the district and county courts of Burleson county. He served in said capacity seven consecutive years, voluntarily retiring in 1877.

He was elected in November, 1886, to a seat in the lower House of the Twentieth Legislature by an actual majority of 2057. Mr. Hunt is a trusted legislator, being chairman of the Committee on Engrossed Bills, and also a member of the committees on Internal Improvements, on Roads and Bridges and Ferries, and to examine Comptroller's and Treasurer's Offices. In 1861, he was married to Miss Adelaide V. Wilson, of Burleson county, and has a family of two sons and five daughters. His complexion is florid and his eyes are a dark hazel. He stands six feet upon the floor, and weighs one hundred and forty pounds. He is a fine specimen of the Kentucky gentleman; converses freely, but gives evidence of respect for the opinions and conveniences of others. He is a fair-minded man, but firm in his convictions; a safe legislator; does not make many speeches, but is a hard worker, always at his post, and ever faithful to his constituency in his present position, as he has always been to every public trust confided to him.

WILLIAM T. HUDGINS.

WM. T. HUDGINS, a Democratic member of the House of Representatives of the Twentieth Legislature, Seventeenth district, composed of the counties of Bowie, Cass, Marion and Morris, was born on the fifteenth of January, 1859, in the county of Northumberland,

Virginia, and was graduated from Richmond College with the degree of M. A., in 1879. He is a lawyer, and served as county attorney for Bowie county, Texas, 1882 to 1884, and an alternate delegate from the Fourth Congressional district of Texas in the National Democratic Convention in 1884. In the Legislature of 1887, he served as chairman of the Committee of Enrolled Bills, and was a member of Judiciary Committee No. 1, and a member of the committees on Towns and City Corporations, and Counties and County Boundaries.

His family emigrated to Marshall, Texas, in 1865, and upon his return from college in 1879, he studied law with the Honorable George L. Todd, of Jefferson, Texas. He was admitted to the bar in 1880, and practiced in Jefferson until 1882, when he removed to Texarkana, where he still resides and is engaged in the practice of his profession, being junior member of the well known law firm of Todd & Hudgins. Mr. Hudgins is a member of the Masonic fraternity, Knight Templar, Knight of Pythias and an Odd Fellow.

At the present writing, Mr. Hudgins is unmarried. He has a compact physique of medium height, is most thoroughly trained in political economy, and has an earnestness of purpose that marks him as a man of conspicuous prominence in the affairs of his adopted State.

The Twentieth Legislature was the first session Mr. Hodgins served as a law maker in his State, and his efficiency was fully recognized by his fellow-members. A bright future awaits Mr. Hudgins, in both his profession and in politics.

J. W. JARROTT.

PARKER county was represented in the Twentieth Legislature by the most youthful looking member of the body, Honorable J. W. Jarrott. He was born in Marion county, Alabama, February 7, 1862, and having immigrated to Texas, entered school at Add Ran College, Hood county, Texas, where he was educated. He is a farmer of Parker county, being quite active and successful in his line of life. His election was declared by a majority of 427 votes. He has been prompt in the work of the Legislature, and is fearless in speech. In the purposes he undertakes to carry out, he is persistent to the last. He shows quickness of discernment and a readiness to take hold of the best interests of the people whom he serves and represents. His labors in the committee room, and in the hall, have been respected and given due consideration. His district embraces Parker county, and is known as the Forty-sixth.

J. W. Jarrott was married to Miss Mollie D. Wylie, of Parker county. He is a member of the Christian Church. He shows a commendable degree of cultivation, and is refined in his manners, small in statue, and of light figure; his action is quick, and his speech rather rapid.

HUGH JACKSON.

REPRESENTATIVE JACKSON is a lawyer by profession, representing the First district in the Twentieth Legislature. His district is composed of Hardin, Chambers, Liberty, Orange and Jefferson counties. He was educated in the common schools; began to read law in 1872, and was licensed to practice in 1879. Prior to his election to the Twentieth Legislature, he had served as county and district

HUGH JACKSON.

clerk, county judge, and county surveyor.. He began life as a farmer, and has continued that interest while engaged professionally. He is thirty-six years of age, having been born February 2, 1851, in Chambers county, Texas, and is a married man, his wife, being the daughter of Major Minter, of Liberty, Texas. He is five feet, ten inches high, weighs one hundred and seventy-two pounds, has dark complexion, jet-black hair, and is a generous friend and pleasant gentleman. He is a working member of the following committees: Roads and Bridges, Judicial Districts, and Enrolled Bills.

WILLIAM CONE JOHNSON.

THE subject of this sketch, William Cone Johnson, a member of the Twentieth Legislature, from the Ninety-third Representative district, composed of Smith and Gregg counties, was born at Dawsonville, Dawson county, Georgia, and was educated at the following schools and colleges in his native State, to-wit, the common schools, the high school at Atlanta, one year at Emory College, Oxford, and was graduated with the degree of Bachelor of Arts from the University of Nashville, Tennesse, 1880. Mr. Johnson first settled in the eastern part of the State, and taught school for five years. In the prosecution of the study of law, he taught in the University of Tyler, Texas, and read law in the office of Hon. W. S. Herndon, at Tyler, and was admitted to the bar in 1885. He had held no office until elected to the Twentieth Legislature, to which he was elected by a a majority of 1400 votes, as a Democrat.

Mr. Johnson's paternal ancestors were from North Carolina, and on the maternal side from South Carolina. His father, the late S. C. Johnson, was solicitor-general in what is known as the "Blue Ridge Circuit," of Georgia, at the time of his death in 1870. It will be seen that W. C. Johnson became an orphan early in life, ten years of age, and to his honor, be it said, he obtained his education solely by his own efforts. He is a member of the Methodist Episcopal Church, South, and, at present writing, is unmarried.

Mr. Johnson is on the threshold of his career, and gives promise of rapid advancement and high position, both in his profession and the broader field of politics. Even before and during the organization of the Twentieth Legislature, Mr. Johnson, upon the nomination of an officer of the House, distinguished himself as an orator of the highest order, and a debater ready for any and all antagonists.

Mr. Johnson is only twenty-five years of age, six feet tall, and weighs one hundred and seventy-five pounds. His splendid physique, admirable manner, and readiness of thought upon his feet, attracted attention the moment he rose in the House of Representatives, and marked him as one of the "coming men" of Texas. He was also known as a working member, and served, to the great benefit of the House, on the following committees: Judiciary No. 1, Judicial Districts, Insurance, Statistics and History, Internal Improvements, and Cities and Incorporated Towns.

Mr. Johnson will yet make a reputation for himself not confined to the limits of his adopted State.

R. J. JONES.

R. J. JONES served as a member of the Twentieth Legislature, from the Seventh district.

T. W. KENNEDY.

DR. T. W. KENNEDY, a native of the city of Philadelphia, Pennsylvania, was born in the year 1838. He is a graduate of Eureka College, Illinois. He began the practice of medicine in Paducah, Kentucky, and has pursued his profession in several of the Southern States. He came to Brownsville, Texas, in 1870, and subsequently removed to Rio Grande City, his present home. In 1884, he was elected to represent the Thirty-eighth district, composed of Webb, Zapata, Starr, Hidalgo and Duval counties, and was consequently a member of the Nineteenth Legislature. He was, by re-election, a member of the Twentieth Legislature.

W. C. LARKIN.

W. C. LARKIN, a member of the Sixteenth and Twentieth Legislatures, from the Tenth Legislative district, composed of the counties of Henderson and Anderson, serving in the Twentieth Legislature as chairman of the Committee on Public Buildings and Grounds, was born September 28, 1836, in Franklin county, Tennessee, and was educated at the Cumberland University, Lebanon, Tennessee, in the classics and belle lettres, and also graduated in medicine from the University of Pennsylvania, Philadelphia, in 1858, at twenty-one years of age. After graduating in medicine, he located in Sumter county, Alabama, and continued in the practice of his profession for two years. He then married Miss Hattie Holloway, of Sumter county, Alabama, and came to Texas in 1860, locating in Henderson county, where he has since resided. He has followed his profession till within a few years. He has lately been paying his attention to farming. He is a member of the

F. W. LATHAM.

Democratic party and the Masonic fraternity; has two sons and two daughters.

Mr. Larkin's legislative experience gave an advantage of training that proved of use to the House and his fellow-committeemen.

F. W. LATHAM.

F. W. LATHAM, a member of the Seventh, Eighth, Eighteenth and Nineteenth Legislatures, from the Eighty-fifth Legislative district, composed of the county of Cameron, was born in Groton, Connecticut, and educated at his native place. He is, at this date, sixty-eight years of age, and at every important epoch in the history of Texas, his adopted State, he has been called to the councils of the best men.

Mr. Latham served under General Scott in the war between the United States and Mexico, and participated in all the engagements of that illustrious general, that were accentuated by the Stars and Stripes floating over the City of Mexico, and an acquisition of almost a continent of valuable territory. With the last division of the army, Mr. Latham left Mexico, but attracted by the mild climate and blue skies of the State, in 1848 he settled near Brownsville, on the Rio Grande, and has since devoted himself to the business of farming and stock-raising upon his ranche, which is one of the largest and best conducted ranches in Southwest Texas. This distinguished citizen served in many important positions of honor and trust in his adopted State. In addition to his services mentioned in four sessions of the Legislature, Mr. Latham was an influential member of the first State convention that framed its organic law, and also a member of the convention of 1861, that attempted to sever the connection of Texas with the Federal government. During the Nineteenth Legislature, he was chairman of the

Committee on Claims and Accounts, and served as a member of other important committees. He has also served as clerk of the court of his county, and as collector of customs for Brazos de Santiago. Mr. Latham's wife was a Miss Mary Anna Sprague, of Providence, Rhode Island. He is a member of the Masonic fraternity. His record as a citizen and legislator is without reproach. Animated by a strong patriotism, he has always favored measures that he believed would forward the material interests of the State and elevate and ennoble his fellow-citizens. Perhaps no other man in the State enjoys such popularily as is evidenced by the fact that in all his political races he has never had any opposition. Coming up to the Jeffersonian principle of letting the office seek the man, in times of trial his people have always called him to the front.

ALEXANDER M. LATIMER.

ALEXANDER M. LATIMER, from the Forty-second Representative district, composed of the counties of Palo Pinto, Eastland and Stephens, was born in Carrol county, Tennessee, January 16, 1836, and came to Texas with his parents in 1839. He was educated at McKenzie College, Red River county, and is, by profession, a temperperance lecturer.

He served as chief justice of Young county in 1862, secretary of the Constitutional Convention in 1875, postmaster at Belknap under the Confederate States government, and collector of the Confederate war tax. During the war between the States, Alexander M. Latimer served in the Trans-Mississippi department, Polignac's division, Confederate States army, and participated in the battles of Mansfield, Yellow Bayou, Pleasant Hill, and several others. Mr. Latimer belongs to the Cumberland Presbyterian Church, and married

Miss Mattie Warren in 1865. They had six children. His first wife died, and in May, 1885, he married Miss Lennie Brittain. They have one child. He is a member of the Knights of Labor, and served in the Twentieth Legislature with ability on the following committees: Constitutional Amendments, Public Printing, and Stock and Stock-raising.

J. W. LIGHT.

J. W. LIGHT, of the Eighty-sixth district, composed of Bexar county, was born in Danville, Illinois, October 24, 1825, and was educated in his native place.

Mr. Light was one of the first bold adventurers to the Republic of Texas. He immigrated to Austin in 1848, at a time when the Indians made frequent incursions upon the then small settlement of Austin, and were often successful in stealing horses on the very limits of the city. Mr. Light is now a farmer, and resides in Bexar county. He resided during the late war "too near the Rio Grande," as he says, to be forced to take either side, and stood neutral as to active service. Mr. Light served as county commissioner in Bexar county after the adoption of the present Constitution.

He has been a Mason for forty years, and is also a member of the Farmers' Alliance. Mr. Light was married to Miss Rebecca Mobley, in Terre Haute. Indiana, who died in 1883. He has by her four children, two sons and two daughters.

JESSE McCALEB.

THIS elderly legislator, from Montgomery county, Texas, is a native of Tennessee, and was born June 26, 1827. He came to Jackson county in 1839, when but a boy, and subsequently removed to Montgomery county, where he now resides. The length of his residence in Texas has given him quite the identity of a native Texan. His education was not collegiate, having attended only the common schools of the country, and from this source laid the foundation, which, with experience and application, added to sound sensé, has made him what he is. He pursues the business of farmer, and has accumulated a competency.

Before his service as a representative from the Fifty-fourth district, he had filled the office of justice of the peace. His election in November, 1886, to membership in the Twentieth Legislature, was by a majority of 1585 votes. Four counties compose his district, to-wit: Harris, Montgomery, Trinity and Walker. He was on the following committees, viz: State Affairs, Revenue and Taxation, Penitentiaries, and Agricultural Affairs. He has been a quiet and laborious legislator, and represented well the people who honored him by election. Mr. McCaleb has been twice married, his first wife being Miss Dorcas Ceade; his second Mrs. Emma B. Chambers, both of whom are dead. His family has numbered fifteen children. He is a member of the Episcopal Church, the Masonic fraternity, and the order of Patrons of Husbandry. He bore himself wisely in the House of Representatives, and was held in high esteem and honor among his co-legislators.

J M! McCLANAHAN.

IN Lawrence county, Alabama, on the thirtieth of May, 1832, the subject of this sketch was born. At the age of fourteen he came to Burleson county, which at that time was accounted the frontier of Texas. In a subsequent division of the county, Mr. McClanahan fell into Lee county, where he now resides. As his name would indicate, he is of Scotch ancestry, and belongs to the Jeffersonian type of

Democracy. In early life, the stirring scenes and daring adventures of Texas frontiersmen inured him to hardships and endurance. Like his ancestry, he possesses a remarkable solidity of character. He is not subject to the mutations that bear on the unstable and light, but is firmly established in the elements of character that abide. Largely taught in the rugged school of experience, his education is broad and deep, and almost altogether of a practical nature. His business is that of a farmer, in which he takes a pride and has been in a good degree successful. He entered the arena of public life in 1884, being elected to the Nineteenth Legislature from the Seventy-third district, composed of Lee and Burleson counties. He was also returned by his constituents to the Twentieth Legislature. Aside from committee work, of which he has done a full share, his record as a wise legislator is above reproach.

W. L. McGAUHEY.

STERLING integrity and outspokon conviction of right are prominent elements of the character of the Represeutive from the Fortieth district. Bold in speech, vehement in delivery, and having a stentorian voice, he makes a telling argument when he comes before the people or the Legislature. He is of stout physical figure, and is an indefatiguable worker in whatever he undertakes. With the positive elements of charater which might graduate into austerity, he happily combines a broad and ardent philanthropy that gives him a well-balanced nature. He is an efficient member of the Legislature, and a gentleman of good nature to all the world. He is a native of Lawrence county, Alabama, born on the twenty-sixth of February, 1837. He is a graduate of LaGrange College, leaving his *alma mater* with honor to himself and credit to the institution. He was ten years a teacher in a private school. In 1869, he came to Tarrant county, Texas, where he lived for three years; then moving to Granbury, Hood county, he has resided there ever since. He was at one time a member of the faculty of Add Ran College, Thorp Springs, Texas, but is now engaged, successfully, in farming and stock-raising. He was a member of Cleburn's Division of the Army of Tennessee, during the late war in the United States. In Church relations, he belongs to the Cumberland Presbyterians, and is also a Mason. He was elected from his district, composed of Hood, Erath, Bosque and Somerville counties, as a Representative to the Nineteenth Legislature, and was also re-elected to the Twentieth. He is one of the most active and efficient members of the House, and has labored on many of the most important committees.

JAMES FOSTER McGUIRE.

THE education of James Foster McGuire, in the preparatory course, was acquired at Tuscaloosa, Alabama. The family having transferred their citizenship to Bastrop, Texas, in 1851, his further and finishing course was pursued at that place. He began the active business of life as a merchant, but has turned his attention to farming, and from this honorable and principal business of life, comes to the Twentieth Legislature of the State of Texas to represent the Seventieth district, composed of Fayette county. His election was by a majority of 255 votes. He is a substantial, reliable member of the House. According to the convictions of his order of mind, the gifts of nature and the direction of his education, he is more inclined to work and vote than to make speeches. He has been assigned to membership on four important committees. In the war of 1861 to 1865, he was a member of the Eighth Texas Cavalry, Company D,

Terry's regiment. He was in a long list of battles, beginning at Bowling Green, Kentucky, to the close of the war. His entire military service was rendered in the Cis-Mississippi department of the Southern army. He was once wounded at Murfreesboro, Tennessee. James Foster McGuire was born on the fourteenth day of December, 1838, in the city of Tuscaloosa, Alabama.

He was married to Miss S. R. Payne, in Washington county, Texas, in February, 1861. He has three sons. He is a Royal Arch Mason and a member of the order of the Knights and Ladies of Honor. Mr. McGuire is of Scotch descent, as his name would indicate. He is of a stout, compact physique, five feet and eleven inches high, weighs one hundred seventy-six pounds, has a blue eye, auburn hair, and a florid complexion. His movement is vivacious, his speeches argumentative, rather than declamatory, and his manners urbane and pleasant.

GEORGE T. McGEHEE.

GEO. T. McGEHEE, member of the House of Representatives of the Twentieth Legislature, from the Ninety-first Representative district, composed of the counties of Hays, Caldwell and Guadalupe, was born in Bastrop, Texas, the fifth day of February, ——, and educated in that county at Seguin. He is a farmer. His popularity is evidenced by the fact that he defeated four opponents for the Twentieth Legislature by a plurality of 2700 votes. He is a Democrat, and served on the following committees: Finance, Public Debt, Revenue and Taxation, State Asylums and Penitentiaries.

Mr. McGehee was not a candidate before the convention, but was nominated for the Legislature entirely without solicitation on his part. He served during the "late unpleasantness," as a private in Company D, Terry's Rangers, Confederate States army, and participated in all the battles of the Army of Tennessee from the first fight on Green River, Kentucky, to the last engagement. He was wounded twice. He is a member of the Methodist Episcopal Church, South, also of the Masonic fraternity. Mr. McGehee married a daughter of Colonel P. C. Wood, of San Marcos. He acquired very considerable influence in the Legislature by his close and intelligent attention to the business in hand, to the entire satisfaction of his constituents.

J. M. McKINNEY.

FEW of the members of the Twentieth Legislature present a finer physique than the gentleman from Milam county. Above the average in stature, and developed symmetrically, he commands respect in the presence of strangers. He is a man above the average in intelligence and moral standing, and is full of the spirit of accommodation and kindness, being a consistent member of the Missionary Baptist Church and a Knight of Honor. He was a soldier of fidelity and trust in the late war in the United States, serving in the Seventeenth Texas Infantry. In 1884, he was elected to a seat in the Nineteenth Legislature of the State of Texas by a majority of over 2300 votes. He was re-elected to the Twentieth Legislature. Having lived in Milam county since he was eleven years of age, and grown to manhood in that county, his popularity is proof of the manner of his life. He filled important places in both Legislatures, on committees, and made a record for efficiency and ability of which his constituents may justly be proud. Mr. McKinney is a native of Alabama, born October 3, 1841; is a farmer and stock-raiser, and has an interesting family. He has accumulated a competency by dint of energy, industry and economy, is not a man of display, but is the peer of any in solid worth. Scholastic training and experience have qualified him for official trust on the part of the people, and in no wise has their confidence been abused.

W. MATEJOWSKY.

W. MATEJOWSKY was born in Bohemia, April 30, 1828; moved to Texas in 1850, and settled in Bastrop county. In 1853, he was married to Miss C. Dietrich, his present wife, and shortly afterwards moved to Fayette county, where he has since resided. By occupation he is a merchant and farmer, though he has held several positions of trust in his county. In 1869 he was appointed postmaster of Nechanitz, in Fayette county, which position he held until he resigned after his election to the Twentieth Legislature.

In politics, he is independent. He was a member of the committees on Education, Roads and Bridges, and Commerce and Manufactures.

He has twelve living children, six sons and six daughters, which entitles him to the blue ribbon as far as the Twentieth Legislature is concerned. He was quite popular among his brother members, and was recognized as a good worker.

SETH P. MILLS.

SETH P. MILLS was born in Dade county, Missouri, August 19, 1841, and educated at Newtonio, in that state, but, the civil war breaking out, he joined that gallant soldier, General Joe Shelby, and participated in twenty-five different engagements. By his gallantry he was promoted from the ranks to that of lieutenant. His command was disbanded in 1865, at Waco, where the subject of this sketch, with nothing but his energy and hands, engaged in the task of reaping from the ground his support. He has been rewarded for his industry and pluck. He married Miss Fanny Steurt on the twenty-second day of October, 1871. They had seven children. He is a Mason. He served in the Sixteenth Legislature, and was a member of the committees on Finance, Constitutional Amendments, and Agriculture and Stock-Raising. He represents district number sixty-one, McLennan county, in the Twentieth Legislature, and served on the Committee on Revenue and Taxation. Mr. Mills is a farmer, and a Democrat, and fully alive to the great interests of the agricultural classes.

ROBERT TEAGUE MILNER.

THE honorable gentleman whose name stands at the head of this sketch makes his debut in the arena of politics as a member of the Twentieth Legislature of the State of Texas. In the primary elections his nomination was hotly contested, but, having got the nomination by the Democrats of his district, he was elected by a handsome majority, and, by his bearing and intense interest in the affairs of the House, promises to be an efficient member.

He is an Alabamian; born in Cherokee county, of that state, on the twenty-first of June, 1851. During the same year, and while he was an infant, his father immigrated to Rusk county, Texas, and engaged in farming. In Henderson, the county seat of Rusk county, and in the adjacent country, Mr. Milner has spent his whole life.

The foundations of his education were laid in home training and the common schools. For a time he was a student of Henderson Male and Female College, presided over by Professor Oscar H. Cooper, now Superintendent of Public Instruction of the State of Texas. The difficulties that disputed every step of his way to the goal of his ambition were only subdued by an inflexible determination to win.

He was raised a farmer's boy, and, until majority, made a hand with the laborors in the field. After he had acquired the necessary qualifications, he taught for several terms. Six years ago he assumed control of the Henderson Times, one of the oldest and best weekly newspapers in the State. That position he still holds. He was happily married to Miss M. L. Hawkins, of Henderson, in the fall of 1883, where the excellent lady had been raised.

His ancestry are of an extraction combining a descent from the English, Scotch and Irish. The Milner family had reached the new world before the days of the revolution. The honorable gentleman from Rusk is of handsome figure, nearly six feet high, and weighing 155 avoirdupoise. His hair is black, having an auburn tinge; his eye is blue, and his physiognomy indicative of intelligence. There is a vein of pleasantry in his mental constitution, and his manners are so gracious as to win even a stranger. He is free in conversation, and respectful to the responses of others. He possesses the power to draw others to him socially—is generous, and of a kind heart. He is logical, but makes no pretentions to entrancing oratory.

R. J. MOORE.

R. J. MOORE, of Washington county, Texas, was born in the year 1844, of a colored mother, in the county which he represents. He is well educated, being, by profession, a teacher. He is intelligent and modest, and by his decorous behavior, has made a good record as a legislator.

He has served as commissioner of Washington county, and in three consecutive sessions of the Legislature, to-wit, the Eighteenth, Nineteenth and Twentieth, as a member from the Seventy-first Representative district. In politics, he is a Republican, and in his legislative work has had membership on a number of committees.

E. T. MOORE.

E. T. MOORE, representing the Seventy-fifth district, Travis county, in the Nineteenth and Twentieth Legislatures, was born in Missouri, November 26, 1846. In 1864, he came to Caldwell county, Texas, where he lived two years, and then removed to Austin for the purpose of studying law. He pursued his legal studies with diligence, and was admitted to the bar after an examination by the Supreme Court. His merits as a lawyer and orator were soon appreciated by his fellow-citizens, and he was soon elected city attorney, then county, and afterwards district attorney. He was first elected prosecuting attorney by the commissioners court, and next by the people, with a majority of 1165, then with a majority of 1756, and fourth, in 1884, without opposition.

Mr. Moore resigned his position of district attorney in 1883, and in 1884 he was elected a member of the Nineteenth Legislature, and again to the Twentieth Legislature, in 1886. He served in the Twentieth Legislature as chairman of Judiciary Committee No. 2, and was also a member of the committees on Constitutional Amendments, Educational Affairs, and Revision of Rules.

Mr. Moore is a Democrat, a member of the Methodist Episcopal Church, South, and is a Royal Arch Mason, and Knight Templar.

Mr. E. T. Moore is fully equipped both as a lawyer and

legislator. He has brought to bear upon the study of law and political economy the powers of a clear and strong mind, and his taste has led him to adorn his ability with the highest literary accomplishments. His education is classical, and naturally gifted with a pleasing presence and a forcible and graceful delivery, in early life, when other men of his age were struggling in the rudiments of the profession, he sprang into notariety as an orator of the finest qualities. As a lawyer, he stands among the foremost of the profession at the Austin bar, and either in prosecution or defense, his speeches before juries rarely fail to effect his purpose.

Amiable in dispotion and thoroughly religious in conviction and practice, he is an object of pride to his fellow-citizens, and his friends regard him as the "rose and expectancy" of the State.

Mr. Moore has merely entered the vestibule of life, and gives promise of entering its most exclusive halls and ministering upon the highest altars of his country.

JOHN McCULLOUGH MELSON.

AMONG the young members of the House noted for their promise and prominence, is the Representative from Hopkins county, Honorable J. M. Melson. He began his education in his native county at Sulphur Springs, under Professor James H. Dinsmore, and was a student at the University of Texas in 1887. He illustrates the truth that there is no excellence without great labor and endeavor. Without the advantages of wealth to make the way to classical training less difficult of ascent, he has found, by experience, the truth, which others have discovered before him, that there is no easy way to scholarship, and that where there are the natural elements of intellectual greatness, even poverty itself cannot long obstruct achievement.

Mr. Melson was the prime-mover in the system of the clubbing of students, for purposes of economy, at the State University, which has since been continued with commendable advantage to young gentlemen struggling to get an education. He is the first student of the University who has come to the capitol as a legislator. He is a member of the Missionary Baptist Church, and is exemplary in his life and conduct. He is of medium height, has black hair and eyes, a fair complexion, and a countenance that betokens studiousness and lines of fundamental thought. His ability as a young lawyer, his fine talent as an orator, and his personal popularity, have contributed to the early honor given him by his constituents. He is modest, of fine physique, and has the capacity to make friends and keep them. He is a Texan, a native of Hopkins county, born in 1862.

A. J. NICHOLSON.

THE gentleman who represented the Twenty-first district is a native of Arkansas. Mr. A. J. Nicholson was educated in Fannin county, Texas, in which county he now resides. He was a soldier in the war with Mexico, and participated in the memorable battle of Monterey. He also served in the Southern army during the war between the States, having the rank of captain. He belonged to the Eleventh Texas Cavalry, and during his confinement as a prisoner, having been wounded, he received the complimentary election to the office of lieutenant-colonel.

Colonel Nicholson received the handsome majority of 2386 votes at the election which honored him with a seat in the Twentieth Legislature. He is chairman of the Committee on County Government and County Finances. He is known to be a true Democrat, and is also a Royal Arch Mason. His wife was Miss T. C. Parish. His family is composed of seven children. He has been active and zealous in his office, and has made a record in conformity to his honest convictions. His business in life is farming and stock-raising, and before his election to the Legislature he had served as deputy county surveyor of Fannin county, Texas.

G. A. NEWTON.

G. A. NEWTON served in the Twentieth Legislature, from Cherokee county, Texas.

E. NEWTON.

THE subject of this biographical notice, Honorable E. Newton, of Tarrant county, was born in Bradley county, Tennessee, on the twenty-third of January, 1845. Having immigrated to Texas early in life, he received his education in the common schools of Tarrant county, Texas, where he now lives. He is a farmer and a minister in the Missionary Baptist Church. In the late war between the States, Mr. Newton belonged to the command of General R. M. Gano, and was active in Arkansas and the Indian Territory. His wife was Miss M. E. White. His family consists of eight children. He is a Mason, and belongs to the Farmers' Alliance. He was elected to a seat in the Twentieth Legislature of the State of Texas from the Thirty-fourth district. He is a quite legislator, and not demonstrative. He does not make many speeches, but is prompt and watchful.

Representatives.

A. J. NORTHINGTON.

A. J. NORTHINGTON, a member of the House of Representatives from the Seventy-sixth Legislative district, composed of the counties of Lampasas and Burnet, was born on the first day of August, A. D. 1840, in Lamar county, Texas (then the Red River district), and educated at Georgetown. He has served as a county commissioner, and as a democratic member of the Fifteenth Legisture. The district at that time composed of the counties of Williamson and Lampasas. In the Twentieth Legislature, he was chairman of the important Committee on Stock and Stock-Raising.

Mr. Northington served in the Confederate army, in Morgan's battalion, Trans-Mississippi department, which was stationed, the principal part of the time, in Arkansas and Louisiana.

Mr. Northington is engaged in farming and stock-raising. He married Miss M. L. Knight, daughter of Dr. D. F. Knight. They have six children, four boys and two girls.

Mr. Northington fully understands what legislation is necessary for the State of Texas, and has fully demonstrated that the interests of his constituents are safe in his hands.

W. B. PAIGE.

IN the year 1851, beyond the smoky summit of the Blue Ridge, in Virginia, Mr. Paige was born. He came to Texas in the year 1873, and settled at Crockett, Texas, where he still resides. He is a finely educated gentleman, and a successful educator. He was principal of the Crockett High School for a number of years, and, under his management, the institution grew and was popular. He is a good debator, speaks fluently and correctly, and presents an argument hard to refute. His legislative activity has been distinctive in the cause of education, in which he shows practical knowledge and a great amount of dilligent research. He was elected in November, 1884, to a seat in the Nineteenth Legislature, from the Thirteenth district, composed of Houston county, and was, by re-election, returned by his constituents to the Twentieth Legislature. His prominence in committee work, and in the House discussions, are proof of the great esteem in which he is held by his co-legislators. He is a Knight Templar, and has held places of trust in the fraternity. His Democracy is not questioned, as he has done much to advance the principles in which he is thoroughly imbued. He is not a man given to vacillation, nor is he so ready to form acquaintances as to form them unadvisedly. His purposes are strong, and he is earnest in advocating them.

GEORGE WASHINGTON PATTERSON.

G. W. PATTERSON, member of the House of Representatives of the Twentieth Legislature, from the Twenty-third Flotorial district, composed of the counties of Delta, Fannin and Lamar, was born in Maury county, Tennessee, first of September, 1820, and educated in the old field schools of that county. He came to Texas in 1860, and engaged in farming, which he has constantly pursued, with the intermission of the war between the States. He served for twenty-two years in Marshall county, Tennessee, and Delta county, Texas, as justice of the peace, and was a member of the Fourteenth Legislature, from the Tenth Flotorial district, then including Delta county. Mr. Patterson had no opposition, and his popularity is evidenced by the fact that he received 6652 votes. He served as chairman of the Committee on Contingent Expenses, and also was a member of the committees on Internal Improvements, and Public Grounds and Buildings.

At the commencement of hostilities, he organized a company of cavalry in Paris, Texas, on the first of February, 1862, and joined General Price, with the First Texas Legion, and was finally transferred to the other side of the Mississippi, and served in Ross' brigade of cavalry; but being relieved from service, on account of sickness, in 1862, he returned home, recovered, and in the fall of the same year, organized another company in Bonham, Texas, and joined the command of Colonel James Bourland, stationed at Buffalo Springs, Clay county, and remained with him until 1865. Mr. Patterson belongs to the Methodist Episcopal Church, South. He was first married to Miss Hardeson, in Tennessee, in 1846; she dying, he married, in July, 1875, Miss M. L. Hogue. He has eight children—four sons and four daughters—living. The youngest son is six feet seven inches tall. In fact, he belongs to a race of tall people.

J. WESSON PARKER.

J. WESSON PARKER, a Democratic member of the House of Representatives, from the Fifty-third Legislative district, composed of the counties of Fort Bend and Waller, was born in Fort Bend county, Texas, September 15, 1847, and was educated at Soule University, Chapel Hill, Texas. He combines the profession of law and the occupation of a farmer. He has served as justice of the peace and county attorney of his native county, and his popularity is evidenced by the fact that he is the first Democratic Representative from Fort Bend county since the war.

Mr. Parker served in the saddle in the Confederate army,

and participated in the battles of Mansfield, Pleasant Hill, Yellow Bayou, etc. He received a flesh wound at Yellow Bayou.

He is a member of the Methodist Episcopal Church, South, and married Miss Ruth E. Wade. They have six children, four sons and two daughters.

BEDFORD PARKS.

BEDFORD PARKS, from the Ninth Legislative district, composed of Anderson county, was born December 8, 1837, in DeSoto county, Mississippi, his parents immigrating to Texas while he was quite young. He was educated at McKenzie Institute, Red River county, Texas. By occupation, he is a farmer, and served one term as a justice of the peace. He is a Democrat, and when the tocsin of war sounded over the land in 1861, he volunteered, and served in the First Texas Regiment, Hood's brigade, army of Northern Virginia, in all the memorable engagements of that brigade until the Battle of the Wilderness, on the Rappahannock river, Virginia, where he was shot through the left lung, and was retired from the service.

He served on the committees on Constitutional Amendments, and County Government and County Finances. It being Mr. Parks' first term of service in the Legislature, he was a modest but intelligent working member, and won the confidence of his co-laborors in the Legislature.

Mr. Parks has been married three times. His present wife was a Miss E. A. Parks. He has five children, one daughter and four sons.

Representatives.

JONATHAN PAYNE.

JONATHAN PAYNE, a member of the House of Representatives of the Twentieth Legislature, from the Eighty-seventh Representative district, composed of the counties of Goliad, Victoria, DeWitt, Jackson, Calhoun, Aransas and Refugio, was born in Corydon, Harrison county, Indiana, on the nineteenth of February, 1829, and was educated at Corydon (Indiana) Seminary. He first engaged in the practice of law, from which he retired about two years since, and is now engaged in farming and stock-raising. He has heretofore been a member of the House of Representatives of the Thirteenth Legislature, in which body he served as a member of the following committees, to-wit: Internal Improvements, Judiciary No. 1, Enrolled Bills, and Finance.

In the Twentieth Legislature he served as chairman of the Committee on Internal Improvements, and as a member of the following important committees: Judiciary Committee No. 1, Claims and Accounts, and to examine Comptroller and Treasurer's Offices.

Mr. Payne has resided in Southwestern Texas, for over twenty-six years. He is a Democrat, and was a soldier in the late war between the States, serving for a time in the Thirty-second Regiment, Texas Cavalry, commanded by Colonel P. C. Woods. The latter part of the war, he had charge of government supplies at the depots of Goliad, Karnes and Wilson counties. He is a member of the Presbyterian Church, is married and has one child.

B. R. PLUMLY.

BENJAMIN RUSH PLUMLY.

BENJAMIN RUSH PLUMLY, Representative from the Sixty-fourth district, composed of Galveston and Brazoria counties, is a life-long Republican. Mr. Plumly was born in Newtown, Bucks county, Pennsylvania, May 15, 1816. Although in his seventy-first year, he is vigorous, active and cheerful, his vitality of mind and body seeming not to have abated. An orphan boy, he was placed in a country store when six years old, and continued in the occupation of a merchant through more than forty years. His only instruction, except by long and laborious self-culture, was received at an excellent private school in his native village. Amidst the arduous duties of his calling, he found time to read medicine and law (not practicing either), to be well versed in history, philosophy and English literature, to keep abreast with all living issues, and to become a speaker and writer of note. Major Plumly was many years in the civil and military service of the United States, and is familiar with the leading men and the measures of the last half century.

Major Plumly has been twice married. He and his present wife, and their one son, live at their homestead at Galveston, Texas. He came to Texas, at Galveston, in March, 1866, and obtained permission from the city council, and built there, the first city railroads in Texas. He has been a member of the Galveston city council, and has been frequently sent as an agent to Washington, D. C., on matters of public local interest. He was a member of the Twelfth Legislature, made Speaker, but declined it, and became leader of the House; was also in the Seventeenth, and is now in the Twentieth Legislature, elected each time by a large majority in a strongly Democratic district. Major Plumly is an able legislator, devoted to Galveston and Texas, and, in the House, is without an enemy.

We close by quoting from one of his distinguished cotemporaries: "Mr. Plumly is an orator, a poet, a philosopher, and a gentleman, and withal, a zealous worker for humanity, wherever is human need, without distinction of race, color, or previous condition."

A. J. POPE.

HONORABLE A. J. POPE, of Harrison county, Texas, was born in Washington, Wilkes county, Georgia, July 15, 1854. He is another instance of a self-taught and self-educated man. Not having the advantages of school discipline, he has gone on hewing his own way to the mines of knowledge and stores of learning. He is a lawyer of fine ability, and an earnest pleader. His influence before a jury is of a resistless character. He has gone up in the legal profession till his practice has grown to extensive labors and remunerative rewards.

He was elected in November, 1886, to the Twentieth Legislature of the State of Texas, the first public trust conferred upon him. His election was a popular one, having a majority of 3025 votes. He next was appointed chairman of Judiciary Committee No. 1, and a member also of the committees on Internal Improvements, on Public Lands and Land Office, and on City Corporations. He makes a speech of telling effect, and argues his points well. He is argumentative, and is not abashed at the greatest opposition. His nature is exceedingly social, and no man can feel offended at the display of wit and pleasantry in which he sometimes indulges.

A. J. Pope was married to Miss Bettie Browning, and has one boy as the treasure of the household. He is a member of the Knights of Honor, and also of the Ancient Order of United Workmen.

Mr. Pope is small in stature, has black hair and eyes, and possesses a pleasing nature for everybody.

A. C. PRENDERGAST.

A. C. PRENDERGAST, the well known leading member of the Waco bar, elected to the Twentieth Legislature House of Representatives, from the Sixty-second district, composed of the counties of McLennan, Falls and Limestone, was born near Springfield, Limestone county, Texas, on the nineteenth of February, 1853. His primary education was obtained in the private schools of his neighborhood, but he was finaliy graduated from Trinity University, Tehuacana, Texas. He studied law and located at Waco, where he at once took high position at the bar. His ability was at once recognized by the people of his section of the State, as is evidenced by a majority of 10,000 votes against his competitor for the Twentieth Legislature. Mr. Prendergast served as chairman of the important Committee on Constitutional Amendments, and gave all his fine powers to a close attention to the issues arising in the House. He is a free and graceful speaker, logical in his arguments and convincing in his conclusions. Always in his seat during the sessions of the Legislature, and watchful of the proceedings, he was a frequent participator in the debates, and proved equal to any member in the House in argument and influence.

With the advantages of a thorough literary and legal education, and thoroughly trained in the art of attack or dedefense, he enforced his measures with such strength and tact, that the statutes of the State of Texas will attest the wisdom of his policy, and bear the marks of his intelligence and industry. He is a Democrat, and a strict party man, because he believes that the machinery of government is safe only under Democratic principles and Democratic men.

Mr. Prendergast is a member of the Cumberland Presbyterian Church. He married Miss Lillian L. Conoly, and has three children—two daughters and one son.

Mr. Prendergast has become identified with all the interests of his section of the State, and is always ready to contribute his energy, influence and means to the development of his section and the interest of all the people of his native State. He is destined, *Deo volente*, to make a prominent figure in the State, both in politics and his chosen profession, the law.

CLEMENT MARSHALL RICHARDSON.

WHEN C. M. Richardson was a boy, at the age of ten years, his father, Captain E. B. Richardson, immigrated to Texas, and settled in Leon county, where they still reside. The family, originally, lived in Bladen county, North Carolina, at which place Clement was born on the tenth day of September, 1856. He has had good educational advantages. Beginning with a course in the common schools, he was one year a student at Southwestern University, at Georgetown, Texas, and afterwards attended Vanderbilt University, Nashville, Tennessee. In the year 1878, he received license to practice law in Bellville, Texas. Besides his profession, he is engaged in farming and merchandising, and resides at Leona. He has never been in public life before his election to a seat in the House of the Twentieth Legislature, from the Forty-ninth Representative district. His nomination was by acclamation in the Democratic convention, and his election by a very large majority over his Republican opponent.

Mr. Richardson introduced a bill to create the office of State Geologist, which has since become a law, and a movement popular with the faculty of the University and other leading gentlemen of the State. He is the prime mover in this direction, and the first to call the attention of the Legislature to its vast importance. His membership on several committees indicates the appreciation of his legislative counsel by his co-legislators. He is small in stature, about five feet and seven inches, and weighs one hundred and thirty-five pounds. He has a light complexion and blue eyes. He shows true cultivation and refined manners. He does not make many speeches, but is found attentive and faithful in the position to which his constituents have called him. He is among the youngest and most respected members of the House.

He is a member of the Methodist Episcopal Church, South, and of exemplary life.

J. C. RUGEL.

MR. J. C. RUGEL, Democratic member from Dallas, of the Twentieth Legislature, was born in Jefferson county, Tennessee, and was educated at Morristown. He married Miss Florence Frierson, and has four children, two girls and two boys. Mr. Rugel is a merchant, and has served as justice of the peace of Dallas county. He is a member of the Cumberland Presbyterian Church. Belongs to the Masonic fraternity and the Knights of Honor. In the present Legislature he served on the following committees, to-wit: State Affairs, Penitentiaries, Education, Internal Improvements and Constitutional Amendments. Mr. Rugel is a staunch Democrat.

JAMES FRANKLIN SADLER.

HONORABLE J. F. SADLER was born in Fannin county, Texas, October 12, 1851. He was educated in the common schools of his native place. His instruction and expeience have tended to a business education rather than literature or professional lore. He is a good business man, and has had a fair degree of success. He is engaged in farming and merchandising, in the management of which he has so demeaned himself as to win the meed of popularity on all sides. His wife was Miss M. M. Wiley, and he has a family of three children. His church relations are with the Cumberland Presbyterians, and he is a member of the Independent Order of Odd Fellows.

Mr. Sadler was elected to the Twentieth Legislature from the Twenty-second district, which embraces the populous counties of Lamar and Fannin, in November, 1886, by a majority of 6500 votes. He is a Democrat of the orthodox school, and has been an active and influential member of the party from early manhood. His work in the Twentieth Legislature, both as a committeeman and a member, has made for him a good record, of which both he and his constituents may be justly proud. He is not given to much talking, but is modest and respectful. He knows how to oppose or to suffer opposition, and yet possess the majesty of an even temper. He is of average stature and spare figure, of light complexion and florid countenance. He is easy and deliberate in his legislative work, just as he would cautiously and accurately balance his ledger or plan for a crop. A man of more than average intelligence, he has made a good legislator.

JAMES H. SHELBURNE.

THE Representative from the Sixty-eighth district, Honorable James H. Shelburne, had the honor to legislate for his native county. He was born in Austin county, on the second day of December, in the year 1845, and appeared in the Twentieth Legislature of the State of Texas as Representative from that county. He received his education in his native county, and in the adjacent portions of the State. He began life by teaching school; he also studied law. He is now a merchant, and has been for thirteen years, doing quite an extensive business, both in Austin and adjoining counties.

His career as a public man has been somewhat varied. He was a member of the police court of his county, also a justice of the peace, and filled the office of assessor of taxes. In November, 1886, he received the unanimous vote of his county for representative to the Twentieth Legislature. His labors in the Legislature have been in harmony with his former record. He has served in the regular committee and legislative work with that degree of fidelity which is both commendable and satisfactory. For four years he has been chairman of the Democratic Executive Committee of his county.

As a soldier, he was prompt and brave, serving in Company F, Parson's cavalry, in the regular Confederate service.

James H. Shelburne was married to Miss Mary A. Perkins, of Austin county, and has a family of six children, one of whom is a son. He is a Royal Arch Mason, and a Knight of Honor.

At an advanced age, his father, Samuel A. Shelburne, and his mother, Adeline J. Shelburne, still live.

Honorable J. H. Shelburne is a man of good intelligence, and considerate in his action. He is of rather large physical stature, and commanding presence.

LEONIDAS LAFAYETTE SHIELD.

MOUNT Moriah Institute, located in Panola county, Mississippi, was properly the *alma mater* of Honorable L. L. Shield. Here his early life was spent, and here he received the rudiments of a liberal education. The trend of his instruction has been toward the practical affairs of life, and the habitudes of his mind have been directed toward business. He was born in Lafayette county, Mississippi, on the twenty-seventh day of August, 1850. In the year 1868, he immigrated to Texas, and settled for a while in Titus county; subsequently he removed to Coleman county, where he now resides. Mr. Shield is a farmer and stock-raiser, having engaged also during a part of his life in merchandising. Conforming to the laws of thrift, he has, in the pursuit of his business, grown from poverty to competency, and now controls a reasonable fortune in the world. He represents the Nineteenth district, composed of Coleman, Reynolds, Concho, San Saba, Llano, and McCulloch counties. His first appearance in the political arena of the State is in his present office as a law-maker in the Twentieth Legislature. He made the race as a Democrat, and was elected over three opposing candidates by a plurality vote of four hundred and fifty. He has rapidly grown in the esteem of his co-legislators, and wields an influence both respected and controlling. He has been appointed to membership on the following committees: Stock and Stock-raising, Lands and Land Office, Judicial Districts and on Public Debt. As a citizen, he sustains an unimpeachable character for loyalty and integrity; as a legislator, he refrains from speculations and utopian schemes, and deals with the verities and vital interests of the people. He makes no effort at ornate oratory, but is an earnest and forcible speaker, daring to advocate his convictions with commendable heroism. Mr. Shield was married to Miss Carrie Hubert, on the twentieth of September, 1877, and has two children, one of each sex. He maintains an upright character. He is of average stature and spare in physical figure, florid complexion, blue eye, and very light hair, almost red. His movement is quick and he converses with great freedom. He would be incapable of betraying the trust of a friend, nor would he take advantage of an enemy surrendered, to whom he would show no quarter on equal terms of warfare. He is full of energy and conservative, but in no sense an obstructionist.

W. SHOWALTER.

HONORABLE W. SHOWALTER is a native of Mason county, Kentucky. He has lived in Texas for several years, and has fully ingratiated himself into the esteem and confidence of the people of his district. He received a collegiate education at Kenyon College, Kentucky, and is thus better qualified for the duties of his office than many less favored. He is a lawyer of fine standing, and is patronized by a large and growing clientage. He entered public life in November, 1886, when he was elected to membership in the Twentieth Legislature. His district embraces six counties, to-wit: Webb, Encinal, Duval, Zapata, Starr and Hidalgo, and is known as the Eighty-third. He made the race as a Democrat, and received a majority of 87 votes. He has fully represented the counties who voted him the honor of a seat in the House, and has acted well his part. He was not indifferent to the current legislation, but discharged promptly and faithfully the duties of his office.

EMORY W. SMITH.

EMORY W. SMITH was born in Brunswick county, Virginia, and immigrated to Texas in 1860, settling in Travis county, of which county he is one of the Representatives in the Twentieth Legislature. Mr. Smith is a farmer, and largely identified with that interest in Texas, being president of the Texas Co-operative Association, and believes that the interests of his class depend upon the supremacy of Democratic principles. Mr. Smith did gallant service in the Army of Northern Virginia, and participated in the battles of Gaines' Mill, Spottsylvania Court House, and the seige of Petersburg, at the first of which he was severely wounded. Mr. Smith's wife was Miss Letitia Bowen, of Georgia. They have six children, and, as he quaintly remarks, "all are girls but five." Mr. Smith is thoroughly acquainted with the needs of the agricultural interests of the State, and by a straightforward and intelligent fidelity to the interests of his constituents, has made himself a useful member of the House. He is a Mason, a member of the order of Patrons of Husbandry, and served on the following committees: State Affairs, Agricultural Affairs, Public Buildings, Revenue andTaxation, and Penitentiaries.

W. M. SMITH.

HONORABLE W. M. Smith, a Democratic member of the House of Representatives, from the Fortieth district, composed of the counties of Bosque, Erath, Hood and Somervel, was born in Hawkins county, Tennessee, August 4, 1832. He came to Texas in 1872, and located in Denton, then moved to Bosque county. He was educated in Kingsport, Tennessee.

He is a farmer and stock-raiser, and never served in any political position before his election to the Twentieth Legislature.

Mr. Smith was in all the battles of the army of Tennessee, serving as major of the second regiment of the Tennessee Cavalry (Ashley's), Second brigade, First Division of the Army of Tennessee, Confederate States.

He married Miss Alice Davis, of Charlotte, North Carolina. He is an Odd Fellow, and a member of the State Grange.

He is a member of the following legislative committees: Finance, Public Debt, Judicial Districts, and State Affairs.

Mr. Smith was elected to the Twentieth Legislatute by a majority of about 1100 votes over his opponent. He was not in attendance upon the local nominating convention of his district at its meeting, but was nominated without solicitation.

GEORGE A. STAPLES.

THE men who are honored by political preferment have a dual history—one which belongs to the people by whom they are honored, and the other to themselves. The public career of Mr. Staples began in 1883, when he served a term as county attorney of Jackson county, Texas. Elected in November, 1886, to the Twentieth Legislature, of the State of Texas, by 2000 majority, his higher office of law-maker increased his resposibility, and the expectation of his constituents as well. He represents the Eighty-seventh district, composed of Jackson, Victoria, DeWitt, Calhoun, Goliad, Refugio and Aransas counties. Indoctrinated in the grand old principles of Democracy, he is a zealous friend and member of that party. He was assigned to the chairmanship of the Committee on Judicial Districts, and was a member of other committees of importance. His record in the Legislature will not be set down for naught, when his constituents reckon with the recipients of public patronage and honor. He has been firm and true according an intelligent survey of the matters brought before the Legislature.

G. A. Staples was born in Amherst county, Virginia, September, 6, 1842, and was educated in his native State. He came to Texas in 1860. His service as a soldier was rendered in Arkansas and the Indian Territory, in the late war in the United States. His wife is the daughter of J. McA. White, Esq., one of the first settlers of Jackson county, Texas. He is a Mason and an Odd Fellow. His disposition is of that kind that wins upon the masses, and brings him into popular favor. He does not thrust himself obnoxiously forward, but is discrete and respectful in the advocacy of his favorite measures. He has made a safe member of the House, having liberal views of true progress, yet sufficiently conservative to insure safety. Being a lawyer by profession, he is ready in the transaction of legislative business.

R. E. STEELE.

NO man in the Texas Legislature has such a reputation for a steel-like character as the distinguished representative from the Fifty-ninth district. His movement, speech, promptness and gallantry, indicate the elements of a true and trustworthy manhood. Strong in his convictions, forcible in argument, and abounding in practical knowledge, his influence in the House is as potential as his character is popular among his constituents. He was born in Alabama, in the year 1840, and at the age of fourteen he came to Texas and settled in Freestone county, where he still resides. He was a trustworthy soldier in Granbury's brigade, Army of Tennessee, in the late war, and behaved himself according to the chivalric spirit he has exemplified in after life. He is a member of the Old School Presbyterian Church, and of the order of Patrons of Husbandry. He was elected to a seat in the Eighteenth Legislature, and re-elected to the Nineteenth and Twentieth Legislatures. He has been the advocate of many of the most important bills of the House, and the author of not a few. His labors on numerous important committees were of the most arduous and grave character. His length of service as a legislator has made him a power in the House accorded to very few. Such representatives are to be trusted, and their wisdom respected.

WILLIAM M. SKINNER.

WILLIAM M. SKINNER, from the Seventeenth Flotorial district, composed of the counties of Morris, Bowie, Marion and Cass, to which he was elected by a majority of eight hundred votes, was born in Cobb county, Georgia, the twenty-first day of October, 1832, and came to Texas with his father's family in 1838. He received the rudiments of his education at the "old field schools" of the neighborhood, but that was limited on account of the fact that, while yet a very young man, Mr. Skinner caught the spirit of adventure in 1849, and went to the land of gold, California, where he lived, with various fortunes and adventures, until 1861, when the clamor notes of war armed his patriotic ardor. He then came back to Texas with General Albert Sydney Johnston, who was placed in command, at Bowling Green, Kentucky, of the Southern troops. Mr. Skinner first did service in the secret service, as a spy in the

"Buckner Guards," under General Johnston. He was offered a commission, with an appointment on General Johnston's staff; but he refused, preferring and believing himself more useful in another capacity, that of the secret service. He was, however, with General Johnston when that distinguished captain received his death-wound at the battle of Shiloh; helped to take him from his horse, convey him from the field, and remained with him until the last.

After the battle of Shiloh, he raised a company of cavalry and joined Medison's Regiment of the Third Arizona cavalry, operating in Louisiana. He was captured at Vandalia in October, 1863, and knowing he would suffer death, if recognized, being falsely charged with killing some negroes on a captured cotton boat, he changed his name, and gave another person one hundred dollars to permit him to go in that man's place to Alton. This ruse was successful. He was then taken, with others, to Fort Delaware, and finally paroled with the sick and wounded. After exchange, he did important secret service in the Federal lines.

After the war, he settled in Morris county, Texas. He has served in that county as justice of the peace and county commissioner. In the Twentieth Legislature, he served on the following committees: County Lines and Boundaries, Constitutional Amendments, Claims and Accounts, and Public Buildings and Grounds. He is a Democrat of the old school, and proved to be a most intelligent and useful member of the Legislature. He has a singularly commanding person, being six feet, two and a half inches tall, weighs two hundred and nineteen pounds, is straight and well proportioned, with a strong and handsome face and head.

Mr. Skinner is a member of the order of Ancient, Free and Accepted Masons, and belongs to the Grange and Farmers' Alliance. In religion, he is a Missionary Baptist, was married to Miss Ellen Williams, of Alabama, and they have seven children, five daughters and two sons.

Mr. Skinner's acquaintance with the organization of the

new State of California, and the operation of the laws there in a new State, brought that knowledge to bear in his course as a member of the Texas Legislature.

JOHN B. STRINGER.

HONORABLE John B. Stringer began his public life by being elected to the office of county attorney of Franklin county, in February, 1876. In November, 1878, he was re-elected to the same office, serving, in all, two terms. He was elected to a seat in the Eighteenth Legislature of the State of Texas in 1882, and was returned to the Twentieth Legislature without opposition. His is the Nineteenth Representative district, composed of Franklin, Titus and Red River counties. As a county attorney, Mr. Stringer bore a fine reputation, and acquitted himself as a successful prosecutor of the lawless. In his office of legislator, he is not obtrusive, but makes a strong and telling speech. He is not forward, but dignified, thoughtful and earnest.

He was chairman of the Committee on Public Debt in the Twentieth Legislature, and rendered valuable service on other committees, as a member.

As a lawyer, he builds from foundations deep and broad, not visionary, but argumentative.

He was born in 1845, in Pike county, Alabama, and was educated in the state of his nativity. In November, 1879, Mr. Stringer was married to Miss Emma Ray. His family consists of three living children. He is a member of the Masonic fraternity, and, in political affiliation, is with the orthodox elements of Democracy. He is rather tall, and of spare but handsome figure; is of ruddy complexion, and strong, vigorous movement. His speeches are characteristic of the man, forcible rather than ornate, and bristling with facts and figures, rather than abounding with the flowers of rhetoric. His place in the House was honorable, and his constituents were ably represented by him.

HORATIO LORENZO TATE.

SUCCESSES or reverses in an individual life have their discernable antecedents. The salient features of an individual biography—not discounting its accidents and hidden combinations, which contribute to the development of character—are handed down as an inheritance to succeeding generations. Such a philosophy underlying individual character and conduct is a legitimate patrimony, invested with personal immortality. Like the flower that perishes under the law of decay, the stalk remaining as an enduring element, the personal glory of one's life may fade out of sight, but the immortality of works remain to the generations that come after. So justly balanced is the well-ordered life of the subject of this sketch, that for what he is and

Representatives.

does, he justly commands a foremost place among his co-legislators. Dr. Tate is a Georgian, and was born on the fourth day of September, 1841, in Elbert county, of that State. He was brought to Texas in company with his father's family while in his early youth. For many years the Tate family have been respected and honored citizens of Smith county, Texas, from which place Dr. Tate is now a Representative in the Twentieth Legislature. The rudiments of his education were acquired in the common schools of the State, as a preparatory course to a broad and thorough acquirement in literature, medicine and general information. In 1861, he graduated from the school of medicine in the State of Louisiana. Declining an appointment of Governor Hubbard on the medical staff of the executive, Dr. Tate, true to the instincts of a patriotic citizen, entered the war between the States as a private. He was at first a member of the Third Texas Cavalry, under the independent command of General Sterling Price, of Missouri; afterward, however, he was mustered into the Confederate service, assigned to Company E, in Colonel Brown's Regiment of Texas Cavalry, and engaged on duty in Texas, especially in guarding the coast. His conduct as a soldier was in harmony with the trend of his life—brave, humane and faithful to the obligations of imposed trust and duty. After the surrender of the Southern forces, Dr. Tate returned to Smith county, and engaged in the practice of medicine near the old homestead established and settled by his father. His first public service was in the Nineteenth Legislature of the State of Texas from the Twelfth Representative district, and his re-election to the Twentieth Legislature is an irreputable endorsement of his public record by his constituency. In the Nineteenth Legislature, he was appointed chairman of the Committee on Public Health and Vital Statistics, besides membership on other important committees. In the Twentieth Legislature, his appointment was to the chair of the Committee on Penitentiaries, and he also rendered good service as a member of various standing committees. Dr. Tate was the author of the bill to create a reformatory and house of correction for youthful offenders against the law. This bill was offered in the Nineteenth Legislature, and failing to become a law, was revived in the Twentieth. He occupies an enviable position in the esteem and confidence of co-legislators. He has a broad and comprehensive view of the needs of the people, and is inventive of the requisite plans of relief. In debate, he is a master; in argument, he is invincible; and in oratory, he is eloquent. Behind a fluency of well chosen lan-guage, there is the warmth of the philanthropist and the resistless torrent of a generous heart that conquers, not to enslave, but to make free.

Dr. Tate is a member of the Methodist Episcopal Church, South, of the fraternity of Ancient, Free and Accepted Masons, and of the Independent Order of Odd Fellows; he has also a membership with the Patrons of Husbandry and the Farmers' Alliance. He was married to Miss Mary E. Terry, of Smith county, Texas, on June 21, 1862, and has a family of five children. He has a ruddy complexion, a blue eye, and is of medium statue. His physiognomy is the undisguised exponent of an extraordinary degree of intelligence. His strongest convictions of justice could never be hardened into cruelty. As a legislator, he devises preventives and restoratives rather than surrender the body politic to amputations and heroic surgery. He is obliging and polite; having the courage of a Wellington, he is yet tracable like a child. He would never abuse the confidence of a friend, nor gloat over the miseries of an enemy.

D. E. TOMPKINS.

D. E. TOMPKINS, Representative in the Twentieth Legislature from the Third district, composed of the counties of Tyler, Jasper and Newton, was born on May 8, 1831, in Monroe county, Indiana. He moved to Tyler county, Texas, on the twenty-ninth day of April, 1847, in which county he obtained most of his education. In politics he is an Independent Democrat, and by profession a farmer. He has occupied the positions of justice of the peace, county commissioner and school director of his county. He served as a private in the army, first at Little Rock, Arkansas, and then at Tyler, Texas.

He was married to Miss S. D. Rawles, of Tyler county, Texas, the result of this union being three children—all girls. He was an efficient law-maker, and served on the following committees, to-wit: Public Debt, Public Health and Vital Statistics, and County and County Boundaries.

JOHN HAYWOOD TOLBERT.

OF English and Irish ancestry, the Tolbert family spread into Virginia and North Carolina at an early period in the colonial history of America. In 1810, the progenitors of Representative Tolbert became established in Tennessee. Maternally, he is related to Sergeant George Watts, whose deeds of valor in the Revolutionary War are an appreciable part of American history. Captain Tolbert was born on the twenty-fifth day of January, 1837, in Jackson county, Tennessee. He began his education in his native place, and continued his course of instruction for two years at Burritt College, Van Buren county, Tennessee, at the expiration of which time he received an appointment to a cadetship at West Point, but, owing to ill health, was forced to decline acceptance. He came to Texas in 1857, and stopped at Bonham until the following year, when he settled in Grayson county, which has been his home ever since. He was married to Miss C. J. Miller, of that county, on the thirty-first day of January, 1866; has a family of two children, and is engaged in farming as a business. In January, 1862, he entered the war between the States as a private in Company D, Sixteenth Texas Cavalry, and in the following May was promoted to the captaincy of the company. This position he held until the close of the war, though placed on the retired list in November, 1864, on account of disability, caused by serious wounds which he had received at Milliken's Bend on the seventh day of June, 1863, and subsequently at Pleasant Hill, Louisiana. He participated in the battles of Cotton Plant, Arkansas; Perkins' Plantation, Milliken's Bend, Mansfield and Pleasant Hill, Louisiana, and other engagements more or less sanguinary. He has never been known in politics until he appears as Representative of the Twenty-seventh district. Having received an unsought nomination from the Democratic party, and without making a canvass, he led the ticket in his district by a majority of 2300 votes. He is an influential member of the following committees: Finance, Constitutional Amendments, Public Lands and Land Office, and Roads and Bridges. Captain Tolbert is a member of the Christian Church, and is possessed of an enviable degree of personal popularity. He is 5 feet 8 inches in height, and has an average weight of 170 pounds. He has a vigilant, blue eye, a florid complexion, and hair that in his youthful days was black. He does not dash into acquaintance and friendship, but with the same gradual movement that measures his natural carriage, he unfolds a confiding and generous nature.

JOHN H. TRUITT.

JOHN H. TRUITT, a Democratic member of the House of Representatives of the Twentieth Legislature from the Fifth district, composed of the counties of Shelby, San Augustine and Sabine, was born in Shelby county, Texas,

February 21, 1848, and educated in that county. He combines the profession of law with that of a farmer.

Mr. Truitt is a grandson of the Honorable James Truitt, who was a member of Congress when Texas was an Independent Republic, and for many years a delegate to the House of Representatives and Senate of the State of Texas from Shelby county, serving his last term in the Senate in 1866. His father, A. M. Truitt, was a major in Colonel Jack Hays' regiment of Texas Rangers. John H. Truitt served during the late civil war in the dismounted cavalry from Texas.

He was reared and trained a farmer, and also studied law, and was admitted to the bar in Shelby county in March, 1878. Mr. Truitt was married to Miss Mary Brown, of Shelby county, in February, 1873, who died October 8, 1879. On September 2, 1880, he married Miss Mary Atkins, of Shelby county.

F. A. UTIGER.

F. A. UTIGER represented the Twenty-seventh district in the Twentieth Legislature.

J. H. VOORHEES.

THIS gentleman represented the Ninety-fourth Representative district in the Twentieth Legislature.

W. A. WILLIAMS.

IN the year 1846, in Forsythe county, Georgia, Honorable W. A. Williams was born. He came to Texas in 1873, since which time he has been a law-abiding citizen of his adopted State. In 1878, he went to Kimble county, and is a resident of that place at the present time. His education began in the common schools of Georgia, but has been a progressive work through his entire life. After his removal to Texas, he taught school for five years, then read law, and began the practice of his profession when he became settled in Kimble county. His life has been an eventful one, and full of work; he has found the world a workshop, and his hands have not been idle in doing his part. Along with the practice of his profession, he has engaged in the mercantile business, and has been so far successful as to enjoy a competency and comfortable living. In the late civil war between the States, he engaged at the age of seventeen years, and remained eighteen months thereafter—until the surrender of Lee. He belonged to the Eighth Georgia battalion of cavalry, and was assigned to duty in Florida.

Mr. Williams was married to Miss Ella, daughter of Dr. McSween, of Burnet, Texas, on the first day of February, 1882. One little girl is the light of the home. He is a member of the Methodist Episcopal Church, South, and also of the Ancient, Free and Accepted Masons. He has always been a Democrat, and as such was elected to the Twentieth Legislature of the State of Texas from the Eighty-fourth district, in November, 1886, by a majority of 135 votes. His district embraces the following counties, to-wit: Mason, Kerr, Kimble, Kendall, Bandera and Medina. He has shown good judgment in his labors as a legislator, and is a safe man.

W. A. WILLIAMSON.

[Name incorrectly printed "Williams" in sketch, on page 190.]

T. A. WILSON.

THE Representative from the Second district is a native of South Carolina, where he was born in the year 1831. He came to Texas in 1860, and settled in Polk county, where he still resides. His education was limited, having been obtained at intervals in the common schools of the country. He is a farmer, and has been prosperous as such above the average of his fellow-agriculturists.

The wife of T. A. Wilson was Miss E. C. Kelley. The family is composed of eight children. He is a member of the Methodist Episcopal Church, South, and belongs to the Farmers' Alliance, and also to the order of Patrons of Husbandry. He served in the late war, chiefly in Arkansas, and was a prisoner three months.

In public life, he has served as county commissioner of Polk county, and justice of the peace. In November, 1886, he was elected a member of the Twentieth Legislature of the State of Texas, to represent the district composed of Polk and San Jacinto counties. He makes no display, but is vigilant and prompt.

LUCIUS ADOLPHUS WHATLEY.

THE Representative from Cass county, Lucius Adolphus Whatley, was born in Newton county, Georgia, on the twelfth day of September, 1838. His education, which was of a preparatory and business character, was obtained in his native State. In the year 1858, he immigrated to Texas, and settled in McLennan county, and, after the war between the States, became a citizen of Cass county, engaging in the merchandise of hardware, which is still his secular business. He served as a private for a part of the time during the war between the States, being connected with the infantry and cavalry service of the Southern army. His military assignment was first to the Tenth Texas Infantry, and subsequently to the Nineteenth Texas Cavalry, Colonel Buford's regiment. His first public service was in the Twentieth Legislature, as a member from the Sixteenth Representative district. He was elected by a majority of eight hundred votes. He was a member of the committees on Judiciary No. 2, Internal Improvements, Educational Affairs, Commerce and Manufactures, and Insurance and Statistics. He is a member of the Masonic fraternity, and of the order of Knights of Honor. He was married to Miss Emma G. Heard, on the twenty-fifth of January, 1868, and has a family of five children. Representative Whatley is not of an obtrusive disposition; is of deliberate calculation in his methods, and has an air of natural dignity and a steadiness of movement which comports with his portly physical manhood. He talks but little, but plans, and works, and votes faithfully.

WILLIAM LEE WOOD.

REPRESENTATIVE W. L. WOOD, of Ellis county, is a modest man, of reticent disposition. He is faithful in duty, but not specially inclined to polemical discussions. He is five feet and eleven inches in height, and weighs one hundred and fifty pounds, avordupois. He was born in Marshall county, Tennessee, December 23, 1850, and in August, 1877, in his native place, was married to Miss Josie Johnson. In January, of the following year, he came to Ellis county, Texas, and engaged in farming, in which business he is now engaged. His education was obtained at the common schools. He is a member of the Christian Church, of the Farmers' Alliance, and of the order of Patrons of Husbandry. He had never served in public life till he was elected a member of the Twentieth Legislature, by a majority of forty-two votes over six opponents.

He is a working member of the following committees, to-wit: Commerce, Agriculture, Public Debt, Stock and Stock-raising, and chairman of the sub-committee of the latter.

J. M. WOOLSEY.

HAVING grown forty-seven crops since he was married, Mr. Woolsey is entitled to be recognized as a farmer. To this honorable business in life he has devoted his best energies, and filled up the measure of a good citizen. He was born in the State of Georgia, September 3, 1819, and is, in consequence, well advanced in the school of experience. He was raised to manual labor, and without shrinking from hardship, he has endured and toiled until a competency has been his reward. He is self-taught and self-educated. Using the dim light of the evening fire, or the limited illumination of the rural cottage, he read at night, and appropriated the spare moments, when not engaged in work, to acquire knowledge, and the result has not been abortive. He is a man of good average intelligence, and has been honored by his countrymen.

The wife of Mr. Woolsey was Miss Matilda A. Blunt. His large family numbering fourteen children, equally divided in sex. He is a member of the Methodist Episcopal Church, South, and is also affiliated with the Masonic fraternity.

Mr. Woolsey was elected to the Twentieth Legislature from the Sixty-seventh district, which includes the county of Colorado, being the first Democrat elected from that district since the days of emancipation, by a majority of 86.

His legislative record has been according to the tenor of his life, solid, and not speculative; staid, rather than adventurously progressive. He is not demonstrative, but has been faithful to his convictions.

JAMES B. WRIGHT.

J. B. WRIGHT, from the Twenty-eighth Representative district, composed of Collin county, was born at Lexington, Kentucky, and received his education at that Athens of America. He studied medicine, and was graduated from the Eclectic College in Cincinnati.

Dr. Wright entered the Confederate army in 1861, as a private in company K, Fifth regiment, Breckinridge's division, then stationed at Bowling Green, Kentucky. He participated with his regiment at the bloody battle at Perryville, Kentucky; but in 1864, he met with an accident on a railroad, by which he had his hip crushed. This occurred when his regiment was en route to relieve General Pemberton, then besieged at Vicksburg. He went to Georgia after partial recovery, and remained there until the cessation of hostilities. He then returned to his home in Kentucky, but being crippled so badly as to prevent his riding horseback, he went over to the prairies of Illinois, and settled in Crawford county, where he engaged in the practice of his profession. While living there, he married Miss Elizabeth Higgins. They have five children, our sons and one daughter.

In 1876, Dr. Wright came to Texas and settled in Collin county, from which he was elected to the Twentieth Legislature by a majority of 238 votes. He served on the following committees: Finance, County and County Boundaries, Stock and Stock-Raising. He is, as he declares, a Democrat "dyed in the wool." He is also a member of the

Representatives.

Christian Church, a Royal Arch Mason, and a member of the Farmers' Alliance.

Dr. Wright is an exceedingly intelligent man, with fine-cut features and a large, brainy head. He is now engaged in agriculture and the improvement of his health in the genial climate of Texas, where he has permanently settled.

OFFICERS OF THE HOUSE.

WILL LAMBERT.

CHIEF CLERK.

WILL LAMBERT was born on Governor's Island, New York, February 29, 1840. His father, Robert Lambert, a native of Scotland, was an officer in the old United States army at the time of Will's birth. His mother was born in Ireland. Both parents died the same week at Fort

Brown, Texas (opposite Matamoros, Mexico), with cholera, in July, 1849. In 1850, he enlisted as a musician (drummer) in Company D, First Infrantry, United States army (his father's old company), stationed at Fort Duncan (Eagle Pass), opposite Piedras Negras, Mexico. He served one year, when his older brother secured his discharge, because of his minority. He joined his brother at San Antonio, and in February, 1852, entered the Weekly Ledger office, owned by Vanderlip & Hewitt, and served five years' apprenticeship at the printing profession. Coming to Austin in 1850, he served two years in a job office, under instructions, and is now an artist in his profession, of which he is proud; for whatever success he has attained in life, he owes it to the education obtained in a printing office, being too poor to go to school.

He served on the frontier, as a Texas ranger, in 1859, 1860, and a part of 1861, under "Rip" Ford, Ed. Burleson and Henry E. McCulloch. He enlisted in the Confederate army in 1861, and served throughtout the war in the Trans-Mississippi department.

At the close of hostilities, he took up the "stick and rule," at Houston, on the old Telegraph, owned and edited by E. H. Cushing.

Mr. Lambert married Miss Fannie E. Black, in May, 1866, and in September, of the same year, embarked in the newspaper business, at Anderson, Grimes county. He was elected mayor of that town, but was removed by General Reynolds, because he was an "impediment to reconstruction."

Drouth, cholera, cotton-worms, yellow fever and radicalism finally forced him to give up his paper at Anderson; so he returned to Houston, where he went on the staff of General W. G. Webb, then owning the Telegraph. He has held similar positions since then on different papers in Waco, Houston, Galveston and Austin.

In 1874, he started the Daily Morning News, at Marshall,

but his Democracy was too ultra for that climate, at that time, so the enterprise did not stick.

In 1875, Mr. Lambert was appointed aide-de-camp on the staff of Governor Hubbard, with the rank of Colonel.

He served as Reading Clerk of the House for the Tenth and Fifteenth Legislatures, was Chief Clerk of the Sixteenth and Seventeenth, and a general clerk of the House of the Eighteenth Legislature, during which session he discharged the duties of every officer in the House, except the Speaker.

He was elected Chief Clerk of the Twentieth Legislature without opposition, receiving every ballot that was cast. He is a good reader, and an accurate clerk. He fully understands the performance of such duties, and, with the aid of his legislative experience, rendered great assistance to the members.

J. C. CARR.

J. C. CARR, Sergeant-at-Arms of the Twentieth Legislature, House of Representatives, was born in Fayette county, Tennessee, July 26, 1833, and came to Texas in 1845, where his education, commenced in his native State, was completed. Mr. Carr has been engaged in several vocations of life; being full of energy, and of an active and progressive enterprise, he caught at everything within the reach of that activity, and worked it for all it was worth, doing his full duty, either as a public officer or private citizen. He has been a farmer, merchant and railroad man, developing in each occupation an ability to stand in the front ranks. He acted as county treasurer of Uvalde county, Texas, in 1879. He resides in the Eightieth Representative district, in the town of Midland, Midland county. He was elected Sergeant-at-Arms of the House of Representatives of Twentieth Legislature by a majority of six votes, over a

J. C. CARR.

popular opponent, Captain H. F. Prater. It goes without saying, that Mr. Carr is a Democrat, and a most loyal party man. He made himself exceedingly popular, not only with the members of the Legislature, but the representatives of the press and the public generally visiting the House of Representatives.

Mr. Carr is of a very striking personage. He is above the average height, and symmetrically proportioned. His face is exceedingly intelligent; and with a long beard and fine head, carried high, with attentive and pleasant manners, he moved through the House, careful of the wants and comfort of every one.

Mr. Carr was in the prime of manhood when the tocsin of alarm sounded through the South in 1861, and, with that readiness that has always distinguished his patriotism and love of his adopted State, he immediately enlisted in defense of the homes and the altars of the South. He was soon appreciated as a soldier, and elected lieutenant of Company I, Thirty-seventh Texas Cavalry, commanded by Colonel P. C. Woods, DeBray's brigade. He participated in all the battles throughout that brilliant campaign, opening at Pleasant Hill, and closing at Yellow Bayou.

In every position and condition of life, whether as a friend, a soldier or a civilian, Mr. Carr has been equal to the emergencies, and conducted himself in such a manner as to win the respect and approbation of his fellow-citizens. He has lived twenty-five or thirty years on the frontiers of the State, and has exhibited all those qualities of prudence and manhood that are so characteristic of the pioneers of civilization. Colonel Carr, being a newspaper correspondent, is well and favorably known throughout the Rio Grande counties as "Locomotive," a pun on his name.

Mr. Carr married Miss Susan Tucker. They have now three children—two daughters and one son. During his temporary residence in Austin, he made many friends.

JAMES D. MONTGOMERY.

ASSISTANT SERGEANT-AT-ARMS.

THE subject of this sketch, James D. Montgomery, Assistant Sergeant-at-Arms of the House of Representatives of the Twentieth Legislature, was born at Anderson, Grimes county, Texas, and educated at Hempstead.

He is a member of the Methodist Episcopal Church, South. He measures about six feet and four inches in his stocking feet, and made an attentive and vigilant officer, as Assistant Sergeant-at-Arms of the Twentieth Legislature.

He married Miss Elizabeth Hooper. They have three sons and a daughter. He belongs to the Knights and Ladies of Honor.

J. SPRINGER BOGGS.

CALENDAR CLERK.

MR. J. SPRINGER BOGGS, the subject of this sketch, was born on February 29, 1849, in the village of Carrollton, in the historic county of Carroll, in the State of Georgia. In the town of Henderson, Rusk county, Texas,

Mr. Boggs received a good education, and has since followed the business of stock-raising and trading. In a great measure he has been successful, and, although a good trader, his transactions with his fellow-citizens have been characterized at all times by such a spirit of honesty and fair dealing that he came to the Twentieth Legislature, as he did to the Seventeenth, Eighteenth and Nineteenth Legislatures, backed by the whole intelligence of his county for any position to which he may aspire. The official experience of Mr. Boggs began when he was Sergeant-at-Arms of the regular and special sessions of the Seventeenth Legislature, and since then he has successfully and creditably performed the arduous duties of Calendar Clerk in the Eighteenth, Nineteenth and Twentieth Legislatures. In politics, Mr. Boggs is a Democrat, true and tried, and has been prominently identified with all the struggles for Democratic supremacy in his section of the State.

A few years ago, he was united in marriage to Miss Alice Anderson, of Terrell, Texas, and one of the fruits of this union now blesses a happy home in Terrell in the person of a bright-eyed, rosy-cheeked boy. The order of the Knights of Pythias in the State looks upon Mr. Boggs as one of its brightest and most upright members. In concluding this sketch, it is but justice to say that, among the young men in public life, none are more courteous and obliging, and few stand higher in the estimation of their friends and associates.

WILLIAM LAFAYETTE McDONALD.

ENGROSSING CLERK.

A SKETCH of a young life is prospective. The deeds that make men great are better seen at the sunset than at the sunrise of life. The subject of this brief notice has the best part of life before him, and the enchantment that lurks in the prospective is glowing with ardor. W. L. McDonald was born in Anderson, Grimes county, Texas, June 29, 1860. His father came to Texas, from Tennessee, in the year 1852, and has brought up his family in the Lone Star State.

Mr. W. L. McDonald was educated at the Southwestern University, Georgetown, Texas, taking the degree of A. B. in 1885. In 1886, he graduated in the law from the University of Texas, going through two years' course in one, and receiving in honor the degree of B. L. Twice, in the Southwestern, he won medals for oratory and declamation.

He is engaged in the practice of law, in Dallas, Texas. He has been Engrossing Clerk of the House of Representatives for two sessions of the Legislature, to-wit, the Nineteenth and the Twentieth.

He is five feet and eleven inches in stature, and weighs one hundred and sixty pounds. He is a bright instance of self-made young manhood.

MONTAGUE JAMES MOORE.

CLERK OF COMMITTEE ON FINANCE.

MR. M. J. MOORE'S father came to Texas, from Georgia, in the early part of the year 1865, and settled in Cameron, Milam county, Texas. The family have resided there ever since. M. J. Moore was born in Cameron, Texas, on the twenty-eighth of March, 1866, and has been educated in the schools of his native town. His intelligence and culture are of a superior character for one of his age. He has been engaged in the newspaper business for three years, having his connection with the Cameron Herald, one of the best county weeklies of the State. He is now reading law, preparatory to entering regularly in the practice at no distant day. He was appointed as one of the clerks of the

Officers of the House.

House of Representatives of the Twentieth Legislature, and served as clerk of the Committee on Finance. He has been found affable and efficient. He is of pleasant and winning manners, five feet and eleven inches high, and weighs one hundred and forty pounds. To him the red light of a rising sun heralds a day of honor and usefulness.

DISTINGUISHED TEXANS.

CURRAN MICHAEL ROGERS.

CURRAN M. ROGERS, the subject of this sketch, was born in Coosa county, Alabama, on the twenty-third day of July, 1841, his father immigrating to Texas in 1849, and settling in Smith county. Young Rogers was educated at McKenzie College, Red River county, in this State. He joined the Methodist Episcopal Church, South, in early life, and, when he attained majority, felt it his duty to preach the gospel of Christ; he, therefore, entered the pastorate of that church, in 1866, and remained an active member of the West Texas Conference for fourteen consecutive years. In 1880, he retired from the active pastorate, and engaged in agriculture and stock-raising. Being a man of education and fine attainments, he occasionally became interested in public affairs, and participated in political matters, rather *con amore* than with any design of holding office; but being pressed by his friends, he became a candidate, and was elected to a seat in the Eighteenth Legislature, from the Eighty-fifth Representative district, composed of Nueces, San Patricio, Bee, Live Oak, McMullen and LaSalle counties. He served on the special committee of twenty, to which was referred the lawlessness in the State arising especially from fence-cutting and kindred acts.

Colonel Rogers, in 1885, purchased a fine estate near Austin, upon which had been erected a handsome residence, and removed to Travis county, where he has since resided. He is now engaged, extensively, in stock-raising and farming, on choice land, and all under fence, consisting of 24,000 acres, and within twenty miles of the capital.

C. M. ROGERS.

His pastures are well-stocked with graded and improved cattle and horses.

His first wife was a Miss Price, of Collin county, Texas. His second marriage was to Mrs. Martha A. Rabb, of Nueces county, Texas. He has a family of six children. He is a man of commanding presence, fine personal appearance, open and intelligent face, and with a fine command of language.

Having been reared in Texas, he manifests the greatest concern in everything connected with the welfare of the State, and especially its agricultural and stock-raising interests. His command of fortune enables him to indulge his propensity to advance the interests of young men of merit. He also contributes largely to all humanitarian schemes that are practical and of use in the elevation and ennobling of his fellow-man.

JOHN HANSEL COPELAND.

CHESTER, the oldest Roman city in England, is the birth place of this elegant gentleman. He was born on the twenty-fifth of July, 1853. He came to San Antonio, Texas, early in the year 1857, and has since resided in that city. His education is broad and varied. From 1873 to 1877, he attended school and college, and traveled both in Europe and America. He was a student in the schools at San Antonio and at St. Chad's College, Denstone, England. At one time serving as a journalist, he was fearless and bold, and is a fluent and graceful writer. He was admitted to the bar in 1880, and has acquired a large and lucrative practice. His success as a lawyer has been exceptional. He has rapidly advanced in reputation, and as an orator, he excels in impassioned eloquence, and bears the masses on the tide of his oratory. He is often called on for speeches on public occasions.

Among the principal questions of study and investigation to him, have been those of political economy. He has openly declared himself on the side of the masses, and aspires to no greater honor than to be a tribune of the people. Not a communist, he is yet a philanthropist, and can be easily touched by the sufferings of guiltless nature wherever found. He was one of the incorporators of the Texas State Society for the Prevention of Cruelty to Animals, and the founder of the Alamo Literary, which has been a great success and blessing in the cause of literature. He has figured prominently as a candidate for the mayoralty of the city, and for Representative to the Legislature, and was a member of the city council in 1880.

He began life with the struggle of dependence—working at eight years of age. The success he has attained has been the reward of personal endeavor. In matters of faith, he is liberal and unrestrained. He holds to an inherent love of truth wherever found, but discriminates between speculations and theories on the one hand, and facts and truth, as attested by human experience, on the other.

Judge Copeland is the Deputy Grand Commander of the American Legion of Honor, and a representative from Alamo Council, to the Grand Council of that order. His wife was Miss Wilhelmina Ludwig, who, with a daughter and son, constitutes the family.

He is stoutly built, and is a lordly specimen of English manhood; of florid complexion, bright hazel eyes, and withal, a ready and entertaining conversationalist. He is progressive—offensively so to the staid order of people who are content to linger in the footsteps and shadows o their grandfathers. He knows how to be a friend, and having tested, by experience, the struggles of life, enters into actual sympathy with the struggling masses.

Distinguished Texans.

RUDOLPH KLEBERG.

IN the political history of a State or country, talent is called forth, that, but for the opportunities afforded, must have remained forever unknown and unrecognized. Trying emergencies are often the crucible in which needed qualities of true manhood and patriotism are sufficiently tested to make them available for the purposes of political place and power. In his career as editor of the Cuero Star, the pioneer journal of DeWitt county, which he established in the year 1873, Honorable Rudolph Kleberg won laurels of unfading hue. During reconstruction days, when the Taylor-Sutton difficulty caused the citizens of Cuero and surrounding country to be in jeopardy of life itself, and terror ruled in the heart of a civilized land, editor Kleberg was defiant of oppression, and fearless in his editorials on the situation. To the heroic stand made by his paper must be attributed, in a controlling degree, the potential agency that restored peace and order. His own life endangered did not abash his courage to defend the right, and for this noble conduct in the interest of peace and order, he has not been forgotten by a grateful people. His public life began by election to the office of county attorney of DeWitt county, in the year 1876. In 1878, he was re-elected to the same office. He received the Democratic nomination, and was duly elected State Senator from the Twenty-sixth district, composed of Wilson, Karnes, Atascosa, Live Oak, McMullen, San Patricio, Calhoun, Goliad, DeWitt, Jackson, Bee, Aransas and Victoria counties, in the year 1882. His senatorial office expired with the Nineteenth Legislature, in which body he was chairman of the Committee on Stock and Stock-raising; was also a member of Judiciary Committee No. 1, and the Joint Committee to Investigate the Penitentiaries. As a Senator, he took a prominent place in the leading issues, and his influence was duly appreciated. He is now filling, with his usual ability, the office of United States District Attorney.

Rudolph Kleberg, a son of Judge Robert Kleberg, a Texas veteran, was born in Austin county, Texas, July 15, 1847, and the following year was taken by his parents to Cuero, De-Witt county, where he has since resided. He has been finely educated, and in the practice of the law has excelled. He took part in the war between the States in the Trans-Mississippi Department, a member of Green's Brigade, Texas Cavalry.

Mr. Kleberg is a gentleman of fine appearance and address, converses freely, and is entertaining. He is compact and stout, physically, and moves himself, both in speaking and in the social circle, with dignity and grace. He was a law partner of Honorable W. H. Crain, now a Texas congressman, and, at the time of his appointment as United States District Attorney by President Cleveland, had an extensive and lucrative practice. Genial as a friend, patriotic as a citizen, zealous and able as a lawyer, and cultivated as a gentleman, he is not only acceptable, but even popular, in the part he takes officially or in the business intercourse of life.

HENRY EXALL.

THE distinguished gentleman whose sketch is briefly given, Colonel Henry Exall, is a typical Texan in many respects. He illustrates the triumph of indomitable energy and push over apparent unsurmountable obstacles. Combined with that, Colonel Exall possesses in a remarkable degree that faculty of always looking upon and presenting the brighest side to every picture; and while others hesitate in doubt and fear of failure, he seems to have derived a peculiar incentive from opposition and impediments, and full of courage, pressed on to the accomplishment of the objects before him. Not only is this sound and healthy condition his own characteristic, but he imparts it to those about him; and many who would otherwise have surrendered to the seeming inevitable, have been animated to hope and effort, by his cheery and hopeful nature. He is not a man to whine over the want of opportunity, or to grieve over failure; he makes opportunity, and gathers from disappointment renewed ardor.

Henry Exall was born in Richmond, Virginia, on the thirtieth of August, 1848. His father, the Rev. George G. Exall, was a distinguished divine and educator of the Old ominion. He obtained the advantage of a thorough classical and literary training at a school presided over by his father near Richmond. He also studied law, but his nature was too active and versatile to be tied to the desk and office of a lawyer, and his life thus far, has been spent in various mercantile pursuits, stock-raising, etc., in which he has been both fortunate and successful. Henry Exall was yet a youth when the cloud of war enveloped the old and historic State of his nativity. He promptly volunteered as a private in Company I, Tenth Virginia Cavalry, commanded by Colonel J. Lucius Davis, and was engaged with his regiment in the battles around Richmond in 1863, 1864 and 1865.

At a late Confederate re-union at Waco, he was called upon to make a speech. He made an extemporaneous address that delighted his old comrades in arms. One of them, who had known Exall in his youth, writing an account of it in the Waco Examiner, said: "Henry Exall was one of the youngest soldiers of the army of Northern Virginia. He enlisted under Colonel Davis, and fought in several battles on Grant's James River line. At Reams Station, he was conspicuous for his bravery, and as a scout, he won encomiums from the regimental and brigade commanders."

With such antecedents, it is natural to correctly conclude that he is a Democrat dyed in the wool. He is now filling the responsible position of chairman of the Democratic State Executive Committee, and to his splendid energy and executive power may be attributed the thorough organization that has made Texas the banner State of the Democratic party. He represented the capital district in the National Democratic Convention that nominated Cleveland and Hendricks, in 1884. He was chairman of the congressional convention that nominated Joe Sayers for Congress, in 1884.

Colonel Exall has also been prominently identified with the cattle interests of the State of Texas, and is a large operator in stock of that kind. He was vice-president of the National Cotton Planters' Association at the New Orleans exposition in 1885.

In 1869, Colonel Exall married Miss Emma Warner, of Owensborough, Kentucky, who died in that State in 1875. His mother and father are both living at an advanced age, in Paducah, Kentucky. Colonel Exall came to Texas to live in 1876; first located at Dallas, but finally settled permanently at Grapevine, Tarrant county, and at once took an active part in private business and public affairs. He has, by energy and prudence, acquired a competency, and is still in full business activity; especially is he valuable as a citizen on account of his ready participation and aid in every enterprise that promises to redound to the good of the State and the elevation of his kind. He is a very ardent and enthusiastic man in everything he undertakes, and imparts his buoyancy and hopefulness to all with whom he comes in contact. He thinks this is a most excellent world, and enjoys it rationally, and as a Christian gentleman ought to do. He is destined, if he lives, to be identified with the development and history of Texas, and to leave the memory of a noble and disinterested life behind him.

CHRISTOPHER COLUMBUS SLAUGHTER.

MORE men of originality and comprehensiveness of thought and mind, develop under the free institutions of this country than under the highest intellectual facilities afforded by the gymnasiums and universities of

Europe. This cannot be attributed to climate or soil, but is attributable to two causes—first, the highest, social, political and intellectual positions of this country, are open alike to the poor and to the wealthy; and secondly, because oppositions and disadvantages serve as a stimulus to a naturally vigorous mind. So far these facts are applicable to the subject of this sketch, Christopher Columbus Slaughter, but there is connected with him an additional characteristic corollary to the same—we allude to the fact that the question of finance is not only broader, but more intricate in this country than elsewhere, and few men understand all the workings of an intricate system that covers the financial policy of the country. His mind, while comprehensive and emulous on account of early difficulties in his way, as he is emphatically the architect of his own fortune, was of a nature that naturally flowed into the channels of finance, and by its adaptation reduced the theories of finance to practical success. There are many men who have become fine financiers in theory, but who failed to reduce these theories to practical advantage. Colonel Slaughter does not belong to this class, finance with him is a science, that he has reduced to utility, both for himself and his associates.

As an illustration of this, we point to the recent organization of the refrigerating system in Texas, and the establishment of the works at Houston, by means of which the cattle men of Texas will derive peculiar advantages. Again, his very eminent success as a cattle man and banker emphasizes his clear understanding of the difficult and intricate workings of financial theories. So strong and clear is his mind in this respect, that his friends regret that the State itself has not had the advantage, in a more direct degree, of his financial ability.

Christopher Columbus Slaughter was born in Sabine county, Texas, on the ninth of February, 1837. When thirteen years of age, his father settled near Prather's Prairie, where Columbus attended to his cattle on the Keechi creek.

He remained there about seven years, when he removed to Palo Pinto county, where he landed with about five hundred head of cattle.

At that time, there were few persons living in that county; and the only stock man then living south of the Brazos river was Robert Sloan, who, after residing in a cedar log cabin for about eight months, sold out to the father of Christopher. This venerable man, now in the seventy-fifth year of his age, resides upon the very spot that once supported the humble home of Robert Sloan, where he leads a retired life.

When Christopher became of age, he, in company of a younger brother, started to Houston, some 350 miles, with an ox team of seven yoke of wild oxen. This adventure proved to be the initial effort of the splendid financial ability that subsequently distinguished Colonel Slaughter as a financier.

He returned from Houston with a load of goods in about three months, which realized him about $300. This money he invested in cattle. For three years, he remained at that place with his herd, and then removed to Young county, near Old Belknap, taking 2500 head of cattle with him, which have multiplied, until now Colonel Slaughter is recognized as one of the wealthiest men in Texas.

With an instinct that is unerring, Colonel Slaughter appreciated his financial abilities. He therefore moved to Dallas, where he organized the City Bank of Dallas, which was an eminent financial success. He is now the first President of the American National Bank of Dallas, which ranks abreast of the first banks in America.

Colonel Slaughter is at present in the very meridian of life, full of vigor and enterprise, and has yet the broadest possibilities for the further exercise of his financial ability.

He is genial in his manners, and of fine conversational powers. He fully appreciates the resources of Texas, and lends his powerful aid to its development.

The following address of the executive committee of the

refrigerating company in which Colonel Slaugeter is interested, will explain itself:

The Executive Committee of the Texas Live Stock Association having met in the city of Austin, March 15, 1887, in accordance with a resolution passed by the last annual session of the State Association, to hear and act upon the report of the committee for the establishment of a refrigerator in Texas, said committee submitted the following as their report:

"Your committee unanimously recommend that the refrigerating, canning and packinge stablishment be located at Houston or vicinity, and that the proposition and plans proposed to the citizens of Houston be accepted by the executive committee. Your committee make this recommendation after having carefully considered all the facts and figures presented, the natural advantages of Houston, its superior railroad facilities, and the great advantages of water transportation, etc."

The above report was received and adopted, and the proposition of the citizens of Houston accepted, as being liberal, and, in our judgment, to the best interest of the live stock business of the State at large. The proposition of the citizens of Houston is here submitted, to-wit:

"In the event Houston or vicinity is chosen as the site where the refrigerator shall be erected, it will donate the land necessary for a refrigerating, canning and packing company, not less than five hundred acres; and, further, will subscribe to a majority of the capital stock of a company, to be incorporated under the laws of Texas, of a paid up capital stock of $500,000, with the right to increase the capital stock to $1,000,000. This subscription to be conditional, as follows: That the members of the Texas Live Stock Association will subscribe the balance of the said $500,000 not taken by Houston and her associates, to be paid in cattle; that is to say, when cattle are delivered in payment of subscriptions of stock by the cattlemen, one-fourth of the value of said cattle at the date of delivery is to be paid in cash, and the remaining three-fourths in the stock of the company, until the subscribed stock is fully paid up.

"And, further, the following plan for the establishment of said plant, or something similar, to be adopted, viz: That a company be chartered under the laws of the State of Texas, under a name appropriate to the business to be conducted.

"Second—That said company be organized by the election of a directory and all necessary officers, including an executive committee, if deemed necessary, and the adoption of by-laws and rules for the government of said association. And the principal office shall be located at the city of Houston, and the officers of the company shall be controlled by such agencies as the directory may choose."

It follows, from this proposition, that the representatives of the live stock interest of Texas are expected to raise two hundred and forty-five thousand dollars ($245,000) to put the enterprise in operation. We deem it necessary to urge upon the citizens of Texas the importance of this move. As all know, we are suffering from a depression in the price of cattle. The depression, in the opinion of your committee, is not because there is no demand for beef, but because there are no adequate means by which we can get the thousands of Texas cattle to the consumers; and this state of things will continue until we have other and cheaper means of transportation. We, therefore, urge the cattlemen of the State to come to the front and take stock with us in this enterprise, and let us make a success of this Texas venture. We are confident that a saving of at least five dollars per head on our cattle, of the average weight of one thousand pounds, will accrue in favor of shipping the animals to market slaughtered or dressed. This fact alone, if we read the signs of the times aright, will place the live stock industry of our State on an independent footing.

H. B. BARNHART.

Distinguished Texans.

H. B. BARNHART.

H. B. BARNHART, the subject of this sketch, was born in Austin, Texas, on the twelfth day of March, 1855. His father, Joseph Barnhart, was one of the early pioneers of the then (Texas) infant republic, having pitched his tent in 1836 where its proud capital, surrounded by a beautiful city, watches the Colorado flow onward to the gulf.

At the proper age, H. B. Barnhart was placed at Parsons' Seminary, where he obtained a liberal education. Possessing a mind of extraordinary capacity, his literary acquirements were rapid, and his mind became well stored with scientific and classical knowledge. He was as courageous as he was bright, and, as an evidence of his bravery, at the age of eleven years he was sent from Manor to Port Sullivan, on the Brazos river, a distance one hundred and twenty-five miles, on horseback, alone, with several thousand dollars, and at a time when traveling through the country was considered dangerous.

At the early age of sixteen, he was promoted to a position of assistant professor of mathematics. Thus thrown among men more advanced in age and experience, his quick mind became companionable with his seniors, and followed them through channels logical and legal in their course of thought.

Great in all of his achievements, and as good as he is great, with a pure, noble and exalted character, he stands before us to-day as one who commands the affection and perfect confidence of the people; for, unwilling to pause on the first round of the ladder of fame in his profession, he has shaken off all trammels, and now stands a glittering star among the brilliant galaxy of Austin's talented young lawyers He generously bestows the secret of his success on his preceptor, the late Colonel A. J. Peeler, one of the most profound and comprehensive lawyers of this State.

Distinguished Texans.

Mr. Barnhart was admitted to the bar in 1876, and met with merited success. By assiduity and close attention to his business, and his reliability, he has won the entire confidence of the community.

On the twenty-seventh day of April, 1881, he married Miss Alice Blanche Millican, a perfect type of pure womanhood.

In 1886, a vacancy occurring in the office of county attorney of Travis county, Judge Z. T. Fulmore, county judge, recognizing the ability and talent of the younger members of the bar, selected from a number of distinguished young men, Mr. Barnhart, and appointed him to fill the vacancy of Mr. Morris. At the next term of the commissioners' court, he was appointed to fill out the unexpired term, and again, he was nominated by the county Democratic convention for county attorney, and was elected by a handsome majority of nearly one thousand votes over his opponent.

His course as county attorney warrants the hopes and predictions of his friends, of eminent success in his profession. With uncompromising firmness, he has made successful war upon evil and wrong-doing wherever and whenever found, and by vigilance and courage brought evil-doers and law-breakers to justice. Crime, under his prudent and sagacious management, is becoming less frequent, and the the law is more and more respected and feared by the dishonest and turbulent classes. The best eulogy that could be pronounced upon this youthful and rising attorney would be a contrast of the condition of affairs to-day in this county and city, and that of a few years since. Not more than sixteen months ago, Austin had a national reputation for midnight murder, with criminals undiscovered and unwhipped by justice. Crimes, the most nefarious and diabolical, were committed with impunity. Then every citizen locked and barred his doors and windows, and slept with arms near at hand to defend his wife and children from the deadly ax of the midnight assassin. Mr. Barnhart has been county attorney for fifteen or sixteen months. Every citizen now feels secure; the law is enforced; the officers are vigilant, and Austin has become an unhealthy place for criminals, and they avoid its neighborhood.

These are facts that give testimony to the completeness of the man and the attorney, and the consciencious and vigorous discharge of his duties as a public officer. Mr. Barnhart is yet a young man, and is destined to become a conspicuous figure in Texas jurisprudence.

As a citizen, Mr. Barnhart is alive to the interest and improvement of the city of his nativity, and in all the social relations of life he fills the measure of a Christian gentleman. With that sympathy and love for his kind that breaks down the artificial barriers of caste in the common brotherhood of mankind, he enters freely into every effort made for the amelioration and elevation of the people in moral and intellectual improvement.

CHARLES GOODNIGHT.

MR. CHARLES GOODNIGHT, who is now frequently spoken of as the "cattle king" of Northwestern Texas, and whose early life and adventures in that section of the State reads more like romance than ordinary history, was born in Madison county, Illinois, March 5, 1836. He is consequently fifty-one years of age, and the plain recital of his life indicates that he is strictly a self-made man of indomitable energy, fearless nerve, possessing a wonderful foresight and native intelligence. He was born in that latitude of the United States running east, embracing Illinois, Indiana, Ohio, Virginia and Maryland, which has a soil and a climate that has produced, among our public men, the greatest statesmen of America, and among our business men those possessing the greatest financial and executive ability, capable of planning and carrying out the most colossal business enterprises. Mr. Charles Goodnight is one of the best illustrations of this class. When but five years of age, his father died in Illinois, and he immigrated, with his mother and two young sisters and a brother, to Texas, in 1846, settling in Milam county, where they remained until 1853, and then removed to McLennan county. Being imbued by nature, with a sturdy, earnest energy to carve out his own career, and being a poor boy, at the age of sixteen he hired out to a farmer, and at odd times, when his services were not needed, he worked for other farmers in the neighborhood, usually earning from ten to twelve dollars per month, which he contributed to the support of his mother and sisters.

In 1855, his mother married again, and he, being about nineteen years of age, branched out in business for himself, still working by the month; and what he made by manual labor, he would invest in cattle, indicating plainly in his youth the bent of his business inclinations. Indeed, it is truthfully related of him that the first pair of work cattle that he owned he paid for by splitting rails for the owner of them. He made it a rule to work for parties and receive his pay in cattle. Here he laid the foundation upon which, as time went on, he accumulated his vast fortune in the cattle business.

After remaining in McLennan county a few years, on June 6, 1856, he gathered together what cattle he had, amounting to some twenty head, and with a young man by the name J. W. Sheek, who owned about the same number, together with about four hundred and thirty head, which they had contracted for with Claiborne Varner, of McLennan county, they started for the frontier of Texas. On their way there, they wintered in Johnson county, losing but a small percentage of their stock. They then moved to Palo Pinto county, where, at that time, there were not more than twenty-five white men. Here he kept his cattle for nearly ten years, until the fourth calf. At the end of the first eighteen months, he and his partner had, in addition to their original forty head, thirty-two calves, but making very slow progress for three or four years. In keeping with that tireless industry and thrift which had always characterized Mr. Goodnight, he used to spend his summer months, while raising cattle at this time, in carrying freight on an ox-wagon, in order always to have a supply of provisions on hand. After the third or fourth year, Mr. Goodnight began to accumulate considerable property, and as fast as he did so, he would invest in cattle, as was constantly his rule, and he soon found himself the owner of several hundred head of cattle, and success began to smile upon all his efforts.

When the late civil war broke out, Mr. Goodnight was in easy circumstances, owning about four thousand head of cattle. Immediately upon the outbreak of the war, he joined Curretson's company, Norris' regiment of Texas Rangers, for the protection of the frontier from the Rio Grande to the Red River, and served during the four years with fidelity to the Lost Cause as a scout and guide, being stationed at Fort Belknap when in camp, which was but seldom the case. While engaged in the service, he moved about three thousand head of cattle to what is now Throckmorton county, but which was then the frontier, he and his associates being the only white men in that section, which was some twenty-five miles west of old Belknap. By the depredations of the Indians, most of this herd was lost, they capturing in one night one thousand head, together with a number of horses.

At the close of the war, he, in common with the rest of the Southern people, suffering from the consequences of defeat, gathered up all of his stock that was left, and determined to drive them to New Mexico, or Colorado. As there was no road or trail, and he had never seen a man who had made the trip, it was a hazardous undertaking, but he had resolved to go, and that settled it with him. Just before starting, he formed a partnership with Mr. Oliver Loving, who was one of the best known cattle-traders in Texas, and who stood high in the estimation of all who knew him. On this drive, they struck southwest to the Pecos river, following it up some four hundred miles, thence through New Mexico and Colorado, until they arrived near the foot of the Black Hills, where the city of Cheyenne now stands, and here the cattle were finally disposed of. This was the first drive ever made from Texas to Colorado, Mr. Goodnight being the first man to have the nerve and hardihood to make this trip and blaze out the way for others. This road has passed into history, and will always be known as the Goodnight trail. To him belongs the honor of taking the first step towards opening up for settlement and civilization a country that was then nothing but a vast waste; not a tame animal nor a civilized person to be found by him as he went through from old Camp Cooper, in Texas, to Fort Sumner, in New Mexico—a distance of more than six hundred miles, eighty-six miles of which his outfit traveled without a drop of water for man or beast.

This first trip was accomplished without any serious adventures or mishaps, save the hardships and privations necessarily incident to such an undertaking.

He did not have the same good luck, however, when a subsequent and similar trip was made in 1867. The Indians, on this trip, made an attack on the herd of cattle, while on the Clear Fork of the Brazos river, just as the trip was about to be begun, and several of Goodnight's men were wounded by the Indian arrows. Shortly before day-break on the following morning, the attack was renewed, which resulted in stampeding the entire herd and wounding one man, some three hundred cattle being lost in this engagement. These attacks were continued by the Indians, at intervals, until the party, consisting of eighteen men, had reached within one hundred and fifty miles of Fort Sumner, New Mexico, when, on the eighteenth day of June, 1867, they were charged upon by six hundred Indians and Mr. Oliver Loving, Mr. Goodnight's esteemed partner and devoted friend, received a fatal wound, and died shortly afterwards at Fort Sumner, to which place they finally made their way with great difficulty and danger. In the death of Mr. Loving, a brave, noble and moral being passed away. After having lost some three hundred head of cattle in this last engagement, Mr. Goodnight sold the rest of his herd at Fort Sumner, New Mexico, and Denver, Colorado, realizing good prices, averaging eight cents per pound, gross. He then decided to remain at Fort Sumner, and contracted with persons to deliver him cattle there, where he bought and sold cattle for several years, until 1871, when he married Miss Mary Ann Dyer, of Rutherford, daughter of General Dyer, of Jackson, Tennessee. After marriage, Mr. and Mrs. Goodnight removed to Pueblo, Colorado, where he engaged in banking, farming and stock-raising. He tried farming by irrigation, but it proved a failure after the construction of railroads. The panic of 1873, in the East, brought on disasters throughout the entire country, and paralyzed business in the West. Mr. Goodnight being the largest real estate owner in Southern Colorado, the decline on real estate alone was so enormous that, after paying all his liabilities, he had but little left. In the midst of these disastrous times, his estimable wife, with that noble spirit of self-sacrifice so characteristic of our high minded Southern women, came to her husband's assistance and generously surrendered all her personal and real property for the benefit of his creditors.

After this panic, he again returned to the frontier of Texas, the home of his youth and young manhood, to attempt to recuperate and build up once more his fallen fortunes. After a careful survey of the field, he decided on locating in that section of northwestern Texas, where, years before, as a scout and guide in the Texas Rangers, serving the Confederacy, he had traversed every hill and valley, ridden over every prairie, and was acquainted with every trail. He established himself on what is now widely known as Palo Duro Ranch, embracing the great canyon, called Palo Duro Canyon, which is in fact the head of Red River, or latterly known as the Prairie Dog Fork of Red River. This grand canyon is 1000 feet deep, and averages, for thirty miles in length, some eleven miles in width, forming one of the largest, best, and most complete cattle ranches in the world. Mr. Goodnight landed at this place on the twenty-ninth of November, 1875, with 1800 head of cattle, and soon afterwards formed a co-partnership with John G. Adair, of Ireland, the latter furnishing the capital at ten per cent interest per annum, and receiving two-thirds of the profits of the ranch. This section of Texas was at this time a wild, unsettled country, unknown, except to the Indians and a few of the old scouts, the nearest civilized spot being Fort Elliott, 100 miles distant, and the nearest settlement in Texas being 225 miles distant, supplies having frequently to be hauled over 400 miles. Mrs. Goodnight, in accompanying her husband to what was then a totally uncivilized and dangerous country, to assist him in gaining a livelihood, has won for herself the distinction of being the first white lady who went to that country, remaining on the ranch for as long as six months at a time, without having the companionship of any of her sex, not even seeing an Indian squaw, the isolation continuing for nearly three years, when the Indians were finally driven from the State, and civilization, over which the refining influence of woman is the reigning power, commenced to draw nearer to Palo Duro Ranch.

In those days Mr. Goodnight was censured for his poor judgment in risking the lives of his family, and those dependent upon him, by locating in a country overrun by savages. Now, however, after using the best efforts of his life to civilize that part of Texas, and substitute for the wigwam of the savage the attractive cottage of the American, he is charged with being a land monopolist.

Many thousand acres of the land that forms a part of his magnificent ranch was purchased at twenty cents per acre, but the land agents made ten cents per acre on these sales, and the public, at that time, were very glad to dispose of them for that price, and for even less. This is the same land that the State now declares to be worth from two to three dollars per acre.

Mr. Goodnight, with Mr. Adair, now owns, on the Palo Duro

ranch, some fifty thousand head of improved cattle, ranging from high grade to thoroughbred Durhams, and many imported Herefords.

Charles Goodnight is just turning fifty-one years of age, and has lived in Texas, the home of his earliest adoption, over forty years. Enjoying, as he does, vigorous health, he is in the prime possession of all those splendid qualities of head and heart with which kind nature has munificently endowed him, and which have distinguished him throughout a varied and adventurous career as a man of indomitable will and perseverance, with a thorough knowledge of human nature in all its forms—a strong, common-sense, practical man, capable of undergoing the severest hardships, as the history of his life shows, but comming out successful in the grand "round up"—and with natural and acquired power to plan, as well as execute, gigantic business enterprises.

Having risen himself from the humblest walks of life, starting as a poor boy on a farm, splitting rails and tending cattle, he can keenly appreciate the troubles of others, as is evidenced by the many substantial acts of kindness and assistance that he has rendered the poor and deserving; and above all, he is noted for standing by his friends when they need his help, and seeing that justice is meted out to them fairly and equitably; and at the same time, he never forgets an enemy who has deliberately and maliciously done him a wrong.

In personal appearance, Mr. Goodnight would strike even the casual observer as a man of solid, substantial attainments and much power. He is above medium height, with a large, well-shaped head, strongly set on broad shoulders. His hair, now with the slightest sprinkle of grey, is very black, as is his rounded beard and moustache. His complexion is somewhat tanned by long out-door life in the Panhandle of Texas, New Mexico and Colorado. His eyes are black and bright, intelligent and quick, but exhibit a very kind and humane expression towards all classes of his fellow-man. He probably weighs about two hundred and eighteen pounds, and his step is firm, active and energetic. If he were met with in any of the large cities of the East or Northwest, he would be taken for a man of comprehensive business talent and remarkable executive ability.

The people of some sections of Texas, principally a few politicians of northwestern Texas, have conceived the idea that, because Mr. Goodnight has large landed possessions there, he is trying to rule that section to suit himself, and they are given to criticise him rather severely on this account, and speak of him as the "cattle baron" and the "cattle king," but the unprejudiced and intelligent people of the State will regard him as one of the few pioneers who has had the courage and been able to secure the means to displace the Indians and the desperadoes from that section, and to open it up for settlement by white people, thus planting civilization, wealth and intelligence in a section of Texas that otherwise would have remained as the hunting ground of the savage and the home of the desperado for many years to come.

Through the instrumentality of Charles Goodnight and a few others like him, the Panhandle of Texas will in a short time become the most productive and largest tax-paying portion of Western Texas. In other words, he has done for northwestern Texas, exactly what the early pioneers, or, as they are called, the "Fathers of Texas," did for this young Republic when they won their independence from Mexico.

The record of his life shows that he has reclaimed the northwestern portion of the State from the Indians and the cow thief, and enabled civilized white men to live there in comparative safety, and posterity will accord him this honor.

Distinguished Texans.

GENERAL HENRY EUSTACE McCULLOCH.

HENRY EUSTACE McCULLOCH is the son of Alexander McCulloch and Francis LeNoir, who married in Nashville, Tennessee, in 1799. He was born in Rutherford county, Tennessee, on the sixth day of December, 1816. About two years after this, his father moved to North Alabama, and in the same year thereafter to Dyer county, West Tennessee, where H. E. McCulloch, the subject of this sketch, was principally reared. The winter he was fifteen years old, Henry, with the consent of his father, was put in charge of a wood yard, on the Mississippi river, under the supervision of the owner, Joseph Mitchell. The next three winters he, with his older brother Ben, spent in rafting and boating on the Obion and Mississippi rivers. In the fall of 1835, when not quite nineteen years old, he accompanied his brother to Texas, but, on reaching Nacogdoches, Ben persuaded him to return and spend a year or two more with their parents. On his return to Tennessee, reaching the mouth of Red River, he met his brother-in-law, W. L. Mitchell, who employed him in examining lands in the Mississippi swamps that winter. He then returned home to aid in making a crop in 1836, but finding a volunteer company making up for the Florida war, he proposed to join it, but his father having spent several months in that section of country with General Jackson during the Creek and British war of 1812 and 1814, and finding it very unhealthy, would not agree for him to muster in as a soldier, but consented to his going as an amateur, making arrangements with the authorities to supply him with arms, rations, etc., as the others, but to serve without pay until such time as he might desire to return home.

In the fall of 1837, he came to Texas to make it his home, and identified himself with her people. He spent his first winter at Washington, on the Brazos, building board houses, hewing the sills, plates, etc., and splitting the four-foot boards out of the red oak timber in the Brazos bottom. In the spring of 1838, he made a trip, with Mr. Hunter, Joshua Robens and Jack Robens, from Robens' Ferry, which was then the upper house on the Trinity, to what was then known as the three forks of that river, their object being to locate and survey lands in that section, but they found the Indians so abundant that they regarded it entirely unsafe at that time, and gave up the enterprise. Returning to Washington, he found Captain Chance, with a party of fifteen men, composed of Captain James Cook, James Shepard, James Evitts, Sam Evitts, McFall, and others, going out to explore the upper Brazos, and he accompanied them. This party, upon reaching the mouth of Little river, took up that stream, and explored a great deal of that country drained by the Gabriel, Lampasas and Leon rivers; and on this trip, while he and McFall were out hunting, they fell in with five Indians, and he got his first shot at a hostile Indian in Texas, and although there were only two white men, they killed two Indians and ran the other three into the timbered bottom on the Gabriel.

Returning to Washington, he spent a short time socially and resting among his friends at that place and about Independence, and, about the tenth of July, struck off for Gonzales, where he joined his brother Ben, and went to work in locating and surveying land and in aiding the settlers in defending themselves against the Indians, who seldom allowed the light of a moon to pass without committing some act of murder or theft upon the unprotected settlers. During the months of November and December, 1838, the brothers, Henry and Ben McCulloch, divided the half league of land upon which Seguin is situated into one-acre, five-acre, and twelve-acre lots, the business lots having been surveyed by Swift and Campbell a month previously.

In January, 1839, Ben planned a raid against the Comanches, with a few Americans and a number of Tonkaway Indians, against which Henry protested, but unwilling to abandon his brother on such a hazardous expedition, he determined to go and share his fate. When the day to march came, there were five Americans, viz: Ben and Henry McCulloch, Wilson Randle, David Henson, and John D. Wolfin, and thirty-five Indians, ready to take the field. Fortunately, after two days, march, they met a band of hostile Waco and Comanche Indians on the head of Peach creek, on their way into the settlements, with whom a battle was commenced at once, and resulted in the killing of five hostiles on the ground, with several others wounded, when they retreated into a large, dense thicket on the creek, into which the friendly Indians refused to follow, and the battle ended, with the loss of one friendly Indian killed. The friendly Indians having lost a man and taken the scalps of the five hostiles, insisted on returning to their camp to mourn over the dead and celebrate the victory with a series of war dances, and while Henry was more than glad of it, his brother Ben had found that while their allies fought bravely, they did so little execution that they were really not valuable in battle.

Winter being unfavorable for surveying, and there being a heavy crop of pecans, the brothers determined to build a small flat boat, 12x24 feet, load it with pecans and take it down the Guadalupe river to the Gulf of Mexico, which they accomplished, and sold the pecans near Pass Caballo. On returning home, they found that Captain Matthew Caldwell (Old Paint) was authorized by the President of the Republic to raise a company of rangers for six months, to defend the settlers at Gonzales and Seguin against the Indians, and they at once agreed for Henry to join the company and Ben to carry on their land business. During the six months a great deal of active, efficient service was performed, and several parties of Indians routed, but not a single battle was fought, nor any depredation committed on the settlements; and, during this period, the brothers surveyed the wagon road from Gonzales to Austin, the newly established seat of government, under the protection of an escort from Captain Caldwell's company.

In November, 1839, Henry McCulloch met Miss Jane Isabella Ashby, a young lady who had been for three years attending school in her native State, Kentucky, to whom he became engaged to be married at a subsequent period; and in order to have bread in the house after the marriage, he rented Mrs. DeWitt's farm, and made a crop of corn on it in the spring of 1840.

At the spring term of the county court, he was appointed assessor of taxes for that year, and as soon as he laid by his crop, he performed that service.

In August of that year, the Comanche Indians made a raid with a force of four or five hundred warriors, passing clear through the settlements, which were very sparse, to the coast, and sacked and burned Linnville, which was then the seaport on Lavaca bay, killing all the men in the place who did not make their escape in boats, and capturing a few families. All the force that could be raised promptly pursued them as they went down the country, and met them in the open prairie soon after they had sacked the town, and, though not strong enough to give battle with prospects of certain success, they were sufficiently strong to hold the Indians together, pursue them on their retreat and prevent them scattering, and thus save the settlers along their line of retreat. Meantime, another force was being raised on the Guadalupe and Colorado rivers, and concentrated where the Indians would cross Plum creek; and about the time the Indians reached that point, Captain Caldwell, with about one hundred men from the Guadalupe, and Colonel Burleson, with about the same number of men from the Colorado, had formed a junction, and as General Felix Huston, who was major-general of the militia, was present, they turned the command over to him. He ordered the attack to be promptly made, sending forward a few men as skirmishers to bring on the battle. The Indians, being on the open prairie, soon discovered the movement and rallied their warriors at a point of timber, making show of fight, while they were rushing off their squaws and plunder. Upon this, General Huston halted and dismounted his force, and for some time awaited an attack, until, at Captain Caldwell's request, Ben McCulloch suggested that it was best to mount his force and charge them. The order was given and promptly obeyed, Caldwell's company charging through and driving the Indians out of the point of timber, while Colonel Burleson charged those immediately in front of his force on the open prairie. The Indians gave way, and a running fight was kept up for several miles. During that run, a party of Indians were overtaken at a boggy branch, where his companions gave Henry McCulloch the credit of killing one Indian, while Ben and Henry E. McCulloch, Alsey S. Miller and C. C. DeWitt, leading the van after this, killed five Indians in single-handed combat, and it is conceded that Henry killed two of these.

On the the twentieth of August, 1840, Henry was married to Miss Jane Isabella Ashby, and settled at a place that he and his brother Ben had improved, four miles above Gonzales, on the road to Austin, and when there was only one other on this road between that and the city. Here Ben opened a small farm that fall and winter, and put in a crop of corn the next spring.

In the fall of 1841, his brother-in-law, Judge B. D. McClure, died, leaving his family very much exposed on Peach creek, ten miles east of Gonzales, which, with other circumstances, rendered it necessary for him to leave his little farm in charge of his brother, while he went to live with her until other arrangements could be made.

While plowing in the field, on the fifth of March, 1842, report reached Henry that the Mexican General Vasques had captured San Antonio with a large force, and that all the families from Seguin to Gonzales were on the move eastward. Knowing that his brother Ben, Alsey S. Miller and others, were west, watching the movements of the enemy, Henry rode hurriedly to Gonzales to try to check the stampede of the families until they could hear of the advance of the enemy from San Antonio; and finding he could not do this, he returned home, packed the wagon, gathered what stock he could hurriedly, and put them in charge of his wife, with a negro boy and her two little brothers, to be taken to the settlements on the Lavaca, off the main traveled road, and wait for instructions from him, while he took the road to San Antonio with what men he could pick up. Just beyond Seguin, he met his brother Ben, and asked him whether it could be an invading force? "Yes," he replied, "we are too weak to attack them, and must necessarily watch their movements and wait for reinforcements;" and before any considerable number of reinforcements arrived, Vasques sacked the place and returned to Mexico. Henry returned immediately to his family, took them back home, and completed the cultivation of his crop.

In September of this year, the Mexican General Adrion Woll, with one thousand regular infantry, a field battery of two guns, and five or six hundred Ranchero cavalry, captured San Antonio again, and with it the district court, which was then in session. As soon as this news reached Gonzales, the McCullochs and others rallied all the force they could and marched to Seguin, where they established a supply camp—sent runners out for reinforcements, and as soon as they had two hundred and two men assembled, organized a company of spies, or scouts, under Jack Hays, with Henry McCulloch as first lieutenant and C. B. Acklen as orderly sergeant, and moved on to the Cibolo, and thence, after night, to a position on the east side of the Salado, about seven miles from San Antonio, and at daylight next morning, Hays' company was sent in to draw the enemy out. General Woll by some means unknown to this force, was about ready to move against it, and when Hays made his appearance, Woll's whole force of cavalry gave chase, which only ended when Hays reached the position of the main body of Texans. Skirmishing was kept up during the day, and the enemy made two bold efforts to dislodge the Texans by charging their line, but were repulsed both times with heavy loss, and, finally, at dark, they retired from the field.

As it rained all the next day, no forward movement was made, but on the next morning, the Texans marched upon the town and found that Woll had evacuated it and commenced his retreat at daylight that morning. They pursued Woll's forces, overtaking him on the Hondo, where he had taken strong position, and placed his battery so as to rake the road upon which the Texans would advance. Without knowing the position of these guns, Hays charged the Mexican rear guard, drove them in upon the main body, and captured the battery before the enemy had fired a half dozen shots; but the enemy, finding he was not properly supported, rallied in force and recaptured the battery. That night the the two commands laid within a few hundred yards of each other, and about three o'clock next morning the enemy continued the retreat and the pursuit was abandoned. Hays had one horse killed and two men wounded in the charge.

The Texans meeting considerable re-inforcements on their return, when they reached San Antonio, it was agreed that they would make a raid into Mexico as early as possible, and all those who could do so were induced to remain at and near San Antonio, while others returned to their homes to get up recruits and gather beef cattle to supply the command on the expedition.

Without the aid of the government, an army of 800 men assembled on the Medina, twenty miles west of San Antonio, in November, 1842, and without a wagon, tent, or breadstuff, marched for Mexico, driving the beef upon which they subsisted with them; took formal possession of Laredo on this side of the river, which had not been done before; moved down opposite Gerreo; crossed and captured that town some miles from the river and returned to this side of the river, where General Alexander Somervell, who was in command, ordered the forces to return to San Antonio.

Disgusted with General Somervell, and desiring to learn more of the country, Henry McCulloch got permission from

Captain Hays and General Somervell to take a portion of Hays' company, of which he was first lieutenant, and proceed down the Rio Grande as far as he thought it safe to go, and return by a route south of that taken by the Texans' main body.

General Somervell's order to abandon the expedition was so unexpected, and regarded as so unnecessary, that over 300 of the men, and some of the officers, refused to obey it, and organized a force under Colonel W. S. Fisher to proceed down to and capture the town of Mier, which was on a small stream a few miles from the Rio Grande. In organizing this force, and before electing Colonel Fisher, the command was first tendered to Ben McColloch, then to Tom Green, and then to Henry McCulloch, but as they had left the command with permission, all refused to accept it, and Henry McCulloch declined to connect his command with it in any way, further than to go in advance of it with his thirteen men, and if he discovered any formidable force to report it to Colonel Fisher.

When opposite Mier, he awaited the arrival of Colonel Fisher, and informed him that while he had seen no formidable force, he had discovered small scouting parties who were watching his movements, and could easily count his numbers as he marched along the river.

He declared his intention was to cross his troops that night and attack the town at daylight next morning; and rather than see him make a reckless attack on the town without any knowledge of what was in it, Henry McCulloch proposed that Colonel Fisher increase his force to twenty-five men, put them across in his ferry boats (having captured two on his way down the river), and place from fifty to one hundred men on the west side of the river to hold and protect the crossing, when Lieutenant McCulloch would make a reconoisance of the town and report to him. This being agreed to, McCulloch marched upon the town at once, and finding no troops there, rode into the main plaza, received the surrender of the place by the alcalde, and was informed by a Mr. Jamison, whom he found there, and an old Mexican friend of the Texans, from San Antonio, that Colonel Canales, with 500 cavalry, was expected there in an hour, and that General Ampudia, with 1500 infantry, was expected that night. After remaining an hour quietly, Lieutenant McCulloch returned, giving no intimation of their future movements, and as he reached the top of the hill, he could see Colonel Canales' command, some two miles off, as they advanced on the town.

He reported the condition of affairs to Colonel Fisher, who said he would move at three o'clock a. m. and attack the town at daylight with his whole force dismounted. Rather than see him do this, without any information as to the locality of the enemy, Henry McCulloch proposed that Colonel Fisher increase his force to fifty men, to act as his advance guard, etc., to which he consented, and he again marched into the town, and found that Ampudia had failed to reach it, though only a few miles off, and that Canales had left at four o'clock a. m., to join Ampudia. The town was again formally surrendered to Colonel Fisher, and he made his demand for money and supplies, which the alcalde agreed to furnish. While his command occupied the town McCulloch kept pickets on all the roads leading into it.

On returning to camp that night, McCulloch found that, instead of Colonel Fisher having the supplies delivered at that place where he had his boats, he had agreed to receive them five miles lower down, and on the west side of the river, whereupon McCulloch said to Colonel Fisher: "You have had a trap laid for you which I do not propose to fall into, but will leave you in the morning, and you will find Ampudia where you expect your supplies." Fisher found this prediction true, and yet he crossed his force in the face of the enemy, driving them before him into the city, fought them in it a day and night, gaining advantages over them, and was finally induced to surrender upon the enemy stating they had received large reinforcements, and offering liberal terms of surrender.

McCulloch, with his small command, leaving Fisher prior to the surrender, struck off through the country, without a a road, and reached the Nueces and crossed it about ten miles above San Patricio, and crossed the San Antonio river at the old deserted town of Sobohea, or Goliad, and reached the Guadalupe river near where Cuero is now located.

When Henry McCulloch arrived at home, he found all well, and that a daughther had been born unto his wife three weeks before, and that during his absence, without consulting him, his friends had placed his name before the people as a candidate for sheriff of the county, and the election being only two weeks off, it was too late to decline, or do anything of consequence to secure his election.

In February, 1843, Henry McCulloch was elected sheriff of Gonzales county, by a handsome majority over C. C. Dewitt, the son of the empressario, and a very popular young man. He held this office two years, unprofitably however, it proving a loss to him of both time and means.

In 1844, he commenced merchandising in Gonzales, on capital loaned him, without interest, by Captain Isaac N. Mitchell, who was one of his old fellow-soldiers, and a farmer of considerable means.

Finding his wife's health failing in Gonzales, he moved to Seguin, in November of the same year, and there finding a stock of goods belonging to General A. W. G. Davis in the hands of Wilson Randle, to be sold on commission, he bought them, and took Randle into partnership with him, opening out under the firm name of Randle & McCulloch. Being remarkably successful, he soon paid his friend the money he had kindly loaned him, and was able to go on with the business.

In February, 1846, Thomas H. Holloman, a young man from Virginia, who had been raised a merchant, and had some ready money, came to Seguin and proposed to go into partnership with the firm. The proposition was accepted, and the firm name was changed to Randle, McCulloch & Co. On the eighth day of June, 1846, McCulloch turned the store over to his partners for their management, and was elected captain of a volunteer company for service in the Mexican war, with orders from the Governor to report to Colonel W. S. Harney, then in command of San Antonio, who had the company mustered into the service of the United States by Liutenant-Colonel T. T. Fauntleroy, and ordered to establish a camp at the head of San Marcos river, where the town of San Marcos now is, and where there was not then a house in fifteen miles.

Having no treaties with the Indians, and fearing the Mexicans would induce them to commit more daring depredations on the frontier settlers then usual, Captain McCulloch's company was kept most of the time on the frontier, but was ordered into Mexico twice, going as far as Monclova on General Woll's line of march, and Monteray on General Taylor's line, and each time, after rendering some service in breaking up guerrilla haunts, was ordered back to his camp on the frontier.

In the fall of 1846, the town of San Marcos was laid off by General Edward Burleson, Sr., and Colonel W. B. Lindsey, proprietors; and by June, 1847, a fine settlement had formed in and around it, extending down the river for several miles, and was regarded sufficiently strong to protect itself against the Indians.

In the early part of July, 1847, a regiment was formed of detatched companies, of which Captain McCulloch's was one, and P. Hansborough Bell (afterwards Governor of Texas) was elected Colonel, who was put in command of all the troops in Texas, with his headquarters at San Antonio, with instructions to place his entire regiment on the frontier to protect the settlers against the Indians.

Upon receiving these instructions, and not being very well acquainted with the frontier, Colonel Bell called Captain Henry McCulloch, Captain Highsmith and "Big Foot" Wallace to his headquarters for consultation as to where the line of defense should be established, and the companies respectively posted, and it was agreed that Fredericksburg was thr outside settlement, and that a line should be drawn about this distance from the main settlements, and Captain McCulloch's company was ordered to take post on it in Hamilton's Valley, on the Colorado river, seventy miles above Austin, with Captain Highsmith's company near Fredericksburg, west of the former company, and Captain Shapley P. Ross east of it, on or near the Brazos, about where Waco is now located. The companies on this entire line of frontier were required to have scouts from each to meet at a designated point between them once a week, with orders to report any failure upon the part of any company to do so, and to keep scouting parties constantly out above this line, which General McCulloch now says, "proved the most efficient protection the frontier has ever had under any other plan that has ever been tried."

About the first of November, 1847, Captain McCulloch established "Camp McCulloch," on Hamilton creek, about three miles below where the town of Burnet is now located, where this company remained until the twenty-second day of October, 1848, which was the end of their term of service. when they were regularly discharged; but a band of Indians having passed down west of Captain Highsmith's company, and committed depredations on the Guadalupe river, both the Governor and Colonel Bell urged Captain McCulloch to hold his company together, reorganize and muster in for an indefinite period, and remain until the arrival of United States dragoons, which he did, and on being relieved by them, his company was finally discharged from the service of the United States in the war with Mexico.

During these terms of service, covering the time from the eighth day of June, 1846, to the eighth day of December, 1848, Captain McCulloch was elected captain four times by the men, one term of over three months, two terms of twelve months, and the fourth for one month and seventeen days, without opposition after his election to the command of the first company. No better evidence could be produced of his popularity with his company, and as no charges or official complaints were ever made against him by his commanding officers, his services must have been satisfactory to them.

As he desired to be retired from the mercantile business and turn his attention to farming and stock-raising, and in order to give his partners ample time to make suitable arrangements therefor, after being discharged from the service, he came to Austin, rented the "Swisher House," and kept hotel from the first of January, 1849, to the last of February, 1850. During this time, over ten thousand dollars were received and paid out, and Captain McCulloch's net profits amounted to just $103.25, with the services of himself, wife, two negroes and a brother-in-law, Travis H. Ashby, who he was raising, thrown in for good measure. During this time, he was made a Mason, in Austin Lodge No. 12, and as far as ascertained, Honorable John Hancock is the only Mason now living who was a member of the lodge at that time.

About the fourth of March, 1850, he returned to his home in Seguin, closed up his mercantile business, in which he found his capital had increased, and that it had, under the management of honest partners, made money, after paying them liberally for carrying on his part of it, during an absence of nearly four years. But before he had time to do much in arranging for his farming and stock-raising, he was again called on by General Brook, then in command of Texas, to take the field for the protection of the frontier settlements, for twelve months, with a company of Rangers, which he raised under an order from him. He was elected Captain, and mustered into service at Austin, on the fifth day of November, 1850, and ordered to report to him at San Antonio, where the company was fitted out for the field, and ordered to protect the settlements between the Nueces and San Antonio rivers, upon which the Indians were committing constant depredations.

Under these orders he established his camp about the upper waters of the Aransas river, above the settlements, and at once threw out his scouts to the San Antonio river, on the east, and the Nueces, on the west, and kept the entire line of same sixty miles constantly covered with scouts; but, as the country was full of mustangs (wild horses), it was difficult to detect the trail of a few Indians that might pass along in the night with bare-footed ponies. Captain McCulloch made an arrangement with the settlers below his line, to report to him promptly if the Indians committed any depredations, or any sign of them should be discovered.

It was only a few days before a party of fifteen Indians passed below the line and succeeded in stealing some horses, but one of his scouting parties under the command of Lieutenant J. R. King discovered the trail and pursued them all day through a heavy rain, overtaking them just at dark encamped in the forks of two deep ravines. King, as was the custom in those days, charged them with his ten men. The Indians dropped precipitately into one of the ravines. where they made a firm stand, and although they wounded the lieutenant, with an arrow at his first onset, and about half the guns of his party (getting wet by the rain) could not be made to fire, he held his ground and fought them until dark, and then came to the company's camp, which was only about four miles from his battle ground. The night was so dark, that nothing could be done, but at day break next morning, Captain McCulloch was on the ground with twenty men, and finding that the Indians had been gone a few hours, began chase at such speed as he thought his horses could hold on a long chase through heavy ground (a good deal of it boggy from the late rain), and at about twelve o'clock, after a chase of many miles, his men who were mounted on the horses of the best bottom, got almost within gunshot of them as they reached the edge of a dense thicket miles in extent, where they abandoned their horses, making their escape on foot, with nothing but their arms. One other party, of two Indians, succeeded in passing below the line and captured a little boy near night at Refugio. The citizens pursued in the direction the Indians took, but not being able to trail them in the night, notified Captain McCulloch of what had occurred, and where they thought he would probably strike the trail of the Indians; and by sunrise the next morning, he had reached that point, and, by accident, found the trail, and followed it, with difficulty, up the Nueces for four days, hoping to find a larger party to which these two fellows belonged, but not doing so, gave up the chase. About two weeks after this, another party of about twenty Indians attempted to pass down near the Nueces, through an open country, and were discovered by a scouting party under Lieutenant Calvin S. Turner, who at once gave chase with fifteen men, but the Indians having a long way the start of him, reached the thickets on Sulphur creek far enough in advance to scatter and elude his pursuit.

The Secretary of War disapproved the twelve months' call, but ordered the company to be mustered out and re-mustered at the end of six months for six months longer, which necessitated a reorganization of the company, and Captain McCulloch was re-elected captain without opposition, and re-mustered into service at Fort Morrill by Captain Gordon Granger, who freed the slaves by a military order, in violation of the Constitution and laws of the United States, on the nineteenth day of June, 1865. In the meantime, General Brook had died, and General W. S. Harney was in command, and as there had been no Indians seen for over two months on or near the line of operations, he regarded them entirely driven off from that portion of the frontier, and, at his request, General Harney ordered Captain McCulloch's company to or near the head of the Llano river, where Kimble county is now located, from where he could completely protect the settlers on the upper Guadalupe, and partially, if not completely, protect those on the upper Medina.

Soon after establishing his camp well up the north fork of the Llano, Captain McCulloch started out with a scout of twenty-two men, intending to pass up that stream to its source, and thence westward to the Nueces, so as to cut across all the Indian trails that traversed that section, and, if no fresh trail was found, to bear northeast to the head-waters of the San Saba, Concho, etc., making a scout of fifteen or twenty days; but, just at the head of the north fork of the Llano, he struck a fresh trail of Indians, going in the direction of the head of the San Saba, which he promptly pursued, and, thinking it likely he would find them resting at the first good water, he placed the detachment under the command of Sergeant Houston Tom, with instructions to move silently, while he took one more with him to go in advance and spy out the Indian camp, in the event of finding it. On approaching the first branch of the San Saba he discovered their camp, composed of some forty braves and two squaws, where the men were all loitering carelessly about in the shade of an oak grove, on the margin of a spring branch, with their horses grazing on a prairie some three or four hundred yards from them. The fact that some of our friendly Indians were permitted to roam and hunt in that section of the country rendered it necessary to use great caution in attacking any party that might be discovered, which prevented his taking all the advantages of them he could otherwise have taken; and, in order to be certain whether they were friends or foes, after getting within three hundred yards of them under cover of the timber on the branch, we advanced upon them in line, at a gallop, but did not open fire upon them until the warriors seized their arms and fired one shot, upon which he charged them, and they fled, scattering over exceedingly rough, broken, rocky and brushy ground, so that he had to turn his men loose with orders to attack them wherever they could come up with them, and in this way four Indians were killed, two squaws taken prisoner, and every horse they had, with all their camp plunder and camp outfit, captured while the rangers' loss was one horse killed, and one man slightly wounded by an arrow shot by a squaw, when he was making her a prisoner. This was a party of

Comanches who had made a raid on the lower Rio Grande, and were making their way back to their main body on the upper Colorado river. After detaining the squaws about two hours, to get them quiet and learn all he could from them, Captain McCulloch allowed each of them to pick a horse out of those captured, take all the plunder they wanted, and then presenting each of them with a good blanket from his own stores, turned them loose to hunt up their men and tell them he was not fighting women, or for plunder, but for peace; that he would remain on the ground until twelve o'clock the next day, and if they would come in and agree to make peace, he would turn over all their property to them; that if they were afraid to do this, if they would hunt up a band of friendly Comanches, and report to the commanding officer at Fort Martin Scott, near Fredericksburg, in a month (a moon), and make peace, he would restore their property.

The property had to be carried back to camp, to be taken care of, and Captain McCulloch's party being too weak to divide and prosecute the scout, after remaining till twelve o'clock the next day, as promised, he returned to camp with his entire party, and was exceedingly careful to have every piece of the plunder captured taken care of, so that it might be turned over to them in case they came in and made peace. In about three weeks, Captain McCulloch received notice from the commanding officer at Fort Martin Scott that they had come in and proposed to make peace, provided he showed good faith by keeping his promise to them through their squaws. They also asked Captain McCulloch to come down and bring the property, if he had it still on hand. In compliance with this request, he carried the property down and turned it over to the Indians, in the presence of the commanding officer of the fort, and they acknowledged that not an article that they could remember was missing. Although no one was authorized to make a treaty with them, an agreement was made for them to commit no depredations on our people, and they to be treated as friends until a proper treaty could be made and they moved to the reservation.

This was the last Indian fight Captain McCulloch ever commanded, although some of his scouts had several little brushes with them while in that section before being mustered out of the service at Fort Martin Scott (on the fourth day of November, 1851) by Captain James Longstreet, and this was the last military service he ever rendered under the United States flag.

Captain McCulloch returned to his home at Seguin, and at once went about making his arrangements to establish his farm and stock business on a solid basis, and invested some money in a piece of land upon which he put a ranch house and built pens. That winter and next spring (1852) he purchased some horses and put them and his cattle (except the milch cows) upon it, in charge of a Mexican, but giving it his personal supervision.

In the summer of 1853, Colonel French Smith declared himself a Whig candidate for the State Legislature. Up to this time they had had no political divisions in the county, but the Democrats got together, informally, and determined to call a meeting and put out their man against him. The Colonel was a fine talker, and the Democrats tackled him with a considerable degree of hesitancy, but they finally determined that Captain McCulloch should make the race against him, and he having never made a speech up to that time, the Colonel laughed at the idea of pitting "Henry" against him. The Colonel made his appointments, and invited Captain McCulloch to meet him. Captain McCulloch never intimated to him or his friends that he intended to do so, but rather intimated that he would not meet him in debate. Captain McCulloch, having business at Austin just before his first appointment, which was at Seguin, purposely stayed away until Smith had gotten well into his speech, which he commenced by asking the Democracy where their champion was, and when might he expect to meet him before the people, if ever? with the remark,

"Henry is a star Indian and Mexican fighter, but you made a mistake when you selected him as a speech-maker," and when McCulloch stepped in and took his seat near the door of the church in which he was speaking, it seemed to move him to his best efforts. As he drew to a close, and before waiting to be called, McCulloch rose to his feet, promptly indicating his intention to reply, and as he walked forward, he was cheered on all sides. Colonel Smith met him cordially, and having occupied the pulpit during his speech, he invited McCulloch to do the same, to which he replied: "No, no, Colonel; I am not only no preacher, but I am not good enough to occupy the pulpit," and as he was a very profane man, while McCulloch was not, this retort he felt to be a pretty hard lick. During McCulloch's ride to Austin and back, alone, he had plenty of time to think, and having about all the manliness that was in him called into requisition, it is doubtful whether he has ever made a better stump speech than he made that day. When he got through, Smith pushed his way through McCulloch's friends to tell him that "if this is a specimen of your speeches, you will prove as good a speaker as you have an Indian and Mexican fighter." The canvass terminated in McCulloch defeating Smith by a handsome majority. Captain McCulloch had no taste for a political life, although, as a patriotic and conscientious member of the Legislature, he did his duty, and was afterwards, as will be seen, drawn into another contest.

In 1855, he was reluctlantly drawn into a canvass (on questions of State policy) against his neighbor and friend, Colonel Thomas H. Duggan, who was a substantial Democrat, and while they both urged Democratic friends to hold a convention and decide between them, they failed to do so, and these gentleman ran the race through, and McCulloch was elected over him by a fair majority to represent the counties of Gonzales, Caldwell, Guadalupe, Hays and Comal, in the Senate, for four years.

In the summer of 1854, Captain McCulloch, purchasing an additional 640 acre tract of land adjoining his ranch tract, on Mill Creek, eight miles west of Seguin, improved it sufficiently to shelter his family, sold his home and small farm in Seguin, and moved his family to his new home. He opened a small farm on it, fenced a small pasture, built good stock-pens, and the next spring invested all his spare funds in good jacks, stallions and mares, with the intention of raising horses and mules extensively.

His brother Ben, had been United States marshal of Texas during President Pierce's administration, and when the State was divided into two judicial districts, President Buchanan appointed him United States marshal for the eastern district of Texas, and as he wished to spend a good deal of his time in Washington, North Carolina, Virginia, Mississippi and Tennessee, and Henry spent a good deal of his time in Galveston, when he could be spared from other interests, managing the office, at the end of the session of the Legislature which was held in the winter of 1857 and 1858, Ben resigned and President Buchanan appointed Henry United States marshal for the eastern district of Texas for four years, which position he held until Texas seceded, when he resigned.

The Secession Convention selected three men, viz: Ben McCulloch, John S. Ford, and Henry E. McCulloch, and appointed them colonels, with authority to raise men and capture the stores at all the military posts of the United States in Texas. As soon as the brothers were informed of their appointment, they hastened home (eight miles north of Seguin at "Ranger's Home") to spend a day with the family, take leave of them, and be ready in every way to take the field, and, impressed with the certainty of approaching war, to make all their arrangements accordingly. As was Captain McCulloch's custom on leaving home for any length of time, he made out full memoranda of all the debts he owed (his brother never had any, as he attended to all home affairs) and all that was coming to them, and then proceeded with what he owed as security for others, and when the last list was made, it being about ten thousand dollars, his brother seemed astonished, and being called on for his liabilities of the same kind, they amounted to about nine thousand, footing up a little over nineteen thousand dollars, and, as they had never had any seperate interest, they felt severally bound for these debts if they had to be paid then.

On carefully looking over the future and calculating the uncertainties of war, and having about $3,000 in gold deposited with R. D. Q. Mills & Co., of Galveston, they placed this, subject to the order of the wife of Henry (Ben never married and the brothers had but the one home), to be used as she saw proper for the good of the family, with the suggestion, as they had plenty of beef cattle, mules and horses of marketable age, that she dispose of these to raise money for present use, and retain the gold for any great emergency that might arise, with the further suggestion, if both fell, and the war closed disastrously, she should do what she thought best for herself and children. Here the brothers separated, to meet no more in life, Henry returning to Austin, and Ben remaining at home awaiting orders and getting everything ready for his move on San Antonio.

The principal military post of the United States being at San Antonio, three commissioners were appointed, viz., Samuel A. Maverick, Thomas J. Devine and Philip C. Luckit, to take charge of the property after Ben McCulloch had captured it. A force of about twelve hundred men had already been raised in the counties of Gonzales, Caldwell, Hays and Guadalupe, for such purposes, by Colonel James C. Wilson, of Gonzales; Colonel Ellison, of Caldwell, and Colonel Henry McColloch, of Seguin, who were called out by Ben McCulloch, and, on presenting this overwhelming force, Colonel Twiggs, who was then in command at San Antonio, surrendered the property. Colonel Ford was ordered to Brownsville, as military commander, accompanied by Colonel E. B. Nichols, as commissioner, while Henry McCulloch was commissioned as colonel and military commissioner, and ordered to raise troops and capture the posts on the northwestern frontier. Leaving Austin without a man, with his rifle, pistols, Spanish blanket, and a change of underclothing in his saddle-bags, and only a few dollars in his pocket, he took the stage for the Salado, where he entered the home of Colonel E. Sterling C. Robertson about three o'clock p. m., and, after telling him of his mission, told him he wanted him to select a man to raise a company hurriedly, to furnish him (McCulloch) a number one saddle-horse (suitable for active, hard, frontier service), with saddle, bridle, etc., and one hundred dollars in gold, and, if possible, to have them all ready by breakfast next morning. Colonel Robertson put McCulloch to bed, saying, "Go to sleep, and I will have everything ready and wake you up to early breakfast." When McCulloch finished his breakfast the next morning, he found everything ready, with Captain Tally waiting for such orders as he might have for him. Having prepared several blank commissions before leaving Austin, he filled one up for Tally, and directed him to raise a company as soon as possible, of from fifty to one hundred men, and report to him at Comanche, where Colonel McCulloch had already sent Captain T. C. Frost to raise a company. Mounting his horse, Colonel McCulloch took the road to Gatesville, where he made arrangements to have men raised to report at Comanche, and passing on through Hamilton county, doing the same, he reached Comanche, where he left orders with Captain Frost to have his company ready to march as early as possible, and to hold all others who might come in squads until Captain Tully arrived with his company, take command of all of them, as senior captain, and report to him at Brownwood.

On reaching Brownwood, he selected a man, and sent him to Camp Colorado, which was then garrisoned by Captain E. Kirby Smith's company of the Second United States cavalry, to make a full examination of the place, make a sketch of it, and return to him at Brownwood, or meet him on the road. Captain Frost soon arrived with the troops, and when those raised at Brownwood were added, they numbered about four hundred men, and with these he at once moved upon Camp Colorado. Placing the troops under Captain Frost, as senior captain, with instructions to reach Jim Ned after night, and camp on the creek four miles below Camp Colorado, he went on in advance of the troops, and demanded the surrender of the post, with all its military stores, including the cavalry horses and arms of every description, leaving it optional with the troops to march peacefully out of the country, via Indianola, with transportation furnished, or take service with Texas. At first, Captain Smith positively refused to comply with the demand, but ultimately consented, with the understanding that while all other stores, arms, etc., were to be turned over on the ground, the horses, transportation and arms of the company were to be turned over at Indianola, where the troops were to be shipped to New Orleans or New York. This arrangement was made, and articles of agreement regularly signed. He left Captain Frost, with his company, to receive this property and garrison the post, and pushed on to Fort Chadburn, with the remainder of the command, under Captain Tally, as senior captain, taking one man and going about a day in advance of the command. Here he found Lieutenant-Colonel Gouvenier Morris in command of the fort, which was garrisoned with two companies of United States infantry; and when the proposition of surrendering the property was made by Colonel McCulloch, without troops to enforce the demand, Morris not only refused but laughed at him. Meantime, Colonel McCulloch found that Captain Bill Burleson had a company of rangers about twenty miles off, which had been called into service by Governor Houston. He rode to that camp at once, and induced him to join the Texas command, and before Colonel Morris knew that there was any body of troops near him, the Texans marched upon the fort with about four hundred well-armed men eager for battle, and made a peremptory demand for an immediate surrender, to which Colonel Morris asked for an hour's time to consult his captains, which was granted, upon condition that during that hour he would make no preparation for defense, and Colonel McCulloch was allowed to place an officer inside the fort to see that this condition was complied with. At the end of the time, Morris notified McCulloch that he would surrender the property, but not the company arms, provided his command was allowed to occupy the fort until transportation was furnished them to Indianola. It was agreed that his command should occupy the fort until transportation could be furnished, upon condition that the stores should be turned over immediately to an officer, to be appointed by Colonel McCulloch, who should, with the approval of Captain Tally, issue to both commands, and that the arms of the companies should be turned over at Indianola, which was accepted by him, and articles of agreement signed to that effect. Upon this agreement, although Colonel McCulloch had not heard from San Antonio, he wrote to the commissioners and asked them, if possible, to furnish the necessary transportation to move this command, and, leaving Captain Tally, with his company, in command, took Captain Burleson's company and the balance of the command and moved at once upon Phantom Hill, which he found deserted, with only a few stores left. Knowing that he would be able to pick up Captain Buck Barry's company of rangers (ordered out by Governor Houston) on the route, Colonel McCulloch left Captain Burleson's company at this place and pushed on with the remainder of the command under Lieutenant Green Davidson, of Captain Tally's company, to Camp Cooper, where he expected to find Captain Carpenter with two companies of the Second Cavalry. Soon after picking up Captain Barry's company, he met Captain Carpenter, who had been compelled to surrender the stores at Camp Cooper to an unauthorized force to whom he could not capitulate, and, in order to relieve him from his embarrassment as far as possible and guarantee his peaceful passage out of the State, Colonel McCulloch entered into articles of agreement with him similar to those entered into with Captain Smith, he passing on to San Antonio with his command and McCulloch pushing on to Camp Cooper, to secure what stores he might find at that place.

On reaching Camp Cooper, Colonel McCulloch found Major Rogers of Waxahachie, in command, with James P. McCord as quartermaster and commissary, taking an inventory of the captured property on hand; and although it had been seized by an unauthorized force, Major Rogers had allowed but little of it, if any, to be appropriated to private use. Colonel McCulloch relieved Major Rogers, furnished his command with supplies for the trip home, placed Captain Barry in command, and appointed McCord temporary commissary and quartermaster to continue to take an inventory of the property under Captain Barry's orders, make issues to the troops, etc., until other arrangements should be made. Leaving Captain Barry in command of Camp Cooper, Colonel McCulloch pushed on with his remaining force, under Lieutenant Davidson, to Fort Belknap, which he found had been deserted by the troops who had left the State for Fort Arbuckle, in the Indian Territory, and if they had left any supplies, they had been carried away by other persons. McCulloch then marched his force back to Camp Colorado, where he disbanded it, furnishing them rations, etc., to their homes, and after a day's rest returned to Fort Chadburn, accompanied by Lieutenant Davidson. On reaching Fort Chadburn, he learned from Captain Tally that Colonel Morris had refused to recognize Tally's authority, suspended the officer whom he had appointed to take charge of the property and given official notice that he did not intend to conform to the articles of capitulation which he had signed, but would supply Tally's company with forage and rations until McCulloch returned. Calling on him immediately, in order to have this affirmed or contradicted by him in person, Colonel McCulloch asked him to invite his two captains who had witnessed the articles of agreement to meet them at his office to witness the conversation. This being done, when called upon by McCulloch, he informed him that upon mature deliberation, he had determined not to comply with the written articles of agreement, and, when ready, would move out of the State in the direction of Fort Arbuckle, if he moved at all. Meantime news had reached there, that in surrendering the property at San Antonio, General Twiggs, as the commander of the forces in Texas, had stipulated with the commissioners (Maverick, Devine, and Luckett) to allow the troops to leave the State at Indianola, where they were to be furnished transportation and supplies, and were to carry their arms out with them, but Colonel McCulloch did not consider that this changed in the least the terms entered into with him, as his was a seperate and distinct command, but agreed that on arrival at San Antonio, that these commissioners might change the agreements made with him, so as to put all the United States troops upon the same footing, if they desired to do so, of which he informed Colonel Morris.

A long discussion of an unfriendly character, more or less, ensued, in which McCulloch accused him of violating his official honor, and of disgracing the flag of his nation, and notified him that he would assemble a force at once to hold his command in the fort until he could get artillery from Fort Mason to batter the houses down over his head, and if he undertook to move out by any route without conforming strictly to the written articles of agreement, he, McCulloch, would fight him at every ravine, creek, branch and river to the line of the State, as long as he had an officer and man to shoot at, and he was left with one to fire a gun or pistol. Upon this, Captain W. W. Wallace, who commanded one of the companies, informed Colonel Morris that he considered the articles of agreement, as signed, binding upon the command, and that his company, while he commanded it, would not participate in their violation if it came to hostilities. Finding his own household divided, Colonel Morris asked two hours further time to confer with his officers before McCulloch took further action, which was granted, and at the end of two hours he invited McCulloch to return, and in the presence of all the officers of his command and Captain Tally, pledged himself to carry out the written articles of agreement on his part, and here the trouble ended. After giving Captain Tally instructions as to his future course, Colonel McCulloch left for Camp Colorado, which he had established as the headquarters of his command.

He remained at Camp Colorado two days, giving orders for the general disposition of his forces for the protection of the settlements on the frontier, as well as the careful management of the captured property; put Captain Frost in command as senior captain in his absence, and returned to Austin to make a full report to the Executive Committee (of which Honorable John C. Robertson was chairman, which had been appointed by the Convention to manage the military affairs of the State until more permanent arrangements could be made) of all his actions, receive their approval or disapproval, and be relieved of the command or receive further orders. On receiving his report, in writing, his course was approved by the committee unanimously, and he was directed to return to Camp Colorado, and give all the protection in his power to the frontier people until more permanent arrangements could be made to that effect.

On the night after receiving this order, and before he had left Austin, he received a commission from his Excellency, Jefferson Davis, President of the Confederate States, to raise and command a regiment of mounted riflemen for the protection of the frontier of Texas. In the absence of any other Confederate officer, and in order that he could control the necessary supplies to fit out this regiment, put it in the field and support it, it became necessary for him to assume command of the Department of Texas, which he did; and upon informing the Executive Committee of these facts, they authorized him to exercise full control of all the supplies captured at San Antonio and the posts north of it, and that he should retain command of the troops which he had placed on the frontier until he could replace them with Confederate troops.

After issuing his first order, assuming command of the

Department of Texas, with headquarters at San Antonio, he granted authority to ten select men to raise companies for twelve months' service in the Provisional Army of the Confederate States, to report to him as early as possible, within the next twenty days, at San Antonio, except those to be raised by Captains T. C. Frost, Buck Barry, and Green Davidson (Captain Tally having informed him that he did not desire to remain in the service but a short time) who were to remain at their respective posts. Each of these ten select men was instructed to receive no habitual drunkard or regular gambler into his company, and all, without exception, with the distinct understanding that no leave of absence would be granted to an officer, or furlough to a non-commissioned officer or private, in the twelve months, unless it should be in case of actual necessity, which the colonel commanding would be the judge. Under these instructions, they had but four married men in the regiment, and it was certainly one of the finest regiments of men and horses ever seen mustered into the volunteer service. Going immediately from Austin to San Antonio, to make arrangements with the State Commissioners to turn over the military stores to him as the representative of the Confederate States, and completing his arrangements with them to that effect, Colonel McCulloch continued the officers in charge of them which they had appointed; and, after granting Captain W. M. Edgar authority to raise a company for artillery service, he took leave of absence to spend a few days with his family, near Seguin, while the mounted companies were being raised and equipped to report.

On the seventeenth of April, the first company of the ten reported, and Captain Sayers, who had been sent from Montgomery by the Secretary of War to muster the regiment into service, having arrived, it was mustered in immediately, and as the other companies arrived, one by one, they were mustered, and, in a few days, the six companies that were ordered to report at San Antonio were regularly mustered into service, and Captain Sayers dispatched, with an escort,

Distinguished Texans.

to the posts on the frontier to muster in the four companies in that section.

It requiring a few days to fit out the six companies fully for the field, as well as Captain Edgar's company of light artillery before any further movement of troops was made, Colonel Earl Van Dorn arrived with full instructions from the Secretary of War to take command of the department, and as the war had actually commenced, capture all the United States troops that had not gone out of the department; and after arresting all the officers that were in San Antonio, he hurried off to Indianola with his staff, to capture the troops that were waiting at that point for transportation, with orders for Colonel McCulloch to follow, by forced marches, with his six companies of mounted men, and Captain Edgar's battery, who were all ready for the field; and, although Colonel McCulloch made fully fifty miles in each twenty-four hours, on arriving in Victoria he was informed that all the troops that had not left Indianola had surrendered to Colonel Van Dorn, and that any further advance of his command was unnecessary.

Here Colonel McCulloch remained for two days awaiting the return of Colonel Van Dorn, on orders from him, which was beneficial to both men and horses; and when he returned, he pushed on to San Antonio, and directed Colonel McCulloch to return to that place with his entire command, as expeditiously as practicable without injury to his horses, as troops were expected to arrive there from Forts Clark, Stanton, Davis and Bliss, under the command of Colonel Reeves. Reaching San Antonio before the arrival of these troops, Colonel Van Dorn directed Colonel McCulloch to establish a camp with his six companies and Captain Edgar's battery on the Leon, at or near the crossing of the Fort Clark road, where he, McCulloch, would receive reinforcements, and await the approach of Colonel Reeves, who was known to be within a few days' march.

This being the first time McCulloch's troops had had any rest, he ordered an election for lieutenant-colonel and major of the regiment; and, although being fully authorized by his commission to command them, as they were volunteers, he submitted his own claims for their ratification or the election of any other person they might think proper to elect to the command, and Captain Nelson, who commanded one of the companies, became a candidate for colonel against him. All of the companies of the regiment were embraced in the order, including the four that were absent as well as the six in camp, and the contest resulted in the election of Captain T. C. Frost lieutenant-colonel, Edward Burleson major, and Henry McCulloch's appointment endorsed by a large majority. Here he was reinforced by temporary troops under the command of Captain Samuel A. Maverick, James Duff and James R. Sweet; and just before Colonel Reeves came in, Captain T. T. Teel reported with his battery. On being informed of the near approach of Colonel Reeves' command, Colonel Van Dorn came out from San Antonio, in person, selected his position, and formed his line of battle to receive Colonel Reeves' advance. This being discovered by Colonel Reeves, he took position at a stone house, surrounded by a yard fence built of the same material, about two miles off, where he awaited Van Dorn's attack. As soon as Colonel Reeves had taken his position, Van Dorn advanced in force, placed his men in line of battle, located his batteries, and demanded a surrender of Colonel Reeves and all his forces, with notice that if the demand was refused, he would open fire with his guns and batter down the walls of the house and fence at once, and then prosecute the fight with his small arms. Seeing that defeat was inevitable, Colonel Reeves surrendered himself and command as prisoners of war, and all his troops were allowed to pass through the Southern lines with their arms (which troops remained perfectly silent), which they turned over to an officer at San Antonio, where the prisoners were furnished quarters.

This service performed, as Colonel Van Dorn had sufficient temporary troops to guard the prisoners and property, Colonel McCulloch was ordered, with his six companies and

Captain Edgar's battery of six guns, to proceed to the frontier and dispose of his regiment to the best advantage for the protection of the frontier. Having performed this duty, which ended by posting three companies of his regiment and Edgar's battery on Red River, at the mouth of "Big Wichita," under the command of Major Edward Burleson, of that regiment, to watch the reserve Indians who had been abandoned by the United States government at Fort Cobb, as well as to protect the settlers on that portion of the frontier against the hostile Indians. Then, returning along the entire line, to inspect the troops, to see how they were performing their duty, and see, personally, to the condition of his supplies, when he reached Captain Fry's command of two companies located on the Concho, he was overtaken by an order from the Secretary of War to leave his regiment under the command of his lieutenant-colonel, proceed immediately to San Antonio, and relieve Colonel Van Dorn, who had been appointed brigadier-general and ordered to Richmond.

Furnishing Lieutenant-Colonel Frost with a copy of the order (which was sent to him at Camp Colorado by courier), Colonel McCulloch proceeded at once to San Antonio, which place he reached about the tenth day of August, 1861, and, in reporting to the Secretary of War, requested to be relieved as early as practicable and allowed to return to his regiment.

In a few days, he was informed by the Secretary of War that Brigadier-General H. H. Sibley had been authorized to raise a brigade of three regiments for service in New Mexico, and directed Colonel McCulloch to fit them out with arms, ammunition, forage, rations and transportation, and to raise and organize other troops.

Soon after this, he was informed that P. O. Hebert, of Louisiana, had been appointed brigadier-general, and ordered to relieve him of the command of the department.

From some cause, General Hebert did not reach Texas until October, and stopped at Galveston to examine the coast, giving directions for its defense, and finally determined to remain at that place and Houston, instead of going to San Antonio. Although McCulloch knew that General Hebert was in the department, as he had issued no orders assuming command or relieving him by any order, Colonel McCulloch continued to exercise the authority as commander of the department until early in December, when, for the first time, the orders conflicted in the use of Lieutenant Sparks, whom McCulloch had directed to muster some troops into the service, and General Hebert had ordered on some other duty. Upon this, the Lieutenant wrote McCulloch, asking whose orders he should obey, and he replied that "he must obey my orders," and sent General Hebert a copy of the Lieutenant's letter, and his reply. On the receipt of this, he wrote McCulloch, requesting him to call on him at Galveston, which he did promptly, and on the meeting, which was quite friendly, he tried to convince McCulloch that the mere knowledge of his presence by him personally was all that was necessary for him to have, in order for him to recognize General Hebert as the commander of the department, while McCulloch rightly contended (and it was so decided by the Secretary of War) that he could only recognize him by an official order, and that if he had retired from San Antonio without such order he would have been liable to arrest and court martial for deserting his post, and to remain there without exercising the command would have been to render himself ridiculous, which he did not propose to do. So, in in order to right up matters, as far as possible, he issued an order assuming command of the department, and validating all the acts of McCulloch from the date of his arrival in the State, and assigning him (McCulloch) the command of the Western District of Texas, with headquarters at San Antonio, where he remained organizing and fitting troops for the field, and sending them to different points as they were needed. until some time in May, 1862, when he was relieved by General H. P. Bee.

In the meantime he had been appointed brigadier general, and just at this time received notice of the fact, with orders to report to General Van Dorn, east of the Mississippi river; and, as it would naturally take a few days to appoint his staff and make suitable arrangements to take the field, he determined to spend that time with his family at his home.

General McCulloch appointed Dr. Jesse Boring, of San Antonio, brigade surgeon, with the rank of major; John R. King, brigade commissary, with the rank of major; W. G. King, brigade quartermaster, with the rank of major; John Henry Brown, of Belton, assistant adjutant-general, with the rank of major; Wm. A. Pitts, ordnance officer, with the rank of captain, and Ben. E. Benton, aide-de-camp, with the rank of captain. Sending his quartermaster to San Antonio for a first class wagon and team, to haul the staff baggage, and an ambulance and team, for his own use and to have along in case of sickness, he awaited his return with the property, to see that the staff was properly fitted out, and after agreeing upon the route they would travel, General McCulloch took leave of his family and took stage for Houston, where he called on General Hebert, who informed him that he had just received orders to forward all the infantry regiments in his department, except Colonel Lucket s, to Little Rock, Arkansas, without delay, which he said it was impossible for him to do, as he had no transportation or means to obtain it, whereupon General McCulloch advised him to seize the war-tax money in the hands of the collectors, purchase transportation, and send them on. The suggestion of interfering with the civil department of the government startled him, and he promptly rejected it, and remarked that "he believed McCulloch had advised him to do what he would not do himself," in which he assured him he was mistaken; and in the conversation General McCulloch, learning that the regiments of Colonels Roberts and Hubbard were in camp only two miles from Houston, suggested that if General Hebert would send these regiments to Millican by rail, with authority to impress wagons to haul their baggage to Tyler, with instructions to remain there until they could get up transportation by further impressment, if it was necessary, that these officers would manage to take their regiments to Little Rock in a reasonable time. Upon this suggestion he sent for the officers, submitted the plan to them, which they said was practicable, and with such orders they could carry it into effect; and the next morning they took the train for Millican. General McCulloch then intended to take the stage at that place for Munroe, Louisiana, thence, by rail to the Mississippi, opposite Vicksburg, where he could cross it and make his way to Van Dorn, wherever he might be. On reaching Munroe, he found a message from Van Dorn, ordering him to take a position in East Texas, favorable to supplies, and organize and forward troops to Little Rock, Arkansas, for a fall campaign into North Arkansas and Missouri, and he determined at once to adopt Tyler as the point, where he would find two regiments already organized, in a good farming country. So informing Van Dorn by his returning messenger, he returned to Tyler by stage.

Reaching Tyler at night on the second of June, 1862, he put up at the hotel kept by Dr. Irvine, and said nothing to any one about his business until next morning, when he issued an order assuming command of a certain district of country, over which he declared martial law for military purposes, without interfering with the execution of the laws by the local civil authorities, to whom he pledged himself to give his support, and the next order was to declare Tyler a military post, and the headquarters of that district. These orders were published in the Tyler papers. Here he found Mr. Yarbrough acting as quartermaster and commissary, without a dollar of public funds, a two-horse wagon, four mules, and twenty-five bushels of corn in his quartermaster department, and thirteen hundred pounds of side babon in his commissary department. The next thing was to dispatch a courier to meet his staff and turn them to Tyler, with instructions to reach it as early as possible, and another to Captain M. M. Boggess, who had just finished a twelve months' service in McCulloch's regiment, from which he had had just about enough time to reach Henderson, his home, with his company, ordering him to reorganize, with what men he could collect, and report to him immediately at Tyler, with instructions for the remainder of his men to come on as early as possible. The next step was to put Mr. Yarbrough to work among the citizens, to get up additional forage and commissary stores (corn, meal, bacon, fresh beef, and salt), for which he directed him to give memorandum receipts, promising that they should be taken up by paying the cash for them within a month.

Learning that Captain Ball's company of Colonel Young's regiment was near them, with measles having broken out in it, General McCulloch took possession of the Federal court-house for a hospital; and having made the acquaintance of Mrs. Robertson (wife of Colonel John C. Robertson), appealed to her, and through her to the ladies of Tyler, to get up bedding, etc., to fit up this hospital for immediate occupation; and they not only did this promptly, but organized a "Ladies Aid Society," which rendered valuable service, which was indispensable in fitting up the troops with tents, clothing, etc., but especially in fitting up hospitals and taking care of the sick, of whom there were a great number, as the measles had found its way into nearly every regiment before they reached Tyler; and they also selected and procured the service of a doctor, a resident physician, to take charge of the sick until the brigade surgeon could reach headquarters. The regular staff arrived in three or four days, accompanied by Hon. A. W. Terrell, and C. L. Robards, Esq., of Austin, and Colonel E. Sterling C. Robertson, of Salado, who tendered their services as volunteer aides-de-camps on the General's staff; and as he had need of their services, he accepted their kind offer and put them on duty at once, aiding in gathering up supplies. In the meantime, he had picked up a squad of mounted men (one at a time), and placed them under the command of Captain Wm. A. Pitts, to be used as necessary. Captain Boggess soon reached headquarters with some sixty men, whom the General directed him to organize with a full quota of officers, to be mustered in at once, with orders to complete the company as early as practicable. With this company and the squad of mounted men under Captain Pitts, the General could see his way clearly for gathering in a supply of money, and he issued an order directing the seizure, by force, of all the war tax money in the hands of county collectors within his district, and dispatched squads of men, under the command of prudent officers, in different directions; and in about two weeks, they had gathered in two hundred and eight thousand dollars in actual cash, which enabled the General commanding to pay for all the supplies he needed to fit out or aid in putting sixteen regiments in the field in Arkansas. Colonel E. S. C. Robertson being a man of means, with many friends in Houston and Galveston to vouch for him, General McCulloch sent him to Houston, with Dr. Boring, to purchase from twenty to thirty thousand dollars worth of medical and hospital stores, to be paid for in from thirty to sixty days, and to hire or purchase mule teams to transport them to Tyler; and in order to carry out his instructions successfully, he, backed by his friends, became personally responsible for the payment of the purchase money, and brought the needed stores to Tyler.

In order that no man should be responsible for this money except himself, the General had it turned over to his aide-de-camp, Captain Ben E. Benton, who disbursed it by turning it over to officers of the different departments (quartermaster, commissary, ordnance and medical), on their requisitions and General McCulloch's orders, and these officers invested it in purchasing supplies for the troops under McCulloch's immediate orders, so that he knew that not a dollar of it was wasted.

This took over three months; but just as soon as it could be done, the General had his accounts made up, charging himself with this money and crediting himself with sums turned over to the officers of the different departments, and made a full report to the Secretary of War of the whole matter, embracing a copy of his orders forming the district, declaring martial law, and seizing the money by force, with his reasons therefor and the necessities of the case, and sent Colonel A. W. Terrell to Richmond to lay it before the authorities, where he succeeded in getting them to pass the accounts (they being perfectly correct), and the Secretary of War to write General McCulloch a letter exonerating him from all blame, and rather commending his course, under the circumstances, although he had interfered directly with one of the civil departments (treasury) of the government.

General McCulloch, having pushed the regiments forward, except Colonel Speight's, left the necessary funds for its aid in the hands of the post quartermaster and commissary; took Captain Boggess' company, and, with his entire staff, went on to Little Rock, where he reported to General Holmes, who put him in command of all the troops at Camp Nelson (twenty-five miles east of Little Rock), consisting of sixteen regiments of Texas and six of Arkansas troops, with Colonel Nelson, of Waco (afterwards brigadier-general), second in command. Unfortunately for General McCulloch and the service, General Nelson soon took sick and died, and the camp was named after him.

These troops were all new in the service; knew but little of discipline, and less of tactics; and, without the necessary army regulations, or works on tactics to distribute among them, the officers were compelled to come to the General's headquarters for such information as they were compelled to have to enable them to understand their duties. This made it exceedingly laborious on the General and his staff, especially as Brigadier-General Nelson and Colonel Horace Randle (West-Pointer) were the only officers he had that had ever exercised any command of troops until a few months before.

At this time, from over work and malarial affection, the health of Major John R. King, chief commissary, and Major John Henry Brown, assistant adjutant-general, on the staff, failed so completely, that they were compelled to resign, and the General appointed Aide-de-Camp Captain B. E. Benton assistant adjutant-general, and secured the services of Major Isham H. Earle, of Waco, as his chief commissary, and appointed Alexander McCulloch, of Colonel Parsons' regiment, aide-de-camp.

As early as practicable, General McCulloch organized these regiments into brigades of four regiments each, except the Arkansas troops, of six regiments, which he put in one brigade, under the command of Colonel McRea, and placed all in one division.

Soon after they were organized, General Holmes ordered General McCulloch to send McRea's brigade to General Marmaduke, in North Arkansas, and his best brigade to the post of Arkansas. As soon as he put these brigades in motion, he preceded Colonel Dishler to Little Rock, where he called on General Holmes, and not only protested against his sending it to the Arkansas post, but begged him not to do so, as it certainly would prove its sacrifice if the enemy attacked it in force, and that the regiment that was there was altogether sufficient to defend it, unless the attack was made in force; but his protest and argument availed nothing, and the command was captured.

As soon as he was placed in command of the troops at Camp Nelson, he urged General Holmes to apply for a major-general of experience to be put in charge of them: and in order that this might be effected as early as possible, he wrote to his friends in Congress to see the President, and urge upon him the necessity of its being done as early as practicable. Notwithstanding this, General McCulloch was kept in command of the division, under the command of General Holmes, doing nothing except marching from place to place about Little Rock, through rain, snow and mud, crossing and re-crossing the Arkansas river without seeming to have any object in view.

Just before General Nelson took sick, General Holmes informed General McCulloch, by letter, that he had received orders to send all the Texas regiments under his command across the Mississippi river, and wished General McCulloch would come in and bring General Nelson with him for consultation; and while Generals Nelson and McCulloch were delighted with the prospect of seeing the command get where it might do something for the cause, when they reached Little Rock they found General Holmes not only opposed to it, but had already made up his mind not to obey the order if he could avoid it, and asked Generals McCulloch and Nelson to sustain him in his objections, which they refused to do; and as he had said, among other things, to the Secretary of War (written before their arrival), that "the Texas troops would not cross the Mississippi and leave their State exposed to invasion without sufficient force to defend it," they insisted that he should change that portion of his letter or permit them to write to the Secretary of War, through him, that the Texas troops in that camp were ready to go wherever ordered. He changed that part of his letter, and as neither General Nelson nor General McCulloch agreed with him, he dismissed them, but fought it out alone with the Secretary of War, and held the command on the west side of the Mississippi.

On arriving at Camp Nelson, most, if not all, of the Texas regiments had passed through the camp measles, in a virulent form, and were still suffering from its sequence; and, coming from a healthy country into one filled with malaria, in an unhealthy location, poorly provided for in every respect, and especially with poor, unhealthy food (poor Texas beef, coarse corn meal, without sifting in many instances, and a sloppy drink made of corn-meal bran), they suffered greatly from sickness, and the mortuary report showed that, for about six weeks, the deaths ranged from ten to twenty-five per day, and one day twenty-seven.

When General Walker arrived, General McCulloch had been first ordered to report to General Henderson, in North Arkansas, and then to General Dick Taylor, in Louisiana, until he had ferried the entire division across the Arkansas river; and at that time it was about equally divided, one-half on one side and the other half on the other side. When General Holmes directed General McCulloch to consolidate it so as to turn it over to General Walker, General Walker was greatly amused when General McCulloch asked General Holmes which side of the river he must place it, and he replied, on the south side. After resting a day or two at General Holmes' headquarters, to have ample time to confer with him, and give him a fair opportunity of preparing the officers and men in the division for the change in commanders, General Walker came out with his staff, was well received, and took command of the division, kindly offering General McCulloch the privilege of selecting the brigade which he preferred to command; and as one of the brigades was composed of regiments from three divisions of the State (Colonel Waterhouse from East Texas, Colonel Fitzhugh from North Texas, and Colonels Flournoy and Allen from West Texas), General McCulloch selected it, so that he could not be accused of sectional feeling in the selection.

Preparatory to breaking up "Camp Nelson," General Holmes wrote General McCulloch to "select his best colonel;" and direct him to report at (Holmes') headquarters immediately, to select, prepare and command a convalescent camp near Little Rock. General McCulloch carefully and conscienciously selected Colonel O. M. Roberts (since Governor of Texas), furnished him with a full copy of General Holmes' letter, and his order directing him to so report, and at the same time informed him that he would meet him at a given time and place, and ride with him to see General Homes with regard to the interest of the command generally. They met, and after an interchange of greetings, Colonel Roberts surprised General McCulloch by remarking, "you have laid me on the shelf," in which he showed a good deal of feeling. General McCulloch assured him that nothing was further from his thoughts or intentions; that he had acted conscienciously in making the selection, and felt that he had really paid him a high compliment in selecting him as the "best colonel" out of sixteen. "Yes," he said, "most like an old woman; make a good nurse, make a good nurse;" and, finding that he was not to be reconciled, and not being willing to undo what he had done, General McCulloch dropped the subject, and still feels that Governor Roberts never forgave him for it, but played for even with him when he dismissed him as Superintendent of the Deaf and Dumb Asylum when he (Roberts) was Governor.

Two days after General Walker took command, General Holmes ordered him to move the division down to Pine Bluff; and it had not been in that vicinity over two weeks, when he was informed by General Holmes that a large force of gun-boats and infantry had attacked Arkansas Post, and to go to its relief at once by forced marches; and in an hour after General Walker got the order, the division was on the road down the Arkansas river in fine spirits, hoping to reach the Post in time to meet the enemy and prevent the capture or loss of the Post to the Confederates; but, as the division was fully sixty miles off, and the roads in wretched condition from the effects of recent rains and snow, it was obvious that the division would be too late; when it arrived within twenty miles of the Post, the command was informed that the Post had been captured, the works destroyed, and that the enemy had retired in his transports down the Arkansas river. Here it halted, rested the tired troops two days, and returned to Pine Bluff, where they went into winter quarters.

About the time that spring opened, General E. Kirby Smith, who had succeeded General Holmes in command, visited them, and after speaking of what he had learned of the corruptions practiced in the cotton trade on the Rio Grande, asked General Walker to spare General McCulloch from his brigade until the next fall, to be sent to Brownsville, on the Rio Grande, to put a stop to it, and place business out there on an honest basis, and also consulted him about his willingness to go. Both General Walker and General McCulloch objected, but General Smith was importunate, and General McCulloch yielded, with the distinct understanding that he was to be returned to his brigade in time for the contemplated movement into Missouri in the fall.

In order to have honest men to aid him in the performance of this duty, General McCulloch was permitted to take his staff with him, and with them, reluctantly started for Texas. On reaching Camden, Arkansas, he found a telegram awaiting him from General Walker, saying: "I am ordered to report to General Taylor, at Alexandria via Camden —expect warm work, and am sorry you can't be with me." Upon receipt of this, General McCulloch telegraphed General Smith, at Little Rock, that he would abandon the trip to Texas, and join Walker. He sent messengers to General Walker, that owing to the overflowed condition of the bottom of Bayou Bartholomew, it was impossible to cross it with his infantry, and to turn down on the east side of it, and he, General McCulloch, would meet him at its mouth, with plenty of quartermaster and commissary stores on steamers.

In order to do this, General McCulloch had to assume command at Camden, order the post quartermaster to furnish the steamers and quartermaster stores, and the post commissary to furnish the commissary stores, and, although they demurred, they obeyed the orders; and, shipping his staff on board one of the steamers, he reached the mouth of the bayou one day before General Walker arrived with the command.

As there was no traveled road on the west side of Black river near this point, General Walker embarked his troops on these steamers, and steamed down to Monroe, from whence he had a good road to Campton, on Red River, and from thence down Red River to Alexandria, where he met General Taylor, who ordered him to march across the country east, to a small stream which empties into Black river on the west, where they were embarked on steamers, ran down this stream and up Black river to the mouth of

Bayou Tensas, thence up that stream to a point opposite Perkins' landing on the Mississippi river, where they debarked, and McCulloch's brigade ordered to march to attack a force at Perkins' landing, which they hoped to surprise; but, being delayed a few hours by a deep bayou, which had to be bridged, General McCulloch found the enemy ready to receive him. Having ridden forward with a small squad of mounted men, General McCulloch made a casual reconnoisance of the enemy's position, arranged his troops for the attack, threw forward his skirmishers with instructions to feel the enemy immediately in front of the main position of his command, while he placed the two guns of Captain Edgar's battery, which he had with him, on his left, with Colonel Waterhouse's regiment to support it, and directed Captain Edgar to shell the camp, which was on lower ground than that occupied by the brigade, and at the same time try his hand on some transports which were lying in the river; but the banks were so high that but little of them was in view. As soon as he opened fire, he was answered by a gun-boat, which was hidden from view by the high bank on the river, but this bank was so high, and it had to lay so close to it, that they could not depress their guns sufficiently to reach the Confederates by direct shots, and the shells they threw passed over them, but bursting so close to them that a fragment of one of them struck and killed Garland Smith, who was, at his request, serving on General McCulloch's staff that day, and of whom General McCulloch says: "He was one of the best men I ever knew." Smith was within a few feet of the General when he fell dead from his horse, without a groan. General McCulloch then ordered the guns and supporting regiment to advance about seventy-five yards nearer the river and await further orders. Then riding to the front to get what information he could from his skirmishers, he returned to the main portion of his command, which was standing in line of battle, anxious for the fray, and was just directing Captain Benton to say to Colonel Waterhouse that he would advance to the attack with his main force, and, when parallel with him, to do the same with his regiment and Edgar's battery, when he received a note from General Walker, who was fully four miles away, advising him not to make the attack, by which his plan was not only frustrated, but he had to retire from the field when he had every reason to believe that a victory was certain.

On returning to General Walker, and asking the cause of his writing the note, he inform General McCulloch that one of General Taylor's staff, who had accompanied him, had returned and informed General Taylor that the enemy were in large force, strongly posted under the protection of gun-boats, and that he was confident, if McCulloch attacked him, he would be repulsed. The next day, they took up the line of march along a road which led up the Mississippi river, and only a few miles from it, until they reached the little town of Richmond, situated on a bayou, about ten miles from Milliken's Bend, on the Mississippi, where they pitched their tents about ten o'clock a. m., and raised camp fires to cook dinner. About two o'clock p. m., General Taylor sent for General McCulloch to come to General Walker's head-quarters. On his arrival, he informed McCulloch that he wished his brigade to march to Milliken's Bend as soon as it was dark (so as to prevent the movement from being discovered by the enemy), and, if possible, surprise and put them to death with the bayonet. He said he was informed by a friend of his, who was perfectly reliable, that he was in their camp at eight o'clock that day; that there was not a gun-boat there, and only about sixteen hundred negro and four hundred white troops. The General said he knew the country well, and that the road McCulloch would travel was a plain one that would lead direct to their camp, and that on either side there were deserted farms over which he would find no difficulty in marching if he found it necessary to march through them ; furnished him with a sketch of the bend, the locality of the enemy's camp, and how his road would lead him into it. and sent a squad of Colonel Harrison's Louisiana cavalry to pilot him into the place. After giving him all the orders and instructions, he asked McCulloch what he thought of it. McCulloch replied, that he was a soldier; had received his orders; had no right to an opinion, or to think anything except carrying out his in-instructions as well as he could; but, in the presence of General Walker, he insisted on McCulloch's giving his opinion. McCulloch told him, if he required, he would give it, and, if he did so, he would give it plainly and candidly; and, as General Taylor seemed to have made up his mind to make this attack, it would not suit him (Taylor); and yet General Taylor said he wanted it, when McCulloch replied: "Seven days ago made I a feint at Parker's Landing: since then we have marched up and within a few miles of the Mississippi river, through a heavily timbered country; have passed by a few farms occupied by negroes, and had no cavalry to scour the woods on our flank's course. The enemy could have watched and counted us every day. We reached here at ten o'clock a. m.; took no precaution whatever to prevent some negro from giving information to the enemy (which, I have no doubt, has been done), so that by the time I reach the vicinity the enemy will have all the troops and gun-boats they want and the route to the bend picketed, and I will have to fight a force assembled to give battle to General Walker's division, and the prospect of success is extremely doubtful."

General Taylor then remarked that McCulloch seemed to "take rather a gloomy view of it," when McCulloch replied: "Yes, and have said about enough to make you think I am a coward; and, if so, I wish you to accompany me, and if I act the coward, or fail to play my part, try and save my command." The General replied, with some warmth of feeling, that he doubted neither McCulloch's courage nor ability, and that he would find an opening on every road to a victory for his command. General McCulloch replied that he could not think so, but would make the fight, and, if possible, whip it; but that it would have to be done at a heavy sacrifice of some of the best men Texas had in the field. At dark, General McCulloch marched across the bayou on a temporary bridge and moved on silently, and without interruption, until within about two miles of the bend, when his advance guard, the mounted Louisiana scouts, were fired on by the enemy's pickets, when they dashed back on his column like all the Yankees in the nation were at their heels. Placing one regiment in line at the head of his column, and sending forward skirmishers, he moved forward, and soon drew another fire from a small force, which retreated, but kept up a random fire; and, from the course of their retreat, he became convinced that the road he was following would not strike their main camp. He pursued this retreating party through an abandoned farm, which was cut up with dry ditches and bois d'arc hedges, while small detachments of the enemy kept up almost a constant fire on his skirmishers, but never made any stand. The night was dark (starlight), and General McCulloch pursued these small parties of the enemy over this rough ground by their fire, and just at daylight, he found that he had evidently reached their main body, which he could not see plainly because of an intervening hedge, which was within some twenty-five or thirty yards of their breastworks, (a levy about eight feet high), upon which they had placed cotton bales, through which there were several openings, but none of them over ten paces wide, so that McCulloch's line could not be formed to make the charge until this hedge was passed. Under a destructive fire his command moved forward, steady and without wavering, up to and through these openings in the hedge, where his men fell in piles, formed a line and charged the breastworks, driving everything before them, but not without the most stubborn resistance by the negroes, so much so, that the bayonet and clubbed guns were freely used. The white troops fled when the charge was made, but the negroes never even struck a trot, but fought like wild beasts until they were driven across their parade ground (about two hundred yards), through their tents, over the river bank, and under the protection of their gun-boats. By the time the

Confederates reached the top of the breastworks, daylight had opened fully, and the General discovered that he had only covered about half their front; that he had only driven back their left wing, and that a large body of negro troops were massed behind a low cross levee, which intersected the main levee at an angle, which, if manned, would expose McCulloch's command to an enfilading fire from that direction. This rendered a recall of the troops necessary, and as soon as this was donn the fire of four gun-boats was directed against that portion of the works from which the enemy had been driven. As soon as he could form his command, General McCulloch made a second charge on their right wing, before they had discovered the advantage the angle in the levee gave them, and had manned it with only a moderate force. It was carried by a gallant charge, with but little loss, comparatively, and the enemy driven under the river bank, which was not so far here as it was at the other point of attack. Although the levee protected the Confederates completely from the fire of the gun-boats, they continued to rake the space between it and the river, which rendered it impracticable to prosecute the fight; and after remaining in possession of the breastworks for several hours, resting the tired men and removing the kilied and woundəd, General McCulloch withdrew his command in good order, and was not pursued by the enemy.

In this fight his loss was one hundred and ninety-two killed and wounded out of 1100 men, and he stated in his report that the killed and wounded of the enemy was 1000. Since the war the General met a Federal officer who was on the ground, who said they estimated their loss at 1200 men, mostly negroes; and the report of the officer who commanded the Federal's published in the war records, estimated his force at about 1200 and admitted that his loss was about half of his command. Moving back only a few miles from the battlefield, General McCulloch encamped his command for the night; and as it was about noon the next day before he reached Richmond, General Taylor had left, and he has never seen him since.

At the time McCulloch was ordered to make the attack on the bend, General Hawes was ordered to attack Young's Point, some few miles lower down the river. He found the enemy so strong and backed by gun-boats, that he declined to attack the place, with which General Taylor was very much dissatisfied; and on reading his book, written since the war, General McGulloch found that he had made only a slight allusion to these movements, and had not mentioned his name or that of General Hawes in connection with them.

General Walker established a hospital at Richmond, in which McCulloch's wounded were placed, and apparantly intended to spend several days, but he had no cavalry force to watch the movements of the enemy, or, if they did move, to give him any idea of their strength, and in a few days he was surprised at finding them within a mile of his command and advancing upon him with infantry and artillery. He threw Colonel Culberson's regiment across the bayou to feel them and hold them in check, and at once commenced moving his wounded and baggage to the rear; and contrary to General McCulloch's advice (which he asked), retreated with his whole command without giving battle.

The command moved to Delhi, where General Walker was called to a sick family, and the command turned over to General McCulloch, with instructions to return to Alexandria by steady but easy marches. He shipped the baggage and troops from Delhi to Monroe by rail, and empty transportation via wagon road. Rested two days at Monroe, waiting for transportation, then took the road for Alexandria via Camden and Nacogdoches. Two days before the command reached Alexandria, General Walker revoked the command, with orders to General McCulloch, from General Smith, to report to General Magruder, in Texas, for service on the Rio Grande. On arriving at Alexandria he took leave of his brigade, directed his staff to take the nearest road to San Antonio, with all the property and baggage, while he traveled by stage and rail to Houston, to report to General Magruder.

On General McCulloch reporting to General Magruder at Houston, he ordered him to proceed to Galveston at once, to suppress rioting among the troops. This service performed, McCulloch asked for orders to proceed to the Rio Grande, but General Magruder detained him on other service at Houston and Galveston, until he had time to correspond with General Smith, to have his destination changed from Brownsville, on the Rio Grande, to the command of the Northern Sub-District of Texas, with headquarters at Bonham, which was as far from the location of the cotton frauds as he could be put within General Magruder's district. General Magruder gave him permission to go by home and visit his family, en route to Bonham, and he sent a messenger to hunt up his staff and turn them to Bonham.

Spending four days with his family, he took stage for Bonham, which he reached before his staff arrived, but issued orders at once assuming command of the sub-district, declaring Bonham a military post, and assigning Colonel Samuel A. Roberts, assistant adjutant-general, to the command of the post.

Here he found himself a brigadier-general in command, without staff or soldiers; but his staff soon reached him, and special instructions from General Smith with regard to the enforcement of the conscript law. In a day or two after reaching Bonham, Captain Emzi Bradshaw arrived with a fine company of mounted men, on his way to join some command in the Indian Territory. General McCulloch ordered him to remain at Bonham until further orders. This gave him one company, with which to manage the affairs of the sub-district and enforce the conscript law. Meantime, he had learned that there was from two to three thousand deserters and disaffected men in squads laying in the brush, all under command of Henry Boren, who was a deserter from Colonel Martin's regiment, and that this vast horde was

Distinguished Texans.

subsisting off the citizens, who dared not refuse them any supplies that they demanded.

This condition of affairs rendered it necessary for him to know the true sentiments of the people, and he called a council of the leading men of both parties (secessionists and unionists), at his headquarters, and found that, owing to the course pursued by Colonel William Young and other secession leaders at the beginning of the war, there was a considerable disaffected element within the limits of his command, who were probably giving encouragement to these men in the brush. After full and free consultation with these men in council, General McCulloch marked out the course of policy he intended to pursue, which had the effect to neutralize this element, and bring their leaders generally to his support.

President Davis had issued a proclamation of amnesty to all deserters who would return to their commands within a given time, and having no troops to use against these men in the brush, General McCulloch obtained an interview with Boren, at his headquarters, under promise that he would not allow him to be arrested until he returned to the brush. He informed General McCulloch that his command numbered about twenty-five hundred men, composed of deserters from various commands, and disaffected men, who had joined them to evade the conscript law; that they were pretty well armed, and scattered in squads in order to be able to get subsistence from the people. The proposition of amnesty was fully discussed, and the fact that his command would be broken up by main force, if it could not be done otherwise, being firmly but kindly impressed upon him, he seemed inclined to accept the amnesty if his men would consent to it, and agreed to have as many of them together as he could assemble in four days, at a lake in the Jernigan thicket, in the upper edge of Hunt county, to confer with him on the subject.

At the time appointed, General McCulloch took Major John W. Wicks, who was a volunteer aide-de-camp on his staff, with him, and, on reaching the ground, Boren informed him that there were about seven hundred men present to hear what he had to say to them. These men being assembled, General McCulloch mounted a wagon, made them a talk of some forty or fifty minutes, in which he laid the disgrace of their course of conduct plainly before them, as well as the penalty of the laws which they had voluntarily incurred, and closed by offering them full pardon for their offenses, with fifteen days' furlough to arrange their affairs, and meet him at that place, provided they would agree and bind themselves to return to their respective commands; and four hundred and eighty-nine accepted the proposition. Having sent forage and rations to the place to supply them for three or four days, on the day appointed he met them, and four hundred and eighty-seven out of the four hundred and eighty-nine who had given their names were present; but Boren told General McCulloch candidly that he had little or no confidence in their promises to return to their commands, and unless he had some means of compelling them to do so, that all that had been done would amount to nothing, but that he had notified these and all the others that had been under his command, that he had accepted amnesty in good faith, and would have nothing more to do with those who did not, and would aid in forcing them to leave the country or submit to its laws.

This ended his trouble with these men (those in the brush) as an organized force, but there were so many places in the district where they could secret themselves in small squads, that their presence was a great annoyance to the commanding general and the citizens of the country up to the close of the war, notwithstanding his constant efforts to have them arrested and punished according to law.

General McCulloch's district embraced the northeastern Indian frontier, upon which the mounted regiments of Colonels James Bourland and Buck Barry were posted, which added very much to the labors and responsibilities of the command, as the Indians seemed unusually hostile.

Having but little well organized, available force at his command, and it being made his duty to watch the movements of the Federals at Fort Smith and other points, and prevent an invasion of our State from that district, as well as he could, by calling out the State troops, or reserved corps, he managed to get spies into both Fort Smith and Little Rock, who kept him very well posted in all the movements of the Federals west of the Mississippi, and who informed him of the plan of Banks' (information from both sources corresponding) campaign, of which General McCulloch informed General Smith in time for him to have all the cavalry from Texas on the ground, and in the battles of Mansfield and Pleasant Hill.

Although asking several times to be relieved from this exceedingly unpleasant and laborious command, which embraced the getting up and forwarding supplies to the troops in the field, as well as all the other duties embraced in the command of a sub-district, General McCulloch's requests were always refused upon the ground of his successful management of the affairs of the district, which General Smith seemed not willing to entrust any one else, so that he was retained in this command until the close of the war; and when he received news of the surrender of the troops ot the Trans-Mississippi Department, he issued a general order disbanding his troops, and returned to his home near Seguin, without a surrender of himself or any soldier of his command to any one.

Before leaving Bonham, General McCulloch was informed that General Joe Shelby intended to go to Mexico with his command, and join Maxamillan, and wished him to join him with what force he could command. McCulloch replied that "he did not know what he would do until he reached Seguin, and if his wife and children were at home he should not leave the State under any circumstances; that he was a strong secessionist, had done what he could to bring the trouble upon our people, had done the best he could to bring success to the cause we had lost, and while he might not be

Distinguished Texans.

able to be of any service to his friends, he would stay with them, share their fate, and try to do them good."

On reaching home General McCulloch found his wife and children still there, with their home and what stock had not been stolen during his absence, and that of his oldest son, Ben E. McCulloch, who was mustered into Captain Boggess' company as a private at Tyler in 1862, when only seventeen years old, and put on detached service by order of General Smith, soon after taking command of the department; was captain commanding a cavalry company at the close of the war, and at present and for the last four years Assistant Superintendent of the State Penitentiary at Huntsville.

During the war General Ben McCulloch had fallen. As the brothers had no separate interest, Henry fell heir to his property and shared his liabilities; and on a careful examination into their financial affairs, the General found that they were involved in surety debts of over nineteen thousand dollars, and he could see plainly that he had these debts to pay, and the stock of horses and cattle, with some valuable property they had in Galveston, the only available means he had to pay with. As soon as it was understood that the United States Government did not intend to confiscate property, General McCulloch called on the parties who held these obligations, and assured them that he intended to pay them if possible, but asked time, and went to work to that effect, and at the end of three years had paid them all. But this had not only taken that much of his time, and prevented his going into any other business at a time when money could have been made, but had taken about all the available means he had to do business on; and when just fairly out of the embarrasments he had a devoted friend who foresaw he must necessarily fail as a merchant, who begged him to accept his assignment, honestly made with preferred creditors, which he believed his creditors would accept, with General McCulloch as assignee, and which all but one did accept; he brought suit, put his friend into bankruptcy, sued the preferred creditors with a proviso that, upon recovery, if the money could not be made out of them, that McCulloch should be held responsible, and obtained his judgment accordingly; and the man (Colonel Frazier)to whom McCulloch had paid most, failed and refused to pay any part of it back, and General McCulloch had to fork over two thousand and seventy-two dollars in that case.

This found him with nothing but his farm that would bring half its value in money, and rather than sacrifice his other property, which was worth but little then, but promised to be worth something more at a future day, he then purchased a place in Seguin as a temporary home for his family to occupy, while educating his children and some orphans he was raising, with the intention of returning to the farm as early as practicable. Although the security debts he had paid amounted to about ten times as much as this one, they had all been paid by the sale of horses and cattle and Galveston property that he had never used, and, consequently, not felt like this one, which forced him to dispose of a place which he and his brother had intended to make their home for life, and which he felt had really left his family without a home, as he had not been entirely without a farm, though sometimes small, after he improved the one near Gonzales.

This loss seemed to render it indispensably necessary for him to try to make some money, and leaving a little money with his wife for her immediate use, he took the balance for which the farm sold, and went into the cattle shipping business from Indianola to every market within reach where he thought he could make a dollar fairly, including New Orleans, Mobile and Havana, and wound up by shipping about six hundred beeves, by steamer and rail, from Indianola to East Virginia, where they were sold at a small profit to farmers who intended to put them on their blue grass meadows (it being in the early part of May) until fall, and then stall-feed and ship them to eastern markets. Prosecuting this business vigorously for three years, he found that he was making nothing, gave it up and returned home with just $333.25 clear profit over all expenses, claiming nothing for his services, or any interest on the money he was using in the business; and although he had to borrow money from friends to aid him in the business, he refunded every dollar that he borrowed, and every dollar that he had contracted to pay for any purpose, and his three hundred and thirty-three dollars and twenty-five cents was, all in clear cash, actually his own money, and against which no man had a claim for a dime.

Just as he was ready to leave for home, he was employed by the managers of the Gulf, West Texas and Pacific Railway Company as their out door or field agent, in hiring men, purchasing wagons, teams, etc., to rebuild their road to Victoria from Indianola. Soon finding that the work of repairing the old road-bed, in that flat country, had to be done with the mattock and shovel, and that neither white men or negroes could be induced to work in the cold water and mud, he made a trip into Mexico and brought out a Mexican force to do this work, and was then kept on duty as paymaster and outside agent until the work reached Victoria; then as right-of-way and land agent until the road reached Cuero. He had superintended the location of the line to Gonzales, and had obtained the right-of-way and secured the necessary depot grounds whereon the stations were to be built. This company paid him a good salary, and continued his services as long as they had anything for him to do in his line.

At this time, Colonel Pearce commenced extending what is known as the Sunset road from Columbus to San Antonio, and employed General McCulloch as right of-way and land agent on that line, with a good salary. He remained in this employment in that capacity until the right-of-way and depot grounds were secured to San Antonio, when his services were no longer needed in that capacity.

While acting as Colonel Pearce's agent, and with his consent, when the road was put into successful operation as far Harwood, opposite Gonzales, General McCulloch opened a lumber yard, in connection with his third son, Sam L. McCulloch, who was placed in charge of it, under the firm name of "McCulloch & Son;" and when the road reached Luling (where it was expected to remain some time), General McCulloch, with his oldest son, Ben E. McCulloch, and Captain W. M. Edgar, of San Antonio, opened a receiving, forwarding and commission house, with family groceries attached, under the firm name of "Edgar & McCulloch," with Captain Edgar and Ben in charge; but they soon bought Captain Edgar out, and as Sam had sold out their lumber yard at Harwood, they continued the business at Luling under the firm name of "McCulloch & Sons," with the sons, Ben and Sam, in charge. When the road reached Kingsbury, they established a branch of this house, with a lumber yard attached, with Sam in charge, leaving Ben at Luling until he sold out, and he and the General sold out to Sam at Kingsbury, and the General took charge of the Deaf and Dumb Asylum at Austin.

After Richard Coke was elected Governor, in 1874, and before the time arrived for the assembling of the Legislature and the inauguration of the Governor, it became pretty well understood that E. J. Davis, then Governor of Texas, intended to hold the office by force, and about two weeks before the Legislature was to assemble, General McCulloch left home and went to Austin to try, if possible, to learn for himself the true condition of affairs, and what Davis' real intentions were; and, as they were what they had been reported to be, upon consultation it was deemed advisable to call the strong men of the State to Austin to consult together, and adopt some plan by which Davis should be defeated in his intentions—the legally elected Legislature organized, and the legally elected Governor inaugurated.

After the plan of proceedings was adopted by the council, of which Governor Coke was president, General McCulloch was selected as the commander of the armed force to be used by the Democrats in carrying out the plan agreed upon. McCulloch then, in order to be clothed with authority to keep the peace, sought and obtained the appointment of deputy sheriff under George B. Zimpelman, then sheriff of

Travis county, under which McCulloch exercised the command of all the armed forces until the Legislature was organized, the Governor inaugurated, and all the State officers put in charge of their respective offices. As soon as Governor Davis commenced assembling and arming his forces (mostly negroes) in the basement rooms and halls of the Capitol, an advantage was taken of him, by suddenly, and to him unexpectedly, taking possession of the Representative hall, Senate chamber, and all the upper rooms of the Capitol, by what seemed to be a gathering of unarmed citizens and members of the Legislature, but which really was a force armed with six-shooters, ready for the bloody work, if forced upon them. This enabled the Legislature to organize; and, when organized, they sent the usual committee to inform Davis of that fact and that they were ready to receive any communication that His Excellency, Governor Davis, might send them, upon which he informed them, in writing, that he declined to recognize them as a legislative body, or hold any official intercourse with them, which was the first official act publicly indicating what his intentions were, and which enabled the Democrats to see most clearly the necessity of promptly organizing a sufficient force openly to meet and overcome any that he might present to prevent the inauguration of Richard Coke, Governor elect, and obtaining full possession of the State offices; and, for the first and only time in the history of our government, the governor of a sovereign State had to be, and was, inaugurated under the protection of an armed force: and that, too, of a governor who had been elected by a very large majority over his opponent, according to the laws of the State, and a proclamation of the very governor who was then trying to keep him out of the office by force of arms; and yet the Republican party of Texas claim to be a respectable, law abiding political party.

On the first of March, 1876, Governor Coke appointed General McCulloch superintendent of the Deaf and Dumb asylum, and, although he had the influence of the Republicans to contend with on the outside, and trouble with dishonorable aspirants to his position on the inside, he was sustained by the trustees, and both Governors Coke and Hubbard, and held the position until dismissed by Governor O. M. Roberts, on the first of September, 1879, when he returned to his home in Seguin, where, with his son-in-law, W. S. Brown, he opened a furniture store; but after a few month's trial, found it would not pay two, and sold out to Stephen Golihar.

Not contented with a life of idleness, General McCulloch bought a small tract of land on the south bank of the Guadalupe river, and improved it with the aid of W. S Brown, and while this improvement was progressing, and the first crop being made on the farm, Colonel W. L. Moody, a large commission merchant in Galveston, employed him as an agent (drummer) to solicit business for his house; and, although he made as faithful efforts in this as he ever did in anything he ever engaged in, he did not succeed to his own satisfaction, and voluntarily retired from his service.

He then sold his home in Seguin, the small farm he had improved on the Guadalupe river below the town, and bought the Sheffield and Oliver farms (adjoining, not even a fence between), which lay in a bend on the south side of the Guadalupe river, about three miles below Seguin, which is one of the most beautiful and valuable farms on the river; and here (on the Sheffield place) his family now reside, having sold the Oliver place to his son-in-law, A. J. Dibrell, in order to have one family of his children near to their parents in their old age.

In August, 1885, he was employed by the State Land Board, as their agent in the management of the public school, university and asylum lands, with Presidio and El Paso counties as his field of operations, with special instructions to examine carefully into the mining and timber interests in those counties. In the discharge of this duty, General McCulloch found a ten stamp mining mill, owned by a California company, in full operation and located in the Chenati mountains, about forty-five miles from Marfa, in Presido county, which was reducing their ore to bullion at the rate of from twenty to twenty-four thousand dollars per month, at a cost of about four thousand dollars, and that a goodly number of leads had been discovered within an area of twenty miles, which promised to be as rich, if not richer, than the mine this company was working. General McCulloch says: "In fact, this range of the Chenati mountains, in which this mine is located, seems to be almost a bed of valuable mineral, and there have been mineral leads found in other portions of this county which are pronounced to be equally, if not more valuable." He also found, in the eastern portion of El Paso county, near Sierra Blanco and Carrizo, a good many partially developed leads of silver which were regarded as very valuable.

In the timber line, he found a section of country in the Davis mountains on the waters of the Lympia creek, commencing within some ten miles of Fort Davis, where a valuable body of pine and juniper timber, covering a area of from sixty to seventy thousand acres of land, once stood, but that all the valuable timber within the reach of human effort, suitable for lumber, had been cut and sawed up (by steam saw mills) by the United States troops in the construction of the houses, etc., at Forts Davis and Stockton, for which a claim could and should be made against the United States Government. When this, and similar agencies, was created by the State Land Board, they paid the agents one hundred and fifty dollars per month and their actual expenses. Called them in on the twentieth of November, 1885, detained them in Austin one month; made a new contract with them for a year, to commence on the fourth of January, 1886, at the same salary, but they to pay their own expenses, and granted them leave of absence until that time (without pay) to go home and arrange their affairs to be absent for twelve months; but notwithstanding this contract (verbal), on the fifteenth day of the next June they discontinued the salary, leaving it optional with the agents to resign or retain the agency for the fees of office, which were worth in McCulloch's district about three dollars per month; but as the board had granted him the privilege of performing the duties through a local sub-agent, to whom applications for leases and purchases could be made, holding him directly responsible to them for his acts, and as he wished to accommodate the people, facilitate settlers, and augment the school fund, he retained the agency until the thirteenth day of March, 1887, when he resigned, having accepted an agency under the Board of Directors of the Confederate Home, to canvass the State and get subsriptions for the present support of the home, where they have already inmates to provide for, and which takes him out of State service and places him in a field of charity, where he can work faithfully, with heartfelt interest, as well as from a sense of duty.

This is a brief narrative of a most eventful life, which is filled with heroism and the performance of manly duty, which cannot fail to impress the reader with the purity of the life of Henry McCulloch, and serve as an example and incentive to the youth of the land.

M. A. TAYLOR.

M. A. TAYLOR, the son of Colonel Matthew Taylor, was born in Columbus, Ohio, on November 12, 1830. Colonel Matthew Taylor was an officer in the army of General W. H. Harrison, and was stationed on the south side of the Scioto, in the old town of Franklin, in command of the army. During the winters of 1811-1812, in connection with a brother and Lion Starling, he laid off the site of the present city of Columbus, Ohio; and through the influence of the father and grand-father of Colonel M. Taylor, the State capitol was located there. M. A. Taylor's early education was had in the common schools of the early day, and when able to enter the Academy school (Covert's), he spent two years there, and then went to Oxford, the location of the University of the State of Ohio, to further prosecute his studies. He began the study of medicine in 1846, in his native town, entered the Starling Medical College, and graduated, with its highest honors, in February, 1849. After graduating, he remained for several months in business connected with the college. In the early spring of 1850, he selected his location in Logan, a town of five thousand inhabitants. Shortly after locating, the cholera made its appearance, and through his early labors during that epidemic, won for himself honors rarely achieved by so young a man. In the early winter of 1851, he married the only daughter of Peter B. Lowe, of Bond Brook, N. J., and, on account of the health of his young wife, moved to Texas in the fall of 1852, accompanied by his father-in-law, and permanently located in the city of Austin. Though blessed with but barely enough money to make a home, with a determined spirit to succeed as well in the new field as the one he had so shortly left, he opened an office in the store of Lethand Townsend, ex-consul of the Republic of Texas, and in a short time a lucrative practice was built up. During the first ten years of active practice, over $100,000 was booked.

In the fall of 1856, losing his wife, from consumption, leaving only one infant daughter and a sorrowing father and mother to mourn the loss, not discouraged, but with a Christian fortitude, moved on in the prosecution of his profession, and in the spring of 1859 married a daughter of Captain O. H. Millican, of Columbus, Mississippi; and at the opening of the question of the South seceding from the General Government, was opposed. Following in the views of General Houston, he thought the question should be settled in, and not outside, the government; though, when the State of Texas seceded, he took sides with the South—right or wrong, was with his adopted State. In the beginning no one was more active in doing all he could, not only by words, but headed a list to furnish the means of support for those families whose husbands had gone, or were preparing to go to the front, and in a few days procured about $7000, and was appointed treasurer of the above fund, and opened a store of supplies in what is now known as the Capitol Hotel, just below the present court-house. This depot was kept open as long as the means lasted, and many can still bear testimony of kindness shown in the way of supplies emanating from that source, and others whose husbands were gone to the war, if not in the best of circumstances, found no long bill to settle for medical services during the war. The copartnership of Drs. Taylor and E. D. Rentfro, formed at the opening of the spring of 1861, was continued till the spring of 1866, when the firm books were divided, and all claims balanced against those in poorer circumstances.

During this series of years, he held offices of honor, receiving his appointment from Governor Sam Houston. In the opening of the Mute Asylum, he was appointed one of the trustees, and, shortly afterwards, was appointed a trustee of the Blind Asylum, and served several years in that capacity, and during the administration of Dr. W. S. Baker, as superintendent, was consulting physician; and during Dr. S. G. Haynes' administration was also consulting physician. After resigning the office of trustee of the Mute Asylum, he was appointed as one of the trustees of the Lunatic Asylum, and served in that capacity. Just before the election of Governor Coke, he was chairman of the board, and was instrumental in having the grounds laid off and beautified; having the first lot of fruit-trees planted, and arranging the general park and play grounds for the inmates. For four years he was physician to the Blind Asylum, during the administration of Mr. E. M. Wheelock.

At the close of the war, nearly all of Dr. Taylor's earnings had been swept away. The first two years after the close of the war, over twenty-five thousand dollars were lost by men failing and bankruptcy. Not discouraged by the loss of so much of life's precious earnings, he moved steadily on in his profession, and began to mark his accumulations by the purchase of real estate in and out of the city of Austin.

After the close of the war, Dr. Taylor did his full share in the support of the government headquarters at the city of Austin, and visited Washington on business of importance for this part of the State. It is to be regretted that he failed to accomplish the end sought by this undertaking, as, had it been otherwise, the wealth and development of Austin would have been greatly augmented.

After the close of the civil war, Dr. Taylor was solicited to enter the field of politics, but persistently declined to accept or compete for any office of a political nature, believing, as he did, that such was not the safest road to wealth and influence. Indeed, it has ever been his aim to shun party ties as an element of his intercourse with his fellowman. On the other hand, in public as in private matters, he has relied alone upon his judgment and his conscience.

The influence of Christian parents was early manifested in the character of Dr. Taylor, and in due time he affiliated himself with the First Presbyterian Church, and has since remained a consistent member.

When the question of the division of the State arose, after the close of the war, Dr. Taylor took a decided stand against the measure, and used both his influence and means to defeat it. Texas as a State, and Austin as a city, have had in him a warm and active advocate in all matters looking to their material and moral welfare. He was one of the first to act in the matter of securing for Austin railroad connection with the world of commerce, and was one of a committee appointed to secure the extension of the Houston and Texas Central Railway from Hempstead to Brenham and Austin. Besides contributing from his own purse the sum of $1000 toward the accomplishment of that mission, it was through him, in connection with J. H. Raymond, George Hancock, Alford Smith and Governor Pease, that a subscription of more than $45,000 was raised for this purpose. The greater part of this subscription was paid when the road reached Austin, and the remainder in the course of a year.

When the permanent location of the State Capitol was submitted to a vote of the people, he was among the first chosen to raise means to conduct a canvass for its location at Austin; and so, latterly, with regard to the location of the State University; in both of which undertakings he did his whole duty to his home city, as, in truth, he does in all matters pertaining to her welfare.

During the administration of Governor Davis, Dr. Taylor was appointed as one of the regents of the University, and, in connection with the Board of Regents, went to Bryan and inspected the foundation of the building there, making a report which led to the condemning of the work of the first foundation. In this connection, he also advocated the appointment of a suitable architect by the Governor, whose duty it should be to superintend the construction of the new foundation, which suggestion was adopted and carried out. He was the means of having the clerk of the University Board to make a report of the true state of the funds and lands of the University up to that date; and presented to Colonel Jack Harris, a member of the Legislature from Galveston, a statement of the clerk, from which Colonel Harris could be fully informed as to the general state of the University lands and money.

After the location of the University at Austin, Dr. Taytor's next step was to have more railroads point to Austin. He was one of the early movers in the Austin and Northwestern Railway enterprise; was a charter member of the company, one of its directors, and first vice-president. He immediately went to work to raise the necessary capital; and, having done this, organized and equipped the first surveying corps to run the line as far as Brushy, to which place the preliminary line had been run, and a general profile of the road, with cuts, fills, etc., ready for inspection by the time of the arrival of the elected president of the company.

In order to still further the interests of Austin, Dr. Taylor caused a number of articles to be printed and circulated, setting forth its surroundings and advantages as a possible manufacturing centre, placing Austin in very favorable comparison with Lowell and other manufacturing cities. He advocated the construction of a dam at the gap at the foot of Mount Bonnell, carrying the water by an acqueduct to Shoal creek, at Seiders, and using Shoal creek as the natural outlet, thus creating a power sufficient to run five or six large factories, the same water being the motive power from Seiders to the point where the creek empties into the river; in short, demonstrating the practicability of establishing one continuous line of factories from the point of entrance, at Shoal creek, to the Colorado river.

As a worker for the advancement of his profession, Dr. Taylor has been zealous and untiring. As early as the winter of 1885, he advocated a law to regulate the practice of medicine in Texas; but a committee appointed to look after the matter of medical legislation declined to act upon his suggestions, declaring, if the same were adopted and a law passed to such effect, it would have been to exclude from the profession many then practicing physicians.

In 1854, Dr. Taylor was one of a number of physicians to organize, in Travis county, a county medical society. This example was followed by the physicians in a number of other counties in the State, and, about a year later, these county organizations were merged into a State society; but owing to the sparsely settled condition of the State at that early date, the organization was bisbanded, and was not revived until some years later, when the city of Houston claimed the honor of its initiatory session, under its new lease of life. Of this, the Texas State Medical Association, Dr. Taylor has been a member since its organization, and has been an enthusiastic worker in all matters tending to promote its welfare. In 1874, he was elected first vice-president of the association, and a delegate to the American

Medical Association, meeting in Detroit; and in 1876 he was elected as a delegate to represent Texas in the International Medical Congress, which met in the city of Philadelphia; which honors his love for his profession is sufficient cause for him to remember with pride.

Dr. Taylor has ever been an advocate for the higher educational standard of the profession, and has looked forward to, and labored for, a good law to regulate the practice of medicine in the State. In the education of his children he sought the best schools of the country, and paved the way for them to attain the highest literary and classical endowments. The oldest, Miss Hattie, was sent for five years to excellent schools in the States of Illinois and Iowa. Edward H. was sent to a preparatory school in Canada for one year, and then given four years at the University of Canada, at the city of Toronto. Mary, the second daughter, after graduating at the Alta Vista Institute, of which Mrs. Kirby was principal, was sent to Elmira, New York, where she took a post-graduate course. Lizzie is now in the University of Texas, while Duzie has just entered the training school for children.

Now, after making and meeting the large outlay for the education of his family, he has the comforting thought that Providence has still further blessed his labors and given him many property interests, in various portions of the State, in the shape of wild lands, farms and ranches; of which latter, one of the largest is situated in Dimmit county. This ranch contains eleven leagues of well watered grazing land, and is stocked with cattle and sheep. The estimated value of Dr. Taylor's estate is variously placed at from one-half to one million dollars.

Distinguished Texans.

JOHN M. MATHIS.

THE careful study of the genealogy of a particular family through a series of generations is a fruitful source of intellectual pleasure to the scientist, the humanitarian and the philanthropist. Truth often robes itself in the habiliments of fiction, and goes out into the anomalous experiences of strangeness and romance, from which fiction borrows its enchantment. The life of an individual is an infinitessimal part with which every other life combines into the sum of all history.

The father and mother of John M. Mathis lived and died in Henry county, Tennessee; the former an Alabamian, the latter a native of Tennessee. In this county and State John M. Mathis was born, on the twenty-eighth day of February, in the year 1831. In 1852, he emigrated from his native place and settled at Gonzales, Texas. His education was obtained in the common schools of the country, and served only to lay the foundations for future expansion and business pursuit. His first active business was that of the sale of tobacco for a house in Tennessee, he being one of the very first drummers in the State of Texas. He was energetic and successful in this line of business life until the breaking out of the civil war in the United States, when he suddenly found himself stripped of his earnings by reason of an extensive credit system, and himself involved in a debt of $6000. He entered the Southern army in 1861, under Major Richard Howard, and served as supply agent for the troops in the Cis-Mississippi department.

After the close of the war Mr. Mathis returned to Texas, and established himself where the town of Rockport now stands, giving the town its name. Recognizing his *ante bellum*, debt he planned at once for a settlement by note and paid off the claim at maturity. At Rockport he made a contract with a steamship company for regular landings and the shipment of cattle to New Orleans and Havana. This business was profitable, and in 1871 Mr. Mathis found himself on the highroad to fortune. In company with his brothers, he owned large ranches in Live Oak, San Patricio and Nueces counties. The firm was very successful.

From 1879 to 1883, J. M. Mathis did a shipping business from Indianola to New Orleans and Havana, and in this enterprise made large sums of money. He and his brother, M. L. Mathis, now own a fine ranch on the San Antonio river, near Goliad, on which fifteen thousand graded cattle and two hundred and fifty horses and mules are kept. In Wharton county he has a large interest in a ranch of thirty-five thousand cattle. His success in the cattle industry of the State has been little less than phenomenal. He has had a fixed determination to go forward, and has conquered difficulties and made them contribute to his success.

His wife was a Miss Mary A. Pollan, daughter of John Pollan, Esq., of Ingleside, San Patricio county, Texas. They have an adopted daughter, Miss Mary E. Mathis.

The present home of Mr. Mathis is Victoria, Texas, and he has also a residence in Austin, the capital of the State.

He is an example of success in business and the accumulation of worldly estate. He weighs one hundred and seventy pounds; is five feet and eight inches in stature, and shows by the conformation of his head that he possesses great energy, courage, and a keen sense of honor. He is highly esteemed by the masses who really know him, and his judgment has great weight with the members of the Texas Live Stock Association. His prominence and frequent official service in that body are noticeable facts in its proceedings.

LEANDER BROWN.

AN historic fact in relation to the ancestry of the gentleman of whom this is a succinct notice, is that his grandfather was a soldier in the Revolutionary War, and his father served in the war of 1812. Leander Brown was born in Chester district, South Carolina, and emigrated from his native State to Illinois, in the year 1833. Subsequent to his first marriage, in 1840, he moved to Missouri, and remained in that State, near Lexington, till November, 1846, when he came to Austin, Texas, and has been a citizen of this latter place ever since. He has served in the capacity of county treasurer for the term of three years, and has also held the office of city mayor for a like term. Mr. Leander Brown has been three times married. His first wife was Miss Sarah A. Horne, of Alabama; his second, Miss Lou Bowles, of Texas, and his present wife was Miss Ella Holman, daughter of Dr. Holman, of Texas, who, by her many charitable deeds, has endeared herself to the people of this city. She is an earnest and consistent Christian, and much of her time and means is devoted to relieving the poor and unfortunate. As a citizen, Mr. Brown is respected on account of his honesty and integrity. In office, he has been faithful and efficient. He has tested the sunshine and shades of an eventful life, in which he has not been an unprofitable experimenter. His stores of experience are rich, and he has not been unwise in a profligate waste of them.

CHARLES BURNSIDE STODDARD.

BEFORE the landing of the Mayflower, early in the history of the Colonies, three brothers, of Scottish nativity, by the name of Stoddard, entered into the fortunes of the New World. The date of their landing in America was in 1619. During the Revolutionary war, five brothers of this historic family participated in the struggle for independence, holding the rank of officers in the army. From this progenitorship, Honorable Henry William Stoddard and his wife, Minerva Hayden, the father and mother of C. B. Stoddard, living for a time after marriage in Rochester, New York, finally became established in Portage county, Ohio, on what was known as the Western Reserve, and were noted in the political history of that new and rising State. The family, in its various branches, has a proud record in literature: H. H. Stoddard, the author, in mathematics; R. H. Stoddard, the poet; and Charles Stoddard, a literary genius of the Pacific coast, and others, have distinguished the family and given the name to immortality. The Shermans and Stoddards, of Ohio, for many generations, have been related, nor is it an insignificant fact that the distinguished General, who discharged the youthful soldier, is a near kinsman of the family.

C. B. Stoddard was born in Portage county, Ohio, on the tenth day of January, 1848, and at the age of twelve, removed, under the care of his parents, to the State of Michigan. At the age of fourteen, being well grown, he entered the United States army, but was subsequently discharged by General W. T. Sherman on account of youth. One year later, however, he re-joined the service, irregularly, and remained at the headquarters of General Thomas, in government employ.

In harmony with the literary culture of the family, Dr. Stoddard has been an heir to a rich inheritance of educational privilege. In the University of Michigan, at Ann Arbor, he took a regular course, both in literature and medicine. He attended, also, the University of Pennsylvania and the Dental College of Philadelphia, and also took a course in the Ohio Dental College, at Cincinnati.

He began the practice of his profession in 1866, at Ann Arbor, Michican, and went to Chicago in 1869. In the great fire in that city, he lost all he had but his profession and his ambition to excel. In the city of New York, in 1873, he resumed his practice, which he continued for five years. He made money rapidly, and had a practice equal to the foremost dentists in the great metropolis. Warned by failing health, he went abroad, traveling for a year, and returning to America, began again the practice of his profession in the city of Galveston, Texas. Subsequently, after two years' sojourn in Europe, he came to Austin, Texas, in 1880, and has continued building up a large and lucrative practice to the present.

Professionally, Dr. Stoddard has a reputation not inferior to the ablest and most scientific gentlemen of the entire country engaged in the practice of dentistry.

As a discoverer, he has won an enviable place in the world of science and art. In 1876, he discovered the application of electricity as a motive power to dentistry. He was also the discoverer of the luminous properties of nitrous oxide gas, the same year, for which he received a high compliment from Henry Morton, one of the most distinguished chemists of America. Recently his genius has been exhibited in the discovery and invention of a small electric illuminator of the mouth, by means of the ordinary battery used in telegraphy. Not the least among the achievements of science, is Dr. Stoddard's painless extraction of teeth, by means of an hypodermic injection into the gums of a fluid known only to the discoverer. Able physicians, and thousands of patients, are ready to bear testimony to this wonderful and philanthropic discovery.

As a traveler, Dr. Stoddard is untiring and intelligent. He has visited almost every part of the world—Europe, Asia, Africa, the islands of the ocean, as well as his native continent. He spends, usually, about one-third of his time in this pleasant way. The javelins of calumny that have been thrust at him have fallen pointless at his feet, or rebounded to pierce the hand that threw them. Elements of opposition have contributed to his distinction, and from the smouldering ruins of fire in worldly estate, and the envenomed atmosphere of the calumniator, he has plucked the laurels of triumph. He is spare in figure, has blue eyes, fair complexion, light hair, is five feet and ten inches high, and weighs one hundred and sixty-five pounds.

JOSEPHUS CUMMINGS.

DOCTOR JOSEPHUS CUMMINGS was born in Austin, Texas, November 30, 1849. His father, Steven Cummings, moved to Texas during the year 1840, and married in Austin, to Miss Nancy L. Rowe, during 1847. His father's family resided in Austin until the beginning of the late war, when they moved to Williamson county. The Doctor received his education in Austin and Round Rock, and began the study of medicine under Dr. M. A. Taylor, of Austin, at the age of eighteen years. Before this period, however, we may state that, when not engaged in attending school, his occupation was caring for stock, and, at times, assisting his father in farming. By this means he learned to work, and was not ashamed to do his part in whatever became necessary to aid in the support of his father's large family, as there were seven children in all to care for.

He showed much energy and tact for business when quite young, and when he began the study of medicine, the same application was made to this as to ordinary daily labor, and day after day he was found studying hard the difficult text books of medicine and surgery, until he entered Jefferson Medical College, of Philadelphia, during the fall of 1869. Now in the City of Brotherly Love, the subject of our sketch might have been found, always at his post, either listening attentively to the professors, lectures, or pursuing his dissecting in the anatomical department. When other students were promenading the city at night, and visiting resorts for amusement, he was ever the same persevering student, until finally, March 15, 1871, he was awarded, with a large class, the prize for which he had labored so hard, the degree of Doctor of Medicine. As a beginner in a grand profession, he was still ready to study and work, which he did by immediately on his return home to Austin embarking in practice. He soon won the confidence of the public, and was rewarded by a fair practice; and in 1872, married Miss Texas Glascock, of Austin, a native of Texas. He has two children, the oldest, a girl, Minnie, now twelve years old, and the other a boy, Josephus, jr., aged seven years.

He has devoted his time mostly to his profession, was city and county physician, and it is said of him that he "made one of the ablest the Capital City has ever had; was in this position when the small-pox infected our city in 1880, and his skillful management during this trying and exciting time was commended by all, and made him very popular." He has paid special attention to surgery, and has performed successfully many of the most difficult operations. It may be said that it is largely due to his effort, and that of his personal friends when he was city physician, the establishment and erection of our magnificent city and county hospital. He was chairman of the first committee appointed on the subject, and wrote the able memorial that still can be found in the city record of proceedings on this subject, and was a member of the building board that supervised its erection. He is a member of Travis County Medical Society and the Texas State Medical Association, and has contributed several articles to medical literature in Texas and elsewhere; is at the present time President of Travis County Medical Society. The Doctor has taken some interest in benevolent societies in Austin, was one of the original charter members of Austin Lodge Knights of Honor, was Deputy Grand Dictator of this Order and instituted lodges in Manor, Lockhart, Luling and Capital City Lodge in Austin; is a member of the A. O. U. W. and K. and L. of H., and is an Ancient Odd Fellow. At the present time he is one of the aldermen of the city, and has evinced considerable ability in assisting in the management of city affairs. The sanitation of the city is receiving at his hands many valuable suggestions. Few men of his age has shown more financiering ability. Within ten years past he has amassed a large property, and he has increased his business more than double in less than one year. Honesty, integrity and fair dealing have been his motto from principle, and his success shows the wisdom of such a course.

GEORGE BERNHARD ZIMPELMAN.

IN Rhine Bavaria, on the twenty-fourth of July, 1832, the respected citizen of Austin, of whom this is a brief sketch, George B. Zimpelman, was born. He received his education at the Agricultural and Latin School of Landau, in Europe. He came to America in 1844, landing at New Orleans, thence to Galveston, where he stayed a little more than two years, making short sojourns in New Orleans in the meantime. In 1849, he moved to Travis county, where he has remained ever since, being a citizen of Austin the most of the time.

In the beginning of the war between the States, he entered the army as a private soldier, and returned at the close of the great rebellion as such, in the meantime doing service with the rank of captain. He entered public life in the capacity of sheriff of Travis county, in 1866, and was successively re-elected for three subsequent terms, ending with the year 1876. He was a victim to the Governor Davis administration, and was deposed from office.

Under Governor Coke, he was appointed one of the trustees of the Institution for the Deaf and Dumb; by Governor Hubbard, he was appointed quartermaster of the State militia, and by Governor Ross, aid-de-camp. Governor Hubbard gave him the appointment of a mission to Washington to collect the funds for the protection of the frontier. This latter appointment, however, he declined to accept.

He entered America a poor boy, receiving only four to five dollars per month for labor. Before the war, he engaged in farming and stock-raising; after the war was over, he resumed farming and stock-raising, and engaged in brick-making; and in 1871 he went into the banking business, but withdrew at the end of five years. He is now, and has been for several years, engaged in surveying in Mexico. He has a strong force there, filling a contract with the government of that country.

In 1856, George B. Zimpelman and Miss Sarah C. Matthews, of Travis county, Texas, were united in marriage. Mrs. Zimpleman died on the the thirteenth of November, 1885. Four living children constitute the household.

Mr. Zimpelman has béen a worthy and trusted citizen, has a kind and generous nature, and has accumulated a competency for declining years. He is a noble specimen of Teutonic birth, and has fairly won the good name he bears. He weighs one hundred and ninety pounds, and is five feet eight inches in stature.

Distinguished Texans.

BENJAMIN C. WELLS.

THIS gentleman, whose life is one of grand success and achievement, arrived in Austin from Coffeeville, Mississippi, April 9, 1871, and shortly afterwards engaged in the jewelery business on a capital of less than $2000. For several years thereafter, he did all of the work for his establishment, which included repairing, watch making, etc. Such was his remarkable business tack and ambition, that he soon found it necessary to secure larger quarters, as his trade had begun to extend beyond the limits of the Capital, which at that time was but little more than a country village. He consequently moved into the large brick building situated on the corner of Bois 'd Arc street and Congress avenue, which, from the time of its occupancy by Mr. Wells, has been known as the "Clock Corner." Here he went extensively into the manufactory of many beautiful and artistic articles of sterling silver ware, mounting of diamonds and other precious stones, and by strict integrity and close attention to business, he soon found himself one of the largest jewelry merchants in the State. For reliability and strict integrity, no man in Texas stands higher than B. C. Wells. He is now located in an elegant house on Congress avenue, which he erected some years since, and where he continues to do a large business in his line.

Mr. Wells was born in the town of Maryville, East Tennessee, April 1, 1841, where he remained until 1862. He was educated at Ewing and Jefferson College, near Knoxville, Tennessee. The school was disbanded at the outbreak of the war between the States, by the students volunteering to go into the army. Mr. Wells being one of them, entered the First Tennessee Cavalry, Colonel James E. Carter's regiment. The war, to him, resulted in the consuming by fire of his homestead during one of the battles. No braver or more heroic soldier served under the flag of the Confederacy. When he returned, and found his home gone and himself impoverished, with naught but an intellect which was by no means limited in its scope, and thinking that he could perhaps lay the foundation of a fortune, he determined on leaving the scenes of his boyhood, and decided on moving to Texas, where he has lived to realize all of his fondest hopes.

Besides his success in finance, he had proved himself an artist of high merit. His skill has found a profitable channel through which to win the meed of popular approval. The genius that has expressed itself in the elegant pieces of silver manufactured from Mr. Wells' establishment can but receive the reward it deserves.

Under the administration of Governor R. B. Hubbard, Mr. Wells received a commission as Honorary Commissioner to attend the Paris Exposition as a representative of Texas. He is at present a member of the board of trustees of the Deaf and Dumb Asylum. Governor Ireland also appointed Mr. Wells, on the part of Travis county, to attend the great exposition held at New Orleans. All these positions he discharged with honor to himself and his State.

Mr. Wells was married to Miss Lou. Tully, of Coffeeville, Mississippi, June 9, 1870. They have no children, save an adopted son, little Claude Walker, to whom both Mr. and Mrs. Wells are devotedly attached.

SPEECH OF REPRESENTATIVE BELL, OF COOKE, IN PLACING THE NAME OF HON. JOHN H. REAGAN IN NOMINATION FOR U. S. SENATOR.

Mr. Speaker and Gentlemen of the Twentieth Legislature:

THIS is no ordinary duty we have met to perform. To select a man who shall go as the mouthpiece of this great State to the national capitol is no trifling affair. The great interests of this young empire will be in his keeping.

Distinguished Texans.

Her rights will be under his guardianship and protection. The performance of this task should rise above all personality; all sectional narrowness should be banished, and a deathless determination to do what is best for the whole State dictate our utterances and determine our votes. In presenting to you the name I shall, I trust I am actuated by such motives alone. The gentleman is not in my section of the State; he is not, in but a limited sense, my personal friend. He never did me the smallest personal favor. Others are asking who have done me many personal kindnesses, and are my friends and neighbors, so far as to live in the same section I represent.

For all the gentlemen who have been mentioned in such eulogistic terms to-day I have but the kindest of feelings, and in what I shall say to-day I have no word of censure for any of them. I admire their greatness. I praise their sincere performance of duty.

No, gentlemen, I would not create one ruffle in that mantle of conscious integrity that now falls so gracefully about the manly form of Maxey, the soldier and statesman. Neither would I cast one blight upon the fair escutcheon of our honored governor, the brilliancy of the eve of whose administration is only surpassed by the halo which surrounds the morning of his successor. Much less would I fail to give that intellectual giant, that able jurist and abler statesman, the Hon. A. W. Terrell, the full meed of praise.

But while I join in the admiration of these gentlemen and their services, when I come to consider the grand character of John H. Reagan, my soul is stirred with a fervent devotion and intense adoration akin to idolatry. While others have been great, he has been greater. While others have trodden the paths of duty, he has been a hero in the performance thereof. While others are his equal in point of intellectual ability, as to moral courage he stands to-day on the political plane like some tall peak, lifting its head above its fellows, up through the clouds of doubt and uncertainty as if to talk with God.

This is a time when men, not measures, are wanted. The demands of the day are well understood—the men to execute those demands are few; men of intellectual ability are plentiful; men of heart and nerve are few and far between.

And while I do not yield to any of the gentlemen named the palm of intellectuality over Mr. Reagan, I can, with full justice to all, claim for him superiority over all in point of determination and will to do the right. While others have had equal ability with him to see what was necessary, they have contented themselves with the knowledge. He has had the moral courage of his convictions, and hurling all the powers of his giant mind at the accomplishment of his purposes, gone far in the lead where others scarcely dared to follow. He has not contented himself with being a private in the ranks of duty, but has sought to scale the walls of the enemy and plant thereon the standard of truth and the banner of the people's rights.

A brief rehearsal of the career of this heroic statesman may not be out of place. He was fortunate, and yet unfortunate in his early boyhood. He was fortunate in being reared amid the rock-ribbed mountains of East Tennessee, the Switzerland of America; that land whose mountains God hath robed in starlit clouds and left the kiss of love upon all her green hills and sunny slopes, where the beautiful rivers and pebbly brooks steal down through the gorges like tear-drops on nature's furrowed cheek, where the humble mountaineers met, and every man's a freeman and the peer of his fellows. 'Twas there he learned that great principle of equality which has clung to him through life; 'twas there he breathed that heroic sentiment of devotion to principles which has made him what he is—the Gladstone of American politics. But he was unfortunate in being the son of a poor tanner. Left in early life to work out his own fortune and fame, he began with the seeming hopeless task of educating himself by working on a farm at $9 per month; but he succeeded. At the period of manhood he cast his lot with the people of Texas, landing here in 1839. His life since is a part of the history of the State. Its history cannot be written without writing his biography. Whether we view him as the judge upon the bench, or the lawyer at the bar, he is the same bold, self-reliant, candid and calm thinker.

Many of the old settlers of Peter's colony remember the little black-eyed man, who, when the darkest hour of their history was upon them, came to their relief. I see now that band of brave men come to him, after all the other lawyers in that section had failed them, and when the attorney-general of the State, and the head of the colonists, had to be attacked, and asked him to speak for them. His friends at the bar advised him to say nothing, but they did not know of what metal he was made. Standing there in their midst, in the then little village of Dallas, he said: "Gentlemen, I understand all about this matter, and will speak for you to-morrow." I see the honest old man, A. H. Latimer, go and take him by the hand and tell him he thanked God one man had the courage to speak his convictions. He did speak, and fired the hearts of those colonists and saved them their homes.

I see him when, as a cabinet officer in the Confederacy, he organized such a system of mails that the great Federal captain was forced to say, "we must break their connection if ever we stop this rebellion," and soon his cannon were thundering at Fort Donaldson, at Island No. 10, and Vicksburg.

And when the war was over, while others were despairing and sitting in gloomy silence, or fretting at an unwelcome fate, he, even from the walls of Fort Warren, forgetting his own miseries, sought to save his distracted and ruined country the horrors of reconstruction. He looked forward with a keen, almost prophetic, eye, and saw the new South, of which Grady speaks, and cast upon the waves of passion and prejudice the pearls of truth which were to be gathered up in after years; and, with an aching heart, he threw around him a mantle of silence and sought to still its throbbing as the snow in the churchyard marbles o'er each aching mound, by repairing to his little farm to earn, by honest toil, his daily bread, and commence anew to repair his shattered fortunes. There he plowed, row by row, with the negro laborers, but his giant mind was not confined to plowing. 'Twas then he saw the great problem for whose solution the last eighteen years has heard so much. He saw that agriculture had been the one great industry which made all others. He saw that the men of the ax and maul, of the plow and hoe, had converted this wilderness into a garden, and that they were still creating annually thousands of millions of dollars worth of produce.

He saw, also, that notwithstanding this toil, year by year, that theirs were the hardest lot. He saw want in their homes and at their humble boards; he saw, on the other hand, the great avenues of trade over which these millions of wealth were carried, all centering at New York.

He saw the few great railroad magnates owning these avenues, sending down their cars to gather in this product of the farmers of our country, as if it were a tribute laid by them upon the tillers of their soil; he saw that product being consumed by these magnates in its transportation, and the money being used in building palaces on the Hudson, and yachts in which to sail; he saw these magnates ride down in their palace cars over their vast extent of roads, in the same lordly style in which the feudal barons used to visit annually their possessions; he saw that each new road built was another link added to the fetters that already bound the agriculture of the country. Others saw the same, but contented themselves with the knowledge.

His great heart was stirred; he could not rest and see the wealth of this country accumulating in the hands of the few. He saw ere long we must reach the point where a moneyed aristocracy—the few—would rule and dominate the impoverished and enslaved many. This is the difference between him and others, that he threw himself, his all, into the struggle to save the people from this thraldom. For thirteen years he has waged the war with all the giant powers which unlimited money could bring to oppose him. By the force of his own splendid genius, by the sublime moral courage he possesses, he has at last succeeded, and now the glad shout is going out from every heart, saying:

"Sound the loud timbrel o'er freedom's dark sea,
For Reagan hath triumphed, the people are free."

Gentlemen, you have heard of the commerce of our country and what has been done by others to improve its condition.

Who has done this? Let the records speak! I ask you to remember that when Reagan went back to Congress, after the war, not one dollar had been appropriated since 1860 to the improvement of our Southern rivers and harbors. I invite your attention to the meeting of the committee when Reagan first was placed upon it.

When the bill was read over and the South passed by, this grand old hero rose in the might of his moral power and said, "Gentlemen, unless you put in that bill the proper proportion due my section, I meet you no more, but I go to defeat your bill." Suffice it to say, it was reconsidered, and the South has ever since been recognized as a part of the Union. But, gentlemen, it is unnecessary for me to dwell longer upon the merits of this great and just man. This is not a fight among men. The real struggle here is between Reagan and monopoly; between Reagan, the friend of the people, and corporate power and plunder.

They do not care who you elect, so you don't elevate the man who has dared the fury of their vengeance.

They are going to use every means to secure his defeat. They have marked him out as the object of their vengeance. Read the history of the past! Where now is Allen G. Thurman, that noble old Democrat who dared to step out with Reagan in this fight for the people? His head has fallen upon the political block! The telegraph now brings the news that Van Wyck, that pure Republican who dared to go with them and brave the fury of the party lash, has met a similar fate. Will Texas Democracy place herself on record in favor of monopoiy or Reagan? That's the question at issue. Maxey has been honored all we can. Ireland and Terrell can wait, but Reagan is the demand of the hour. In the name of the old settlers of Peters' colony; in the name of the millions of humble tillers of the soil of this country; in the name of Texas manhood; in the name of our free institutions, whose grand exemplar he is, I nominate John H. Reagan, the able statesman, the pure patriot and moral hero; he who has stalked like a Samson amid the entrenchments of corporate plunderers and smote them right and left; he who, by the force of his moral courage, paralyzed to dumbness the tongues of Northern hate and prejudice, and wrung from unwilling hands the rights of his people. Remember that each vote for Judge Reagan is a blow for freedom and a death stab at monopoly!

SPEECH OF HON. H. M. GARWOOD, OF BASTROP.

[Bill under discussion: Senate Bill No. 219, known as the Land Bill. Mr. Garwood had offered an amendment eliminating the lease features of the bill, and repealing the act of 1883]

MR. SPEAKER: This amendment is offered in no spirit of factious opposition, and with no desire to delay the majority in the exercise of its constitutional prerogatives. It has been introduced that this question may be placed fairly before this House, and before the State. The duty of a legislator in a commonwealth so vast in its extent as Texas, is both difficult and dangerous. In no legislative body is the member so often called upon to sit in judgment upon the claims of different sections, and decide between the demands of separate funds and clashing interests. But, sir, by as much as the task imposed upon us is delicate and laborious, by so much more should we feel encouraged in our labor, and, rising to the full height of patriotism and statesmanship, decide these great questions in accordance with those fundamental principles of right and justice that have secured the happiness and the prosperity of every government that has had the courage to recognize and apply them.

This question of land legislation, like the unwilling ghost that will not "down," comes up before each succeeding Legislature. It is no new one, but is almost as old as government itself. William, the Norman, like that "master mind," the real author of this iniquitous measure, was an advocate of this lease principle, and when he crossed the Channel, and leased up the lands of merry England to his feudal dependents, the foundation was laid for the trouble now agitating the people of Great Britain. There, the question is, what shall be done with public lands, made private by extension of lease and withdrawal of rent. Here the feudal system, engrafted upon our laws by the act of 1883, has not progressed so far, and we are this day to decide whether we will deliver the miserable remainder of our lands, left after that saturnalia of land grabbing so graphically described by Commissioner Walsh in his last report, into the absolute control of the feudal barons now monopolizing the land and cattle interests of the northwest.

If this land, Mr. Speaker, was public land, and was not specially set apart by the Constitution to special funds, there could be no doubt as to the disposition of this matter. The people would condemn this relic of feudalism, the lease system, as a thing strange and unholy, foreign to the spirit of our institutions and unknown to our history and our organic law. But when members from the west contend for that right which is as old as English liberty, the "right of common" and tell you in tones almost pathetic, that you are enacting the great west into a veritable desert, the specious cry of "school fund" is raised, and they are charged with wishing to rob the school children of the State. Thus, for two hundred thousand dollars a year lease money, you are retarding the development of the State, driving back the actual settler, and fastening upon Texas a system foreign to every tradition of our race, and in direct opposition to the Constitution of the State.

In the consideration of questions of public moment, we should recur often to first principles and fundamental law. Members have recently developed an attachment for the Constitution, which is highly commendable. Those gentlemen who, some days since, reasoned so eloquently against the delegation of its powers by a legislative body, will, it is presumed, join hands with us in abolishing the Land Board. We invite their consideration further upon this question.

IS THIS LEASE SYSTEM CONSTITUTIONAL.

A State Legislature is omnipotent, save in so far as it is governed by the Constitutution and treaties of the Federal government, and restrained by express inhibition in the State Constitution. Does the Constitution of 1876 contain these express inhibitions? We believe that it does. Section four, article seven, contains these words: "The lands herein set apart to the public free school fund shall be sold under such regulations, at such times, and on such terms as may be prescribed by law." The language is mandatory—"shall be sold." Test this by all the rules of constitutional construction known to the technicalities of the law, and it does not confer the power to lease. Judge Cooley, in his celebrated work on Constitutional Limitations, lays down several approved rules governing the construction of State constitutions. As that (first) "the intent shall govern" (page 55), and that "to ascertain this intent, the first resort in all cases is to the natural significance of the words employed in the order of grammatical arrangement in which the framers have placed them," and "that which the words declare is the meaning of the instrument; neither courts nor legislatures have the right to add to or take away from that meaning" (page 57); (second) "The whole instrument is to be examined with a view to arriving at the true intention of each part" (page 57); (third) "the common law is to be kept in view" (page 60); (fourth) "the proceedings of the constitutional convention may be inquired into with a view towards ascertaining the objects to be attained," etc. (pages 65, 66, 67). Now apply these rules. The plain, simple, unmistakable words are "shall be sold." An examination of the entire Constitution discloses this pertinent fact, that wherever it is intended that the Legislature shall have power to dispose of public land, otherwise than by sale, it is so declared. For instance, section six, of this very same article, provides, "that each county may sell, or dispose of, its lands, in whole or in part," etc. The word "lease" occurs in the Constitution but once. In section thirty-four, article sixteen, occurs the phrase "lease or sell." These two sections show conclusively that the distinction between sale and lease was clearly drawn in the minds of the framers of the Constitution, as it was definitely expressed in unmistakable terms. Reference to sections two, four, six, nine, eleven, twelve and fifteen, of article seven, will strengthen this view. Could there be the slightest doubt upon this point, that doubt would be removed by a study of the proceedings of the Constitutional Convention of 1875.

On page seventy-nine, we find that Mr. Wade, the member from Hunt county, introduced the following:

"Resolved, * * * that the lands heretofore set apart for school purposes be utilized under a proper system of lease, which will raise a distributive fund for the support of free public schools, and that the title to said lands never be permitted to pass from the State." Here was the feudal idea absolute. The land was never to be sold, even to the actual settlers, but the State was to remain perpetual landlord. Here was an approach to the theory of the land reformers, who would abolish private property in land, that would have delighted the heart of Henry George. The resolution was referred to the Committee on Education, and on page 245, they brought in as their report the present section 4.

On page 326, Mr. Wade having modified his resolution so

as to allow sales, again introduced his lease idea as a substitute for section 4; and on page 329, the lease idea was overwhelmingly defeated. But Mr. Wade was persistent. On page 782, the University article was under discussion, and he proposed to amend as follows:

Section 2, line 25, after "sale" insert "or lease." Section 4, line 40, after "sold" insert "leased." Also, in line 44, after "sold" insert "leased."

Again the Convention expressed its disapproval of the lease idea, and the amendment was lost.

The practical and contemporaneous construction of this Constitution, as of others for years, was that the Legislature had no power to lease, but that, in accordance with Anglo-Saxon ideas, and the precedent set by the Federal government in the disposition of its public lands, all lands, the fee simple of which had not left the State, were free. From this common law of Texas the Legislature of 1883 cut loose, and it is sought to defend the system then inaugurated, and now sought to be perpetuated by this means, upon the theory of "implied powers," so often invoked to sustain dangerous measures. Mr. Cooley says, page 64: "It is therefore established as a general rule that when a constitution gives a general power, or enjoins a duty, it also gives, by implication, every particular power necessary for the enjoyment of the one or the the exercise of the other." But he further says that "the implication under that rule, however, *must be a necessary, not a conjectural or argumentative one.*" And it is further modified by another rule, that "where the means for the exercise of a granted power are given, no other or different means can be implied as being more convenient or effective."

In section 4, as in other sections concerning the asylum and university lands, the whole subject matter is definitely and clearly set out.

The means of exercising the power conferred are distinctly and clearly given, even to the disposition of the funds arising from the sale thus provided for, "and no other or different means can be implied as being more convenient or effective."

Can it be argued that the power to sell necessarily confers the power to lease? Were that true, when a power of attorney to sell land is granted, the recipient of that power has also granted him the right to defeat the intention of his grantor, for, by leasing for a long number of years, the power to sell could be rendered nugatory. This is our relation to the lands belonging to these special funds. We are trustees of an express trust, and the terms of that trust must be strictly construed. The people, by the Constitution of 1876, gave us power of attorney to sell land, and neither law nor precedent can justify us in extending that power, as did the Legislature of 1883, and as this body is about to do.

What, sir, is our duty in cases where the constitutionality of a measure is a matter of grave doubt? "In such a case it seems clear that every one called upon to act where, in his opinion, the proposed action would be of doubtful constitutionality, *is bound upon the doubt to abstain* from acting. A doubt upon the constitutionality of any proposed legislative enactment should, in any case, be sufficient reason for refusing to adopt it; and if legislators do not act upon this principle, the reasons upon which are based the judicial decisions sustaining legislation in very many cases will cease to be of force." (C. C. L., p. 74.)

Can any advocate of this system say that it is not at least of doubtful constitutionality? Our duty, then, is plain. The absurdity of the construction contended for is made manifest by considering the possible consequences. Our Bill of Rights, section twenty-six, contains this provision: "Perpetuities and monopolies are contrary to the genius of a free government, and shall never be allowed." Yet, notwithstanding the Constitution demands that these lands shall be sold, by renewal of leases immense bodies of land (this bill does not limit the amount) can be given over to the control of cattle kings and corporations for year after year, thus creating the very perpetuities and monopolies contemplated by the Constitution and defeating its plain intent.

And just here, I will call your attention to a letter that has been kindly given me by the Senator from Wheeler. There had been introduced in the United States Senate a bill "to provide for the leasing of the desert or arid lands of the public domain lying west of the one hundredth degree of longitude." The bill provides for the leasing of said lands for periods not exceeding ten years, in bodies of not more than 250,000 acres. In this latter respect, the bill was less dangerous than the present bill, which places no limit upon the amount to be leased. Senator Plumb, chairman of the committee on public lands, had referred the measure to the Department of the Interior, with a request for an expression of opinion upon its merits. Commissioner Harrison, in discussing at great length and with unanswerable force the evils of the land system, says:

"The bill provides that at the expiration of a lease, the party leasing may remove his fence, but it is not provided that leases may not be renewed. A renewal of leases once made must become inevitable. The capital invested would demand such protection, and the ultimate effect would be perpetual control, even if future legislation should not be invoked to invest the parties with titles in fee. By the fourth section sub-leases are not allowed, but this restriction would not prevent an assignment of lease, nor the control of any number of leases by single persons or corporations by power of attorney, nor such unity of action among lessees as would allow a single or combined interest to dominate over any part, however large, of the region to which the act would apply. The allowance of such a quantity of land as 250,000 acres to one person or corporation, makes, of itself, a monopoly at variance with the spirit of the land laws and the institutions of the country, and in sharp conflict with popular views respecting the appropriation of the public lands. Should the leasing system be adopted, a vast territory would become subject, directly or indirectly, to the monopolies the act would create. Settlements for homes, town enterprises and the improvement of the country would be discouraged or rendered impossible. Travel would become difficult and dangerons. Present holders of small farms, unable to compete with the large cattle owners, would be hemmed in by the fences of the latter, and their communication cut off. Instead of looking forward to the improvement and filling up of the country, by an increase of inhabitants, they would see a decreasing population. Immigration into cattle districts would necessarily cease. Existing towns and cities must inevitably decay, and civilization be destroyed in a region given up to such desolating influence. These results are already beginning to be in New Mexico, the small farmers and country population retiring, and general business diminishing, as great cattle companies absorb the land."

Here, sirs, we have the whole matter in a few words. The lease system creates a wealthy, powerful and well organized class, vitally interested in driving back the actual settler, and retarding the settlement and general development of the country. Having invested vast capital in the construction of fences and other improvements upon their lesae-holds, powerful influences will be brought to bear upon each succeeding Legislature to renew and extend leases. The danger to be apprehended may be easily seen by tracing the history of this question. In 1883, the present lease law was passed. The cattlemen were not then so bold. The lease was conditional, and the land still open to actual settlers. In 1885, they were still modest, and did not ask for more. In 1887, by this Senate bill, which the gentleman from Goliad (Mr. Payne) tells us is the production of some "master mind," and supposed to reflect the sentiment of the administration, they demand the absolute and unconditional lease of unlimited amounts of land. Do not deceive yourselves; these leases will inevitably be renewed. The step from a long lease to a fee simple title is a very short one. History shows us that it is easily taken. By a systematic renewal and extension of leases, public sentiment will be educated up to the point of selling these vast leased bodies to those who have so long controlled them, just as it saw no wrong in selling three million acres to one syndicate, and in allowing one foreign corporation to acquire four million acres of land in this State.

Another fundamental objection to the lease system is, that it permits the greater cattle corporations and land owners to secure control of the ranges, and thus prevent other owners of herds from engaging in the business, and shutting off competition—a monopoly in the cattle business, compared to which all other monopolies in this State shrink into insignificance. None see this so clearly as the cattlemen themselves. We are told, by eloquent gentlemen upon this floor, that free grass will build up the cattle barons to the detriment of the small stockman. Why is it, then, I would ask, that every great cattleman in this State, and in the territories, is in favor of the lease? The opening prayer of every stock convention is, "Oh, Lord, preserve the lease law." They lobbied for it in the Eighteenth Legislature, and endorsed it so soon as it was passed. Every convention that has met since that time has spoken in terms of admiration of the system. The National Stockmen's Convention, which met in 1884, at St. Louis, asked for a national lease law. This, however, Congress, true to the settled land policy of our government, has hitherto refused to do. These men understand their interests, and appreciate the power which such a system gives them, and are now asking for a lease law stronger than any that has yet graced our statute books.

The Nineteenth Legislature passed a bill, similar in many respects to this. The third section of that bill permitted any person or corporation, for five cents per acre, to lease any amount of land desired. In vetoing the measure, after commenting at some length upon the recent land troubles that had caused so much injury to the State, Governor Ireland said: "By no act of mine will I ever sanction the acquisition of these vast tracts of land by one management. It is not a correct public policy, nor is it justice to the great mass of our citizens." These were wise and statesmanlike words. The bill now under consideration, like that which received this well merited rebuke, places no limit upon the number of acres that may be acquired by one person or combination of persons, and it is to be presumed that were Governor Ireland now at the helm, it would not receive the executive approval. The great powers hitherto exercised by this Land Board are here vested in the Commissioner of the Land Office, clothing that official with an authority and discretionary power too great to be given to any one man. Should he care to do so, under the provisions of this act, he can convert the northwest into a desert.

Again, sir, the lease herein contemplated is absolute. The poor privilege given the actual settler under the act of 1883, of entering upon a lease and there erecting his little home, should he so desire, is taken away. True, as has been said by Messers Swain, Walsh and others, this privilege amounts to but little, as there are but few poor men so bold as to enter these feudal domains and attempt to preserve their rights and maintain their independence. Nevertheless, this mere privilege is something, and the actual settler and the homeless squatter should never be deprived of the right of choosing an abiding place upon the vacant lands of Texas. The law of 1883 was bad. That of 1885, though an improvement, was properly vetoed. This measure, more dangerous in its possibilities for evil than either, will probably pass. By a method which is the evil outgrowth of an overwhelming political majority, grave questions of public moment are decided, not deliberately, in the halls of legislation, but amid the turbulent scenes and clashing ambitions of a political convention. The fiat of a convention has gone forth, and notwithstanding this system has been on trial for four years, and proven a miserable failure; notwithstanding every non-political convention that met during the past year, in which the agricultural and working classes were represented, has demanded its abolition; notwithstanding the policy of the general government has ever been against it, the system must be perpetuated.

Sir, if such a measure, instead of this miserable pittance of two hundred thousand dollars a year, poured into the lap of our treasury the wealth of all the mines of earth, I could not, in conscience, give it my support; for Bastrop county can never lend her sanction to a measure that allows unlimited areas of land to fall under the control of one management, that encourages the monopoly of a great industry, that retards the development of the State, drives back the actual settler, and is enacted in violation of the plainest provisions of the Constitution.

CALVIN SATTERFIELD.

THIS gentleman is one of the proprietors of the Austin Statesman, and has had especial charge of the legislative department of the paper during the Twentieth Legislature. Mr. Satterfield was born in Caroline county, Maryland, August 4, 1861. He attended several schools and colleges, and was graduated in law from the University of Virginia before he was twenty-one years of age. He practiced his profession in Baltimore, Maryland, until two years ago, when he moved to Austin, and shortly afterwards embarked in the newspaper business.

S. B. HILL.

THE cuts in this work were all executed from photographs by Mr. S. B. Hill, the leading photographer of Austin, Texas.

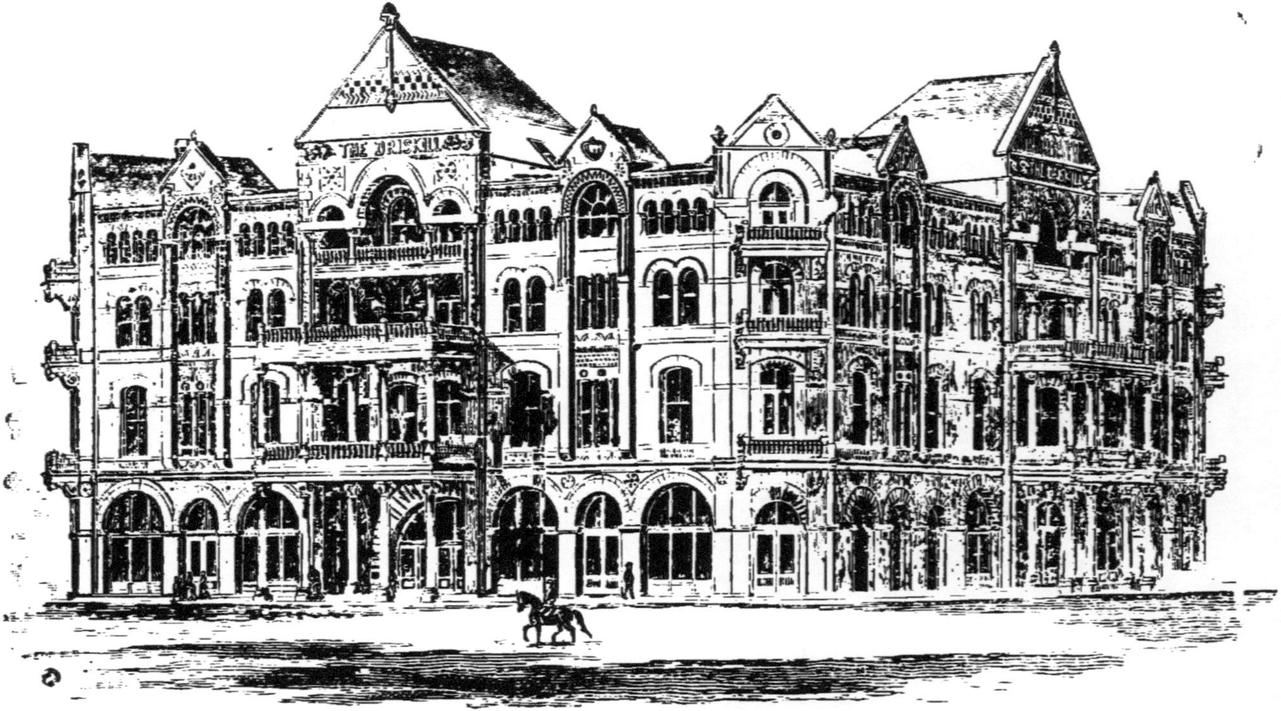

THE DRISKILL HOTEL, AUSTIN, TEXAS.

www.ingramcontent.com/pod-product-compliance
Lightning Source LLC
Chambersburg PA
CBHW031417230426
43668CB00007B/341
* 9 7 8 3 7 4 4 7 2 7 6 8 6 *